RACING POST
ANNUAL 2012

Racing Post One Canada Square, London E14 5AP.
020 7293 2001

THE IRISH
RACING POST
ANNUAL 2012

Irish Racing Post Suite 413, The Capel Building,
Mary's Abbey, Dublin 7. 01 872 7250

Editor Nick Pulford
Art editor David Dew
Cover design Jay Vincent
Chief photographers Edward Whitaker, Patrick McCann
Other photography Mark Cranham, Getty,
John Grossick, Martin Lynch, Caroline Norris
Picture Editor David Cramphorn
Graphics David Penzer, Stefan Searle
Picture artworking Stefan Searle, Nigel Jones, Jenny
Robertshaw
Illustrator David Penzer
Feature writers Scott Burton, Steve Dennis, Alastair
Down, Nicholas Godfrey, Jessica Lamb, Lee Mottershead,
Julian Muscat, Brough Scott, Peter Thomas, Johnny Ward
Contributors David Baxter, Richard Birch, James Burn,
David Carr, Paul Curtis, Dave Edwards, Simon Giles, Bruce
Jackson, Jon Lees, David Milnes, Jonathan Mullin, Tony
O'Hehir, Stuart Riley, Laura-Jayne Roberts, Peter Scargill,
Martin Smethurst
Statistics Mark Bowers, Andy Smith, Craig Thake

Advertisement Sales Racing Post, One Canada Square,
London E14 5AP. 020 7293 2001
Cheryl Gunn, cheryl.gunn@racingpost.com,
Lucy McKermitt, lucymckermitt@racingpost.com

Archant Dialogue Prospect House, Rouen Road,
Norwich, NR1 1RE. 01603 772554
Andy Grant, andy.grant@archantdialogue.co.uk
Kay Brown, kay.brown@archantdialogue.co.uk

Distribution/availability 01635 89878
help@racingpost.com
www.racingpost.com

Published by Racing Post Books, Compton,
Newbury, RG20 6NL. 01635 577603
All rights reserved. No part of this publication may be
reproduced, stored in a retrieval system, or transmitted in
any form by any means, electronic, mechanical,
photocopying, recording, or otherwise without the written
permission of the publishers.

Copyright © Racing Post 2011

The Racing Post specifies that post-press changes may occur
to any information given in this publication. A catalogue
record for this title is available from the British Library

UK Edition: ISBN 978-1-905156-98-6
Irish Edition: ISBN 978-1-908216-16-8

Printed in the UK by Buxton Press

The big st⟨
so much more . . .

**Welcome to the Racing Post Annual 2012 – a
brand-new publication from racing's No.1 newspaper
that celebrates the best of 2011 and looks ahead to what
2012 may hold in store.**

All the big stories of the year are here – Frankel's fabulous Flat
campaign, Long Run's ascent to chasing's summit, another McCain
family triumph in the Grand National, Pour Moi's incredible Derby,
Ireland's phenomenal Cheltenham, the first Champions Day at
Ascot, Hayley Turner's Group 1 breakthrough, Ruby Walsh's
domination of the hurdling scene, and much more.

The Racing Post's best writers are here too, to tell these stories
in fresh, insightful detail. And throughout The Annual you will
marvel at award-winning photographer Edward Whitaker's
stunning images, along with those of Irish Racing Post
photographer Patrick McCann.

It has been quite a year, one we could hardly dare to dream of
when we started to put together plans for the launch of the Racing
Post Annual. To have one star for the ages seemed too good to be
true when Long Run lived up to all his promise at the incredibly
young age of six, but then we were truly spoiled to have another
as Frankel blazed across the summer like a comet.

Their exciting exploits are brought to life again in The Annual,
along with many other tales of human and equine triumph, not
least the story of how the hugely popular Monet's Garden won
the ultimate battle after being close to death late last year.

This unforgettable year has been a reminder of all that is great
about racing and why we all love it so much. When racing is as
good as this, it makes you think the sport doesn't have to change
too much. Here's hoping for more of the same in 2012.

**Nick Pulford
Editor**

CW00551800

BIG STORIES

THE BEST OF 2011

SPECIAL OFFERS

Ascot aces
Page 22

National tradition
Page 38

Long story
Page 64

Queen of the weighing room
Page 30

"This is the people's horse. If someone asked me to sum up my season it would be one word – Frankel"
Tom Queally Page 6

"I didn't think she could win – not judging on her work, on the other horses in the race. But in my dreams, when I went to bed, I said 'maybe this is my chance to win the Arc' "
Andrasch Starke Page 52

"In the darkest days I remember thinking about where we'd bury him. Oh, it doesn't bear thinking about now"
David Wesley Yates Page 72

"I don't know how I felt exactly when I stood up. I had all these emotions and that's just what happened. It was the Epsom Derby"
Mickael Barzalona Page 76

"I'm not daft enough to think it's going to come easily but, dare I say it, I would love to be champion trainer"
Tim Vaughan Page 84

FRANKEL
THE WONDER HORSE

Brough Scott has had unrivalled access to Sir Henry Cecil's stable during the most remarkable season of the trainer's 42-year career and here he tells the inside story of the horse of a lifetime

*T*he great horses have a magic about them; there is both a wonder at what they do and a worry that they might lose it. Frankel was already a spell maker that first morning in March.

It was not just what he had done, although his four victories had got Henry Cecil quoted as saying he was the best two-year-old he had ever trained. It wasn't even the limitless potential of what Frankel might do. It was the stalking presence of his walk, the sense of hidden but explosive power in those hindquarters that converted at the gallop into

Continues, page 8

that huge, forward-reaching stride as he stretched the reins up Warren Hill.

For with Frankel that stride – that rippling, rolling rocket of blood and bone and muscle – is at the heart of everything. It is what sets him apart from all the horses who have opposed him. It is what made him the premier pick among the 2008 foal crop at Prince Khalid Abdullah's famous Juddmonte Farms breeding operation. But it also set Sir Henry Cecil and his training team their biggest challenge as they tried to harness the stride without breaking the temperament. And on the racetrack the world has already seen

times when Tom Queally has found that power almost too explosive a weapon.

Let it never be forgotten that the trainer can't teach the horse to go faster than the genes and limbs and lung capacity allow. A trainer's job is to prevent the physical and psychological pitfalls that lie in wait for the young equine athlete as it goes through the rigours of race preparation. Frankel, arguably the apogee of 300 years of thoroughbred selection, has, touch wood, been a wonderfully healthy physical specimen but don't doubt there have been moments when, in the

wrong hands, his mind could have blown it.

There was a brief stage before he even got on a racecourse last summer when all he wanted to do was to let his stride loose and bolt into the distance in any direction. There was an ugly incident later when he was moved into a box nearer the trainer's house and set about trying to kick it to pieces before getting back to his old lair and lying down in relief. Even this year the early horsebox trips from Warren Place across Newmarket to work on the racecourse side would be accompanied by some ferocious pounding from

11.02.2008
The date he was foaled

14.01.2010
The date he went into training with Sir Henry Cecil

13.08.2010
The date of his first race, a half-length win over subsequent King George winner Nathaniel in a 1m Newmarket maiden

£1.37m
Prize-money earned

139+
Racing Post Rating, the highest recorded on turf

5
Group 1 races won

9
Career races without defeat

45½
Cumulative winning distance in lengths

7-4
SP on his debut, the only time he has been odds-against

1-4
Winning SP in the Greenham, the shortest of his career

Frankel's hooves. When Cecil says his champion is "not entirely straightforward" he is quietly paying tribute to the diligence of his team from dawn to dusk with a horse who doesn't need aggravation. From Chris Russell feeding him, to Sandeep Guatharam grooming him, to Shane Fetherstonhaugh riding him, the group around Frankel act with quiet and practised discipline. "Oh no you won't," said Cecil when Racing Post photographer Edward Whitaker jokingly suggested he might take some flash pictures of Frankel in his box, "I can be very nasty when I want to be."

Back in March the routine was already set. Russell would be on Frankel's half-brother, the 2010 Lingfield Derby Trial winner Bullet Train, leading Fetherstonhaugh on Frankel at the top of the string. Bullet Train was the slightly taller, maybe even more conventionally handsome of the two. Frankel would give the occasional buck of wellbeing but he is neither a bouncing ball of energy like Motivator was, nor one of those sunny, ears-pricked colts who make you whistle of a morning. He is not that big, a size smaller than Sea The Stars, **Continues, page 10**

The hype 'It's the moment we've waited for all winter,' said the Racing Post front page as Frankel returned to action six months to the day since his Dewhurst win had confirmed him as joint-champion two-year-old with Dream Ahead and the hot favourite for the 2,000 Guineas. Expectation levels had been raised with reports that Frankel had outrun the Newmarket-Cambridge passenger train on the gallops during the build-up to his return.

The race Five lined up against him and Frankel went off the shortest price of his career at 1-4, with Strong Suit 9-2 and the rest 18-1 or bigger. Picture Editor was in as pacemaker for Frankel, who looked for a moment or two in the early

stages that he might not settle. He looked more comfortable once he took over just inside the 3f marker and was not troubled as he came home four lengths clear of Excelebration – at the time the lowest-rated in the field. "Workmanlike, not spectacular," the Racing Post analysis said, while Henry Cecil was his usual insouciant self: "Very satisfactory," he said.

RPR view Frankel didn't have to match his two-year-old form to win comfortably and the performance appeared nothing more than satisfactory at the time. It turned out rather better than that, with runner-up Excelebration developing into a top-grade miler, and Frankel's initial RPR of 119+ was upgraded to 124+ in light of the front pair's subsequent form, making it the best Greenham-winning figure since RPRs began.

Totesport.com Greenham Stakes (Group 3)

Newbury, April 16, 7f, good to firm

1 Frankel 1-4f
2 Excelebration 25-1
3 Shropshire 18-1
Distances 4l, 6l
6 ran

his neck is set a bit straight in front of him, but his whole being emanates a sense of purpose and power as those great hindquarters bend the legs beneath him. And that is only at a walk.

At the canter it is even more obvious. As Bullet Train led Frankel towards the four-and-a-half-furlong Warren Hill Polytrack that was their daily

work bench you would notice the care with which assistant trainer Mike Marshall shepherded them on to the track, the gentlest of ways that Frankel would move from trot to canter and then the stillness on the Frankel rein so controlled that, as they came gunning past us, one wag laughed and said, "if Shane as much as coughs he won't pull up till Moulton".

Everyone already knew they were housing something exceptional and the first gallops were awesome enough for the Racing Post's David Milnes to spawn a headline saying 'Frankel overtakes a train'. But what they did not know was what would happen when that stride was really let loose on a racetrack. All the emphasis on settling at home meant Queally actually

had to roust Frankel before storming clear first time out at Newbury and, when the colt came past us up Warren Hill on the eve of the Guineas, he seemed so settled that Fetherstonhaugh's reins were almost slack. Then we saw Bullet Train absolutely flat to the boards ahead of him. "I am not going to worry about the others, **Continues, page 12**

or the draw or the pacemaker," said Cecil as we drove back to Warren Place. "He's got this enormous stride. I want him to use it. I don't mind if he goes all the way."

The world now knows that what followed was the most astonishing, trail-blazing 2,000 Guineas any of us has ever seen. The satisfaction glowed up at Warren Place as the family standard flew on the masthead and Cecil pulled back Frankel's rugs to run his big hands lovingly over the horse's flank and quarters. But what had been done needed to be undone. The sense of "we won't use those tactics again" was so palpable over the next six weeks that it almost backfired at Royal Ascot. My personal view is the problem with the near debacle of Frankel's scrambling St James's Palace victory was that the emphasis on settling the horse had worked so well that it surprised Queally, who, with the pacemaker escaping over the horizon, pressed the 'Go' button far too early and the rocket was rapidly running out of fuel at the winning post.

It was a very public embarrassment; Cecil wincing on camera and Queally fudging away about that being the plan and the horse having plenty left at the finish. Closer to the action, Marshall shook his head as 'Sandy' led Frankel back. "I hope we can put that behind us," he said carefully. Truth be told there were some difficult days but Cecil has 40 years of experience and Queally is old before his years. The jockey put his cause right with an inspired ride on Timepiece to win the Group 1 Falmouth Stakes at the July meeting, led in by a beaming Fetherstonhaugh, who has groomed her since she was a two-year-old.

Best of all, Frankel was beaming. "This is my favourite gallop," said Cecil one morning on the Limekilns as we waited alongside the Bury Road for the horses to come winging out of the rising sun. You could only get glimpses against the glare but there was that familiar set of the neck and the rapacious reach of the stride. The Hannon camp were saying bullish things about Canford Cliffs before the Sussex Stakes showdown, the 'Duel on the Downs'. But that was as it should be. Frankel had a point to prove. If he was half the horse we thought he was, he was going to prove it however and wherever Canford went about his business.

So it happened on what remains the most golden day of them all. Newmarket may have been the most thrilling, Ascot's Champions Day the

Continues, page 14

FRANKEL'S YEAR Race two: 2,000 Guineas, Newmarket, April 30

The hype Thirteen runners made this easily the biggest field Frankel has faced at the top level and he was opposed by three Group 1 winners, but he was the only one people were talking about. 'King in waiting' declared the Racing Post front page on Guineas day. Having been 5-6 for the Guineas before the Greenham, he was sent off at 1-2 on the day – shorter than 1970 Triple Crown winner Nijinsky (4-7), though not as short as 1934 Guineas winner Colombo (2-7). Richard Hughes, in his day-of-race column in the Racing Post, echoed the thoughts of many when he said, "I think we should sit back and enjoy this one because he is something special."

The race Intriguingly, three days before the race, Henry Cecil revealed he was ready to send Frankel to the front, even though Rerouted was in the field as pacemaker. "He has an extraordinary stride and when you take a pull you take him out of his stride," Cecil said. "On the other hand, if you let him go and allow him to use himself he relaxes. Why not just let him relax in front?"

Cecil's words were the prelude to the most jaw-dropping Guineas triumph in living memory. Frankel did indeed go off in front and he did more than relax; he tore the race to shreds. That extraordinary stride soon took him clear and he was ten lengths ahead at halfway. "He was so far clear I thought he was the pacemaker," said Johnny Murtagh, who was fifth on Fury. It was apparent a long way out that Frankel wouldn't be stopping and

The wow factor Dave Edwards (Topspeed) clocks that amazing Guineas	The wind is 'fresh half against' the runners on the Rowley Mile, which will conspire against front-runners and fast times	**13.5sec** A relatively gentle opening furlong but strip out the standing start (circa 1.80sec) and Frankel is ticking over nicely in front	**11.5sec** He begins to tighten the screw with minimum effort and covers the first quarter in a sensational 25sec. Bold and brilliant, or has his cork popped too soon?	**11sec** This furlong is even quicker as Frankel continues to devour the ground with his long, raking stride. It's astonishing to see other Group 1 winners already struggling
	START	**7f**	**6f**	**5f**

at the line he had six lengths to spare over Dubawi Gold – the second-biggest margin in the Guineas after Tudor Minstrel's eight-length win in 1947.

Figures hardly begin to convey Frankel's brilliance and superiority on the day – one of those rare 'I was there' moments for the lucky 16,000 racegoers at Newmarket.

The greats of racing lined up to pay tribute: "breathtaking" (Sir Peter O'Sullevan), "staggering" (Walter Swinburn), "amazing" (Willie Carson), "the best Guineas winner I've seen" (Pat Eddery).

Cecil, meanwhile, knew his mighty colt had done all the talking. "It worked out exactly as I wanted it to," he said. Quite an understatement.

RPR view This was an outstanding performance on both form and the clock. Few of the others showed their form on the day as Frankel's blistering pace took his rivals well out of their comfort zone. His winning margin was a firm pointer to his brilliance and pace analysis indicated he could be rated better than the bare form. Although not his peak figure, his RPR of 133+ still ranks him the best Guineas winner since RPRs began. Few races, let alone Classics, are won in such dominant fashion and the 2,000 Guineas was Frankel's signature performance.

Qipco 2,000 Guineas (Group 1)

Newmarket, April 30, 1m, good to firm

1 Frankel 1-2f
2 Dubawi Gold 33-1
3 Native Khan 16-1
Distances: 6l, ½l
13 ran

11sec
Wow, that's back-to-back splits of 11 dead – he's covering almost the length of a cricket pitch each and every second. He's about a dozen lengths clear

4f

11.5sec
This is high-octane stuff. Cumulatively his time is faster than that clocked by the 5f Palace House winner earlier in the day, albeit over a 'different' five

3f

12.5sec
Slowing down now, not surprisingly, but the race is already over. It's clear this is exceptional and the crowd know it as they break out in spontaneous applause

2f

12.8sec
Frankel decelerates further but still he's in splendid isolation and there's no chance of the others getting anywhere near him. Awesome

1f

13.5sec
His absolute dominance is maintained as he eases to the line. This has been an exhilarating display of raw speed and power that burnt off his rivals by halfway

FINISH

1min 37.3sec
The final time is 1.8sec slower than standard, but that does not do justice to one of the all-time great Classic performances. Frankel's time, especially his mid-race sectionals, is staggering when the wind factor is taken into account

FRANKEL'S YEAR
Race three: St James's Palace Stakes, Royal Ascot, June 14

The hype By now, with his Guineas demolition taking him to a perfect six races, the Frankel factor was an irresistible force. Talk of sending him to the Derby had been swiftly dismissed and this marked the next step in a mission to make him champion miler. There was an extra frisson of excitement at the royal meeting as Henry Cecil's knighthood had been announced in the Queen's birthday honours the previous weekend. 'Hold on to your hats!' proclaimed the Racing Post front page as Royal Ascot opened with a bang. Frankel wasn't the only attraction on a day that also featured Goldikova v Canford Cliffs, but he was the main one.

The race Ascot's turning track and short straight presented a different challenge to Newmarket's wide-open spaces, although Frankel had won the Royal Lodge there by ten lengths as a two-year-old. Lee Mottershead, previewing the day in the Racing Post, said "to remain invincible he must display tactical versatility". How right he was, and how close Frankel came to being caught out.

This time Rerouted did make the pace but so far removed from the rest of the field that the main effect was to leave Frankel exposed. In a move that was widely criticised afterwards, Tom Queally sent Frankel in pursuit a long way out and, in front with more than three lengths to run, was six lengths clear at the 2f pole. This time, however, he came back to the field and hearts were in mouths for Frankel's supporters as Zoffany cut into his lead. Frankel was all out to hold on by three-quarters of a length: unbeaten record preserved, but only just.

"That was nerve-wracking, it didn't quite go to plan," Cecil said. "He wasn't tired, he was going to sleep, wasn't he? The race just went wrong for him. If you ran it again, the result would be very different. He's exceptional and hopefully he'll prove it again."

RPR view Frankel's RPR of 122+ was his lowest since running away with a conditions race on his second start as a two-year-old, but race tactics masked his ability here and he showed determination to hold off the late-closing Zoffany. Both Frankel and third-placed Excelebration — who had been ridden closer to the pace than the other frame horses — looked better than the bare form in relation to the patiently ridden and somewhat flattered Zoffany and fourth-placed Neebras, as evidenced by the rest of their form.

most finally fulfilling, but for sweet proof that we were into dreamtime there may never be anything to match what Frankel did when those gates whacked open at Goodwood. I had walked every yard of the course that morning trying to imagine how Queally would feel as he rolled his rocket off the turn and let that stride reach out where all the great ones had gone before. No dreams could have matched the real thing: the control, the speed and that raw power, which saw Queally still poised while Frankie Dettori was scrubbing furiously on Rio De La Plata and Richard Hughes and Canford Cliffs finally cracked and veered off line in defeat.

Marshall and I stood whooping madly by the winning line. Afterwards we ran up and hugged Sandy and travelling head man Mike McClagan and danced round in those silly little jigs of winning happiness. You didn't need to be a form analyst to know what we had seen. Those three hundred years of selective breeding and two hundred years of racing horses across these downs had not all been in vain. The Thoroughbred's boast of being England's greatest gift to the animal kingdom and the fastest weight-carrying creature the world has ever seen, has never been more gloriously proclaimed.

As he hosed Frankel off afterwards Guatharam was generous about the horse who has transformed his life since he left his earlier career as

St James's Palace Stakes (Group 1)

Royal Ascot, June 14,
1m, good

1 Frankel 30-100f
2 Zoffany 20-1
3 Excelebration 10-1
Distances: ¾l, 1½l
9 ran

Qipco Sussex Stakes (Group 1)

Goodwood, July 27, 1m, good

1 Frankel 8-13f
2 Canford Cliffs 7-4
3 Rio De La Plata 22-1
Distances: 5l, 2½l
4 ran

FRANKEL'S YEAR Race four: Sussex Stakes, Goodwood, July 27

The hype 'The Duel on the Downs' was the billing for Frankel v Canford Cliffs, a clash of the generations that set pulses racing. This was Frankel's first test against older horses and in the four-year-old Canford Cliffs, who had matched his personal-best RPR of 130 with victory over Goldikova in the Queen Anne at Royal Ascot, he faced a rival of the highest class. There were only two other runners, both priced at 22-1, and all eyes were on the big two. 'The race we've all been waiting for,' said the Racing Post front page on raceday.

The race The duel turned into a no-contest, with Frankel repeating the pulverising front-running style of the Guineas. He had the advantage of the 8lb weight-for-age allowance, but even at level weights it's hard to see how the outcome would have been any different. With no pacemaker, Frankel was in the lead from the start and was more tractable this time, taking a keen hold but not fighting Tom Queally. He was always travelling well within himself and there was no repeat of the mid-race burst that had almost cost him dear at Royal Ascot. Canford Cliffs stalked him in second but had no answer when Frankel quickened before the furlong pole and powered to a five-length win. Hanging badly left in the final furlong, Canford Cliffs was hugely disappointing and was retired to stud soon afterwards.

"Definitely the best horse I've seen in my lifetime," said Sir Henry Cecil, before offering an intriguing insight into his confidence in Frankel's powers. "I hate predicting things, but I was going to put a piece of paper in an envelope with 'by five lengths' on it and then produce it after the race. It was the worst thing you could do, though."

Not the worst thing, as it turned out.

RPR view Canford Cliffs clearly wasn't at his best – he'd beaten Rio De La Plata twice as far in the Queen Anne – but he was beaten before hanging badly under pressure and there's no doubt the best horse won as Frankel recorded a new best RPR of 137+. While very different from the Guineas, this was another visually impressive performance, albeit in a small field in which his only realistic rival disappointed. His wins here and in the Guineas put him among the very best in the 25-year history of RPRs.

FRANKEL IN WORDS

"Quality colt, tall with size and scope. Strong hind leg. Very good foal"
Banstead Manor Stud manager Simon Mockridge's notes after Frankel had been foaled

"I think Frankel is the best horse I've ever seen, with Blushing Groom and Shergar. I can't go further back than that as I wasn't around"
Sir Henry Cecil after the Sussex

"I think after another winter you're really going to see a better horse next year – and he's pretty good as he is"
Cecil after the Queen Elizabeth II

"It doesn't look like he's going to get beaten"
Tom Queally in confident mood about the future too

"Many people think he's the best horse there has ever been and I am glad to have that horse"
Owner Khalid Abdullah

"He's like a Ferrari against a field of Austin Sevens"
Joe Mercer

"He's the greatest over a mile I've ever seen and one of the few horses in my life I've heard people clap before a race"
Willie Carson

"We've tried to beat him three times and it has been no different each time. He tried his best but he was second to a great horse"
Marco Botti, trainer of Excelebration

champion apprentice in Hyderabad. "He's growing up all the time," he said. "We came down yesterday and he settled and ate all his feed with not a bother. He wants to please. He wants to get on with things. He can only get better. I am sure he will stay a mile and a quarter. To be honest I think he would have won the Derby."

TALK of trying a mile and a quarter at York was quickly dismissed and, while Frankel went on to the easy routine, the stable had one of its greatest days with Twice Over and Midday running first and second in the Juddmonte. Champions Day was a full two months away and it was time to take stock. Fetherstonhaugh explained how Frankel's stride reaches out so far in front of him that you have to position yourself half a length further behind your leader than on a normal horse, head girl Dee Deacon showed the enormous feed tub as proof that Frankel eats more than anything else, a super-relaxed Cecil took us to his wardrobe and displayed the rows of silk shirts and cashmere jackets, which, like the trees and flowers in the garden, are his out-of-stable delight.

But climaxes always have countdowns and as Ascot closed in the strain began to tell. Frankel was odds-on favourite but potential disaster was there to dog the team every day. One silly move, one frustrated kick, any little thing, could end the game even before we got to raceday. The trainer was still padding round the stable long before dawn, his face now drawn as the extra pressure of the yearling sales doubled up on the hassle of a long season, not to mention the minor matter of cancer maintenance.

But the systems were all in place. Frankel still stalked round behind Bullet Train before his work each morning. Close up he seemed to have packed on even more muscle behind the saddle. On Newmarket's watered gallop he stretched out as ruthlessly as ever. In the last week before Ascot two promising two-year-olds impressively broke their maidens. The scene was set but only the best would do.

It happened sure enough. If you had never heard anything about Frankel's running style you would have wondered what all the fuss was about as he anchored off a pretty moderate pace. Queally admitted afterwards his biggest worry was some crashing crate or stray spectator startling him on the

FRANKEL'S YEAR Race five: QEII Stakes, Ascot, October 15

The hype Many of the racing headlines in the days before the race were stolen by the intensifying row over the new whip rules, but Frankel had top billing on raceday. 'An extraordinary horse for a special day' said the Racing Post front page as Ascot prepared to open its doors for the first Qipco British Champions Day and the other national newspapers joined the fanfare. 'Frankel can ride to the rescue' said the Daily Telegraph, in reference to the whip furore, while the Sun made a simple prediction: 'Walkover'. No red-button coverage either, with BBC1 devoting two and a quarter hours of mainstream coverage to the big day.

The race This time the pacemaker in the eight-runner field was Bullet Train, Frankel's half-brother who had also been his regular companion on the gallops. He was ten lengths clear after two furlongs, with Tom Queally's first priority being to settle Frankel. That was achieved more readily than in the past and Queally showed great confidence in Frankel as he began to take him through the gears. Frankel moved effortlessly into second by halfway and, with Bullet Train as a target, Queally was in the perfect position.

Some of Frankel's army of fans might have worried as Excelebration tracked his run and Immortal Verse started a move from the back, but any fears were quickly allayed. Frankel took the lead well over a furlong out and, as he stretched, it was clear the others were already close to breaking point. The final furlong was a procession as Frankel cruised home by four lengths.

"I know him so well and have great belief in him," Queally said. "The biggest job I have is getting him to the start, keeping him relaxed and

SIX STEPS FROM LONG RUN TO FRANKEL

Long Run, trained by Nicky Henderson and ridden by Sam Waley-Cohen, won a vintage Cheltenham Gold Cup at the age of six

▶▶ A six-year-old had not won the race since **Mill House** in 1963. He won by 12 lengths, almost twice Long Run's winning margin

▶▶ 1963 was the year of the Profumo scandal, which saw the resignation of **John Profumo**, secretary of state for war, over his affair with Christine Keeler

 ▶▶

Queen Elizabeth II Stakes (Group 1)
Ascot, October 15, 1m, good

1 Frankel 4-11f
2 Excelebration 6-1
3 Immortal Verse 7-1
Distances: 4l, 3½l
8 ran

talking to him, making sure everything is okay. This is the people's horse now. If someone asked me to sum up my season it would be one word – Frankel. He's amazing. I'm very lucky."

RPR view Another outstanding performance from Frankel and his best in terms of figures, confirming his place among the greats and making him the highest-rated turf performer in RPR history with 139+. This was the strongest field Frankel faced but the result was a familiar one as he ran out a powerful four-length winner from the unfortunate Excelebration, the latter having recorded a level of form (RPR 129) good enough to have won all but two of the previous ten runnings of this championship race. Remarkably, despite recording such an extraordinary figure, Frankel again left the impression that it wasn't his limit.

ALL-TIME BEST RPRS

139	Frankel
139d	Dubai Millennium
138	Daylami
138	Sea The Stars
137	Generous
137	Peintre Celebre
137	Zilzal
136	Dayjur
136	Mark Of Esteem
136	Montjeu

d=dirt

RACING POST ON SUNDAY
LEGENDARY BOOKMAKERS
THAT'S WHY THEY CALL HIM
THE FREAK
Breathtaking Frankel provides a wondrous centrepiece to a brilliant Champions Day at Ascot. Reports, plus Alastair Down, pages 2-7
LONDON CALLING

FRANKEL
THE FORM LINES

What those beaten by Frankel in 2011 won when he wasn't there

Excelebration
Against Frankel: 2nd in Greenham, 3rd in St James's Palace, 2nd in Queen Elizabeth II
Other races: Won German 2,000 Guineas (Group 2), Hungerford Stakes (G2) and Prix du Moulin (G1)

Strong Suit
Against Frankel: 6th in Greenham
Won Jersey Stakes (G3), Lennox Stakes (G2) and Challenge Stakes (G2)

Dubawi Gold
Against Frankel: 2nd in 2,000 Guineas, 6th in St James's Palace, 4th in QEII
Won Celebration Mile (G2)

Native Khan
Against Frankel: 3rd in 2,000 Guineas
Won Craven Stakes (G3)

Casamento
10th in 2,000 Guineas
Won Prix du Prince d'Orange (G3)

Roderic O'Connor
Against Frankel: 11th in 2,000 Guineas
Won Irish 2,000 Guineas (G1)

Dream Ahead
Against Frankel: 5th in St James's Palace
Won July Cup (G1), Haydock Sprint Cup (G1) and Prix de la Foret (G1)

Canford Cliffs
Against Frankel: 2nd in Sussex
Won Lockinge Stakes (G1), Queen Anne Stakes (G1)

Rajsaman
Against Frankel: 4th in Sussex
Won Prix du Muguet (G2), Prix Daniel Wildenstein (G2)

Immortal Verse
Against Frankel: 3rd in QEII
Won Prix Jacques Le Marois (G1), Coronation Stakes (G1), Prix de Sandringham (G2)

Dick Turpin
Against Frankel: 5th in QEII
Won Premio Vittorio di Capua (G1), Summer Mile (G2), Bet365 Mile (G2)

Side Glance
Against Frankel: 7th in QEII
Won Sovereign Stakes (G3)

way to the post. A couple of us had suggested the champion had not looked quite as gleaming as usual in the paddock. "I don't think you would have said that," he said in that quiet way of his, "if you had felt what I felt underneath me when I let him stretch that stride at the three pole."

Ah yes, that stride, that Frankel stride. Burn it in the memory. For it's a fair bet you will never see its like again. That's until the next year, which brings us to the greatest bonus of all. At a time when racing as a whole and Flat racing in particular was getting quite embarrassingly desperate for a star turn to interest the public, what happens? The most charismatic Flat racing trainer produces the horse he has (probably prematurely) described as "the best we have ever seen" and now we are invited to see Frankel as a four-year-old. What's more, just about all the indications are positive.

For a start the trainer is really looking forward to it. "He should be even better as a four-year-old, shouldn't he?" Cecil said. "He's been growing up all the time and he would get a mile and a quarter now. We can have a nice quiet winter and he should be better than ever." He was speaking in September before any of the Ascot hassle bit in and, as so often, the points were made almost flippantly but there was a real edge in the message he was delivering.

He and his staff really love their older horses. Twice Over is the most popular animal in the stable and Midday would be second if she wasn't so insistent in kicking anybody except her close numbers out of the way. For all his brilliance Frankel has not always looked an entirely happy horse but the longer the year has gone on the more settled he has seemed. If he continues this progress there is no reason why he should not be even more amenable in a racing situation, in which case events like the Eclipse, the Juddmonte and the Champion should be well within his compass.

To match the 20th century's greatest miler Brigadier Gerard, winner of 17 of his 18 races, Frankel ought also to win the King George VI and Queen Elizabeth Stakes over a mile and a half. We might excuse him that, but it would be great to see him fly the flag overseas. By next November his huge stride might even be up to tacking the dirt at Santa Anita in the Breeders' Cup. With Frankel as a four-year-old the best is yet to come.

RACING POST ANNUAL 2012

Person of the Year

Sir Henry Cecil

IT'S a pertinent question – what do you give the man who has everything? Another Hermes tie, another pair of Gucci loafers? Too easy, and anyway it's supposed to be the thought that counts.

Perhaps . . . no, he's already got one of those. The news of Henry Cecil's knighthood was greeted with universal acclaim. It's hard sometimes to think of the great man as 'Sir Henry' after so many decades on first-name terms with the whole spectrum of the racing public.

His knighthood was a lasting tribute to go with the ephemeral ones, the ones uttered in betting shops and on racetracks across the land, all the 'good old Henrys' that spring almost unbidden when the occasion demands. Few men on the turf or under it have been held in such widespread and unstinting affection as Cecil.

What about . . . oh yes, he's got one of those too. Six years ago Cecil's career was at its lowest ebb, now he trains the best horse on turf in the mighty miler Frankel. Cecil won't rank his great horses, won't reckon one above another, but this explosive colt may be the best of them all and his performance in the 2,000 Guineas provided the most potent image of the season, of many a season.

And throughout this season Cecil has balanced the demands of training a champion with the constant intrusion of the media and done so with grace, openness and no little humour at a time when his health still requires constant monitoring. At certain requests a weariness may steal across his face but in its wake come the words "you've got your job to do just as I have", and he has done that job immaculately.

Undiminished by his previous travails and unbowed by the arbitrary bloodiness of life, Cecil's extraordinary and uplifting renaissance has reached full bloom in this memorable year.

So it was an easy choice – Sir Henry Cecil is the Racing Post Annual Person of the Year. It's a small gift in comparison with others but sometimes it's the thought that counts and we're all of one thought. Good old Henry.

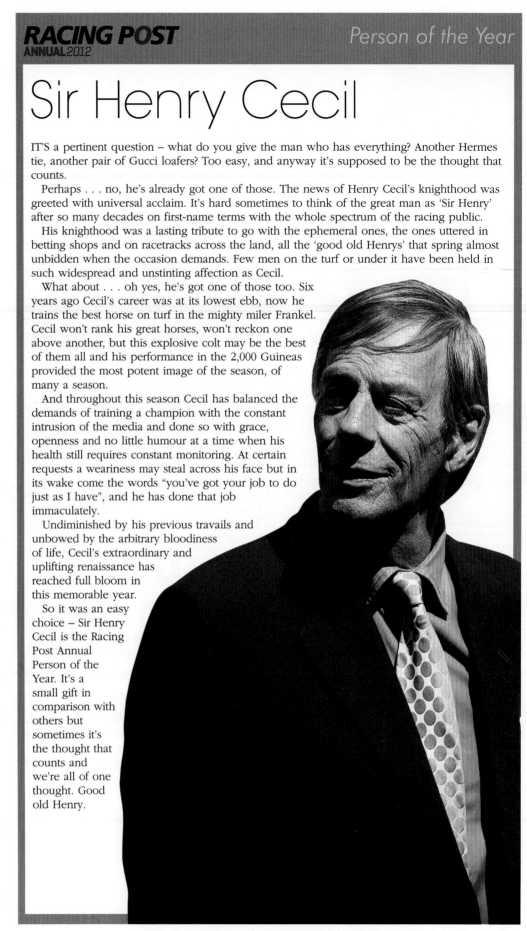

Bloodlines and Powerlines.

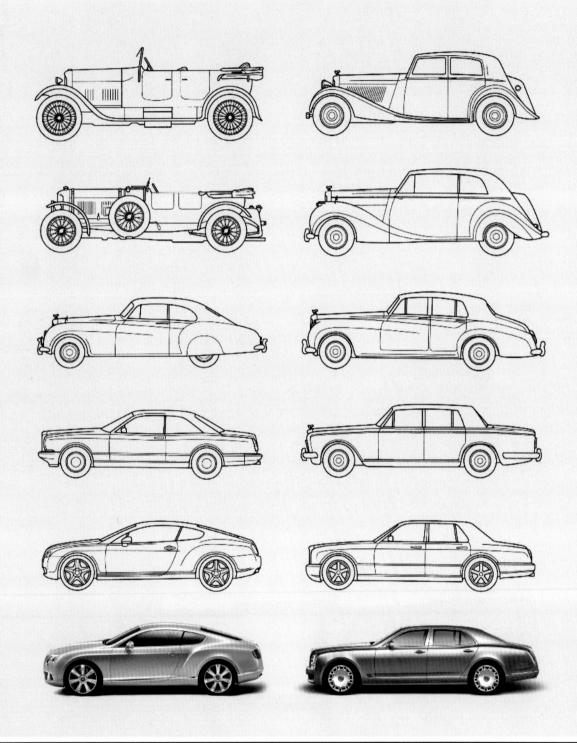

Since the first Bentley burst to life in 1919, we have introduced an evolving series of acclaimed and refined motoring vehicles. Some are more extreme machines; others more classic. Yet all have that sense of timeless, refined style that sets us apart. Our design lineage also reflects a sporting tradition that's closely intertwined with British motoring and the racetrack. Whether it's the Continental GT or the Mulsanne, their bloodlines are pure Bentley. Those classic British proportions are unmistakable: a long bonnet, short front overhang and long rear overhang. Whatever the era or model, design and style are at our core.

BENTLEY

THE
BIGGER
PICTURE

Dawn breaks over Sir Henry Cecil's Warren Place yard during an unforgettable season in which Frankel etched his name among the greats **Edward Whitaker**

Big day comes to life at last

Frankel, a supporting cast of high-class winners and a knowledgeable crowd combined to make the inaugural British Champions Day a success, despite the avoidable own goal over the whip

Words by Julian Muscat

Never has such a difficult gestation preceded such an easy birth. British Champions Day, more than ten years in the starting stalls, was delivered to great fanfare at Ascot on October 15 and pretty much everything went the organisers' way, not least balmy autumnal sunshine that allowed racegoers to enjoy outdoor facilities which are the envy of every other British racecourse.

It was equally invigorating out on the racetrack. Trainers who kept easy-ground horses in reserve for the most valuable day's racing staged in Britain did not withdraw them when the ground came up unseasonably fast. The whole day saw the sport's oft-feuding factions pull together to serve up a treat, in the process showing what can be achieved with a spirit of co-operation.

There was a great deal on the line. It seemed incongruous to set aside £3 million in prize-money at a time when levy receipts are in freefall and when

Continues, page 24

horsemen and racecourses faced off for much of the Flat season over minimum prize-money levels – or tariffs, as they came to be known. Traditionalists had sharpened knives at the ready. They would gleefully have plunged them into the backs of organisers whose restructuring of the autumnal programme was so comprehensive as to render it unrecognisable from what had gone before.

Newmarket was plainly the loser in the switch of races that saw it hand over to Ascot the Champion Stakes, the Jockey Club Cup and the Pride Stakes for fillies and mares. It was never an enviable prospect for Newmarket to promote 'Future Champions Day' around the Dewhurst and Middle Park Stakes for the simple reason that two-year-olds do not draw the crowds.

Conversely, Ascot had a priceless commodity in Frankel, a horse unbeaten in eight previous starts – among them his sensational victory in the 2,000 Guineas, itself the first race in the Qipco Champions Series. Having raised the curtain in April, it lent symmetry to the occasion that he was there to bring it down.

But Champions Day was no one-horse show. In terms of quality the cast compared favourably with Prix de l'Arc de Triomphe day and that was a huge boost for the organisers. Champions Day attracted 17 individual Group 1 winners compared with the 20 drawn to Longchamp, which hosted two more Group races in the Prix Marcel Boussac and Prix Jean-Luc Lagardere. Field sizes held up well at both venues, allaying fears that two major racedays within a fortnight of each other would dilute the quantity as well as the quality.

Just about the only gulf between Ascot and Longchamp was in the domain of prize-money. The gap was significant: the £1.97 million won by connections of Arc winner Danedream comfortably exceeded the sum paid to the

Continues, page 26

Soumillon whips up a storm

"If the winning jockey goes one stroke over the permitted five in the final furlong of the Champion Stakes and forfeits his share of the prize, Frankel will end up as a footnote in the news reports and Sunday papers," wrote one racing commentator on the morning of British Champions Day. It was, unfortunately, a prescient viewpoint, even if Frankel still grabbed his share of the headlines the next day.

In winning the Qipco Champion Stakes on Cirrus Des Aigles, Christophe Soumillon did indeed go one over the maximum five strokes of the whip in the final furlong permitted under new rules introduced by the BHA just five days earlier. As a result, he was banned for five days and forfeited his £52,390 share of the prize-money. "I feel sorry for British racing," was one of Soumillon's more restrained comments afterwards, and it was hard to escape the feeling that the sport had scored an own goal.

British participation – both in triumph and disaster – has played a major role in building up the Breeders' Cup and Arc weekend and a similar sense of adventure from other countries is one of the vital ingredients if Champions Day is to become another mammoth event in the global racing calendar.

What a godsend, then, for the Qipco Champion Stakes to be won by a French-trained gelding who is hugely popular back home, has a romantic backstory and is ridden by one of Europe's best and most entertaining jockeys. But all that – and to some extent Frankel too – was overshadowed by Soumillon's whip ban.

"They changed the rules five days before this big meeting. Do you think in France we would change the rules five days before the Arc?" fumed Soumillon. "In no other sport in the world – football, Formula One, tennis or whatever – can you be banned for such a little mistake."

The pity was that here was a race to rank with the best in the world. Cirrus Des Aigles may have been winning for the first time at Group 1 level, but he was followed home by the Australian champion So You Think, the Classics and Far East star Snow Fairy, Breeders' Cup winner Midday and Nathaniel, this year's King George victor.

Cirrus Des Aigles has won the hearts of the French racing public in his improbable rise from winning on the sand at Cagnes-sur-Mer to top-class Group-race performer, but he will never have the chance of Arc glory because geldings are not allowed in France's premier race.

This was a winner the Arc could not have had, yet with all the whip furore there was no sense afterwards that the French were in any way jealous of British racing's biggest day.
Words by Nick Pulford

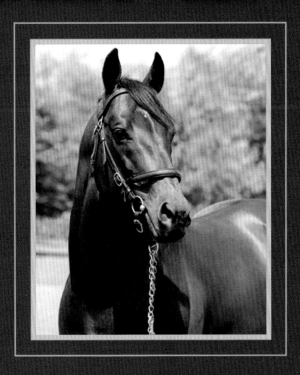

Strong supporting cast From top, Fame And Glory takes the Qipco British Champions Long Distance Cup, Johnny Murtagh salutes the crowd as he returns on Qipco British Champions Sprint winner Deacon Blue and Murtagh lands another victory with Dancing Rain in the Qipco British Champions Fillies' and Mares'

combined winners of Ascot's five Group races, which weighed in at £1.7 million.

As important as prize-money is, the bigger question for now concerns Champions Day's broader ambition to widen racing's public appeal. Only time will yield the definitive answer, but in this respect racing's rulers did the inaugural Champions Day no favours at all. What should have been a positive, week-long media build-up was clouded by the introduction of new whip rules that saw Richard Hughes quit race-riding and other jockeys threaten imminent strike action. The BHA may not specialise in marketing or public relations but those at Racing For Change, who have driven the Champions Day project on their skills in such fields, should have anticipated the furore and stepped in. Hindsight is a wonderful thing, but this could and should have been avoided.

That aside, the early portents for Champions Day's long-term mission are encouraging. The early stated crowd target of 30,000 was quickly revised downwards to 25,000 and Ascot duly delivered, with a little bit more on top. With a substantial promotional and advertising budget spent in pursuit of a young, affluent crowd, there was a danger that the occasion would be hostage to people with less interest in racing than a good day out, but this turned out to be another misplaced concern. The vast acreage either side of Ascot's giant grandstand was shut down and there was no temporary village on the lawns of the old paddock, as there is at the royal meeting. As a result, the near-27,000 crowd brought vibrancy to the central area around the parade ring without the feeling of discomfort that can accompany Gold Cup day.

To be there was to feel that you were attending a major event. There was an energy within the throng that Royal Ascot lacks and the risk of a sterile Shergar Cup crowd never came to pass. These were no day-trippers keen to have their faces painted but people who genuinely wanted to see Frankel in all his majesty. They got a lot more besides, because another fear was laid to rest once the action got under way. Fame And Glory set the ball rolling by bringing his Gold Cup form to bear in the Long Distance Cup, after which Deacon Blues picked up the baton in winning the Sprint.

Here were two winners who had held their form into a mid-October date that might have led to horses running poorly after a long season. After two races, it will have pleased Ascot and punters alike that both winners were well-fancied runners who had been victorious at the royal meeting in mid-June. Yet previous course form was not imperative. Dancing Rain was next into the winner's circle after making all in the Fillies' and Mares' Stakes. Like the previous two winners she had shone in June, winning the Investec Oaks, and yet was still able to show her form four months later.

Continues, page 28

Qipco British Champions Series Roll of honour

	SPRINT 5-6f	MILE 8f	MIDDLE 1¼-1½m	LONG 1¾m+	FILLIES & MARES
MAY Newmarket		**2,000 Guineas** Frankel RPR 133			**1,000 Guineas** Blue Bunting 116
York				**Yorkshire Cup** Duncan 117	
Newbury		**Lockinge** Canford Cliffs 126			
Haydock	**Temple** Sole Power 121				
JUNE Epsom			**Coronation Cup** St Nicholas Abbey 126 **Derby** Pour Moi 123		**Oaks** Dancing Rain 114
Royal Ascot	**King's Stand** Prohibit 121 **Golden Jubilee** Society Rock 119	**St James's Palace** Frankel 122 **Queen Anne** Canford Cliffs 130	**Prince of Wales's** Rewilding 130	**Ascot Gold Cup** Fame And Glory 121	**Coronation Stakes** Immortal Verse 115
JULY Sandown			**Eclipse** So You Think 132		
Newmarket	**July Cup** Dream Ahead 124				**Falmouth** Timepiece 116
Ascot			**King George VI & QE** Nathaniel 126		
Goodwood		**Sussex** Frankel 137		**Goodwood Cup** Opinion Poll 114	**Nassau** Midday 121
AUGUST York Ebor	**Nunthorpe** Margot Did 118		**International** Twice Over 127	**Lonsdale Cup** Opinion Poll 120	**Yorkshire Oaks** Blue Bunting 120
SEPTEMBER Haydock	**Sprint Cup** Dream Ahead 122				
Doncaster				**Doncaster Cup** Saddler's Rock 117 **St Leger** Masked Marvel 123	
Newmarket		**Joel** Ransom Note 119			
OCTOBER Ascot	**Brit Champ Sprint** Deacon Blues 123	**Queen Elizabeth II** Frankel 139	**Champion** Cirrus Des Aigles 130	**Long Distance Cup** Fame And Glory 115	**Fillies & Mares** Dancing Rain 118

Frankel's deeds in the Queen Elizabeth II Stakes, for which Her Majesty was present, require no further amplification. The only sour note came when Christophe Soumillon lost his £52,390 share of the prize-money after the stewards had no option but to ban him for his whip use in winning the Champion Stakes aboard Cirrus Des Aigles. Soumillon's riding was perfectly within the bounds of the morally acceptable face racing is obliged to show a public increasingly alienated by whip use and the punishment was harsh in the extreme.

Thankfully, the incident could not overshadow a compelling afternoon on which two clear messages shone through. The first is that the organisers of Champions Day should persist with efforts to secure an earlier date in the calendar. Such an ambitious concept needed a little help from the fates and received it when the day dawned to a glorious sunrise. Any rain would have rendered this a very different parade.

The second message is one that those who promote British racing should take on board. Champions Day was beholden to one horse; the best of racing always is. Great racehorses make great races; it is never the other way round.

Horses like Frankel carry the occasion with a frisson that animates crowds and, most of all, Champions Day emphasised that racing must have confidence in the ability of its champions to inspire.

BLOODLINES

LEADING THE FIELD IN BLOODSTOCK INSURANCE

The most competitive insurance for all racing and breeding horses.

It is a sad fact that owning a racehorse does not just involve the winner's enclosure or success in the sales ring.

There is the sad reality that sometimes, things take a turn for the worse and you lose what you hold most dear – your horse's life.

At Bloodlines, we provide a first-class insurance service to owners of racehorses, whether it be Thoroughbred or Arabian. Our service is fast, fair and highly responsive.

With our flexible approach, we can arrange immediate cover over the telephone. We like to work with clients to formulate the most suitable cover for them geared to the size and extent of their equine interest. Furthermore, we guarantee that all policy documentation is processed and issued within 48 hours as well as offering a fast and fair claims service.

We offer the right policy at the right price – without any fuss or bother.

Bloodlines Thoroughbred Insurance Agency Ltd is authorised and regulated by the Financial Services Authority.

www.bloodlines.co.uk
Email: enquiries@bloodlines.co.uk
Tel: +44 (0) 207 938 3033

'Being a girl has helped big time'

Hayley Turner made history with a pair of Group 1 sprint wins, proving she could beat the men at the highest level, and not even a broken ankle could dim the excitement of a sparkling year

Words by Lee Mottershead

ACCORDING to Kirsty Milczarek, Hayley Turner has ugly feet. Micky Fenton relates that she is rubbish at golf and has been seen to pick her nose when driving. Frankie Dettori is more charitable. He offers no views on Turner's nose or feet but points out simply: "She has a nice bottom."

Turner will not be troubled by the revelations given that the character assessments of her best and worst bits first appeared on her own website, hayleyturner.com, in which the 'about me' section is more like an 'about her'. Perhaps through modesty, Turner prefers to say little about herself and instead lets others comment on the most successful female jockey in British racing history, a rider who in 2011 became the sport's queen of speed.

At the start of the season, Turner, the joint-champion apprentice of 2005, had barely ridden in a Group 1 race, let alone partnered a Group 1 winner. Her career was hardly in the doldrums, but nor was she succeeding in taking the next step up the ladder. But then, in a glorious summer spell, all that changed. Two rungs were climbed in no time at all – or more precisely, the short space of time it took Dream Ahead and Margot Did to sprint to Group 1 glory. She became only the second British female jockey to ride a Group 1 winner after Alex Greaves, who forced Ya Malak to a dead-heat with Coastal Bluff in the 1997 Nunthorpe Stakes. Turner did it outright, not once but twice.

"I was half thinking my career had levelled off," she says. "I was wondering **Continues, page 32**

Continues, page 32

White van woman
Turner Q & A

Age 28
Place of birth Nottingham
First ride Markellis in 2m Southwell handicap on March 27, 2000. Sadly I only got halfway round. He broke his leg and was destroyed
First winner Generate in a Pontefract apprentices' race on June 4, 2000
First Group winner Lady Deauville in the Group 3 Lando-Trophy at Hanover on November 16, 2008
First Group 1 winner Dream Ahead!
Biggest influence My Mum, Dad and elder sisters
Jockey you admire most Ryan Moore
Best mate in weighing room Robert the tea man
Best ride Bonus in a Kempton Listed race in December 2007. I was drawn widest of all, missed the break, dropped him in and then steered a good run through the field to win. I don't say it often but I was pretty damn good!
Worst ride Bouncy Bouncy in a Warwick handicap in July this year. I made the running, which is totally the wrong way to ride her, but to make matters worse I also crossed over to get the rail, taking a couple out with me, which was very unnecessary. Durr!
Favourite horse Efistorm
Favourite track Ascot
Least favourite track Carlisle
Funniest thing seen on racecourse Liam Jones. On a number of occasions
Favourite food Cinder toffee
Car A white van (Vauxhall) and a Merc
Favourite designer Tretorn
Matt Chapman or Nick Luck Nick Luck! I'm in Matt's bad books anyway
BBC or Channel 4 BBC. Clare Balding is just different class
Strictly or The X Factor X Factor
Graham Norton or Jonathan Ross Jonathan Ross
Music R&B, hip hop
Holiday destination My favourite was South Africa. Next stop Atlantic City!

if I had reached as far as I was going to go. I've been on a gradual upward curve from the beginning of my career but, for me, it's been about raising the bar in small steps. I was very focused at the beginning of the year but I wasn't thinking about winning Group 1 races. At the same time, it wasn't an unrealistic aim."

The aim proved to be wholly realistic but, as so often in sport, its realisation was partly down to chance. The Darley July Cup was, for the first time, staged on a Saturday, a busy afternoon that also featured high-class fixtures at Ascot, York and Chester. Leading riders were spread thinly across the venues and, with Dream Ahead's regular jockey William Buick required by John Gosden on the Knavesmire, trainer David Simcock was forced to look elsewhere. Only on the morning of declaration did he settle on his replacement – and the chosen lady was certainly not expecting to be picked.

"I was in Superdrug when I got the phone call from my agent," she says. "I was very excited by the news but David never made a big deal out of **Continues, page 34**

Dream double Turner scores her first Group I victory on Dream Ahead in the July Cup (top left) and six weeks later wins another with Margot Did in the Nunthorpe Stakes, much to her delight

Trailblazers *Women riding high*

Hayley Turner leads an increasingly successful band of female Flat jockeys, who collectively passed 200 winners for the year in Britain for the first time.

The next-best is Cathy Gannon *(left)*, 30, who started as an apprentice with John Oxx and is now established in Britain as number one to David Evans. When she broke her leg in October she was in the top 20 for winners ridden in Britain in 2011, ahead of former champions Frankie Dettori and Seb Sanders.

The apprentices include Julie Burke *(right)*, 22, who is based with Kevin Ryan's powerful Yorkshire stable, having moved from her native Ireland last year. Another apprentice is Lucy Barry, 20, a former amateur over jumps who switched to the Flat last season and is now based with Clive Cox.

But they all have a long way to go to match Julie Krone *(left)*, the most successful female jockey of all time. The American legend rode 3,704 winners and was the first woman to win a Triple Crown race (1993 Belmont Stakes on Colonial Affair) and a Breeders' Cup race (2003 Juvenile Fillies on Halfbridled). Krone retired in 2004 but showed she hadn't lost it by winning the Leger Legends charity race at Doncaster in September, at the age of 48.

booking me and that helped massively. It meant I was able to ride the horse as if we were taking part in an ordinary race, which I think is the way to approach any big contest. If I'm honest, the huge number of high-quality fixtures that day played into my hands a bit, but everyone needs chances like that to break through. I went into the stalls in an extremely cool frame of mind. Afterwards, though, I was like an overexcited, annoying little girl."

The same sort of chance was not required in the Coolmore Nunthorpe Stakes. As York beckoned, nobody but Turner had ever steered Margot Did in a race. Together they had combined for four victories but also many narrow defeats, following some of which the rider was criticised. However, Margot Did's owners and trainer Michael Bell – the jockey's long-term boss – retained their belief in the value of the partnership. That belief was rewarded, as were those who backed the filly at 20-1.

"Winning on Margot was special," Turner says. "For a start it was for the guv'nor but also the owners had stuck by me. There were occasions when people accused me of giving her bad rides. In racing owners will very often decide to try someone different but they kept faith in me."

When Margot Did next appeared in the Prix de l'Abbaye, Turner was missing. A broken ankle, sustained prior to a race at Bath on August 31, forced her on to the injury sofa for the rest of the year. As a blow it was unfortunate and untimely but also undeniably less serious than the head injury that sidelined her for much of 2009. And the metaphorical mental scar left by that injury proved valuable in helping Britain's Shergar Cup captain cope with the setback.

"The head injury was such a big deal for me," she says. "I was on a high when it happened and then all of a sudden my job was taken away from me. I took it so badly. I felt very sorry for myself.
Continues, page 36

Trading places

All year the top sprinters took turns at beating each other in the Group 1s, which made for some thrilling – if somewhat confusing – results

King's Stand Stakes
Royal Ascot, June 14
Prohibit wins by half a length from Aussie raider Star Witness. Sole Power eighth, Monsieur Chevalier 11th and Tangerine Trees 19th

Golden Jubilee Stakes
Royal Ascot, June 18
Society Rock beats Monsieur Chevalier by half a length. Star Witness third, Bated Breath fifth, Hitchens 11th

July Cup
Newmarket, July 9
Dream Ahead wins by half a length from Bated Breath. Hitchens third, Star Witness tenth, Monsieur Chevalier 15th

Prix Maurice de Gheest
Deauville, August 7
Moonlight Cloud scores by four lengths from Society Rock. Dream Ahead seventh

Nunthorpe Stakes
York, August 19
Margot Did beats Hamish McGonagall by three-quarters of a length. Prohibit third, Hoof It sixth, Bated Breath ninth

Sprint Cup
Haydock, September 3
Dream Ahead beats Bated Breath and Hoof It by a nose and a head. Society Rock sixth, Hitchens ninth, Sole Power 12th

Prix de l'Abbaye
Longchamp, October 2
Tangerine Trees wins by a short neck from Secret Asset. Prohibit seventh, Margot Did 15th

I was a right diva but I've learnt from what happened and on this occasion I've handled things much better. This injury has been no big deal. You have to take the bad with the good and not get too fussed. Feeling sorry for yourself doesn't help."

But looking to the future does and Turner's looks bright. Bookmakers are already betting on her becoming the first British woman to win a Classic. The mere prospect of her landing a first ride in a Classic has triggered talk, a reflection of a gender-driven novelty value that Turner freely admits has been beneficial.

"Being a girl has helped me big time. My profile has been raised because of my sex. I generally get more publicity than the lads do and my name stands out because I'm slightly different. I wouldn't say it has helped me get rides because trainers aren't stupid, but in terms of the wider audience being a girl has undeniably helped me become more popular.

"Looking to 2012, I don't see why I couldn't ride in Classics but they are the other extreme and winning them is really difficult. If it happens, it happens. It's all about finding the right horse, which isn't something you can plan. What I am planning is to crack on in January in the same way I did this year. Come the start of the year I'll be ready to work hard. In fact my desire to do well will probably be even stronger because I will have been off for quite a long time."

In the build-up to her return expect to read plenty of Turner tweets. Whether through her website or Twitter, Turner is invariably active on a social media platform, partly because she enjoys it, partly because she knows it boosts her profile. Yet while she rejects comparisons with some of racing's biggest names – "I would never call myself a top jockey" – she is fully aware of her celebrity status and unashamedly loves everything that comes with it.

"I'm very lucky. I went to the British Racing School in Newmarket the other day to give a little speech to 16 students. Before I started they showed a DVD of my Group 1 winners and it gave me goose bumps. Everyone started applauding. I just thought: 'Oh my God.' I love it. I just love it."

Bill Selwyn

Award-winning horse racing press photographer

Working for the top titles, the premier eacecourses, and industry leaders in racing.
Equally at home at the Breeders' Cup, Japan Cup, morning gallops and the studs.

T: 0117 9651596 | **M:** 07771 904024 | **E:** billselwyn@blueyonder.co.uk
164 Park Road, Stapleton, Bristol BS16 1DW
racinginfocus.co.uk

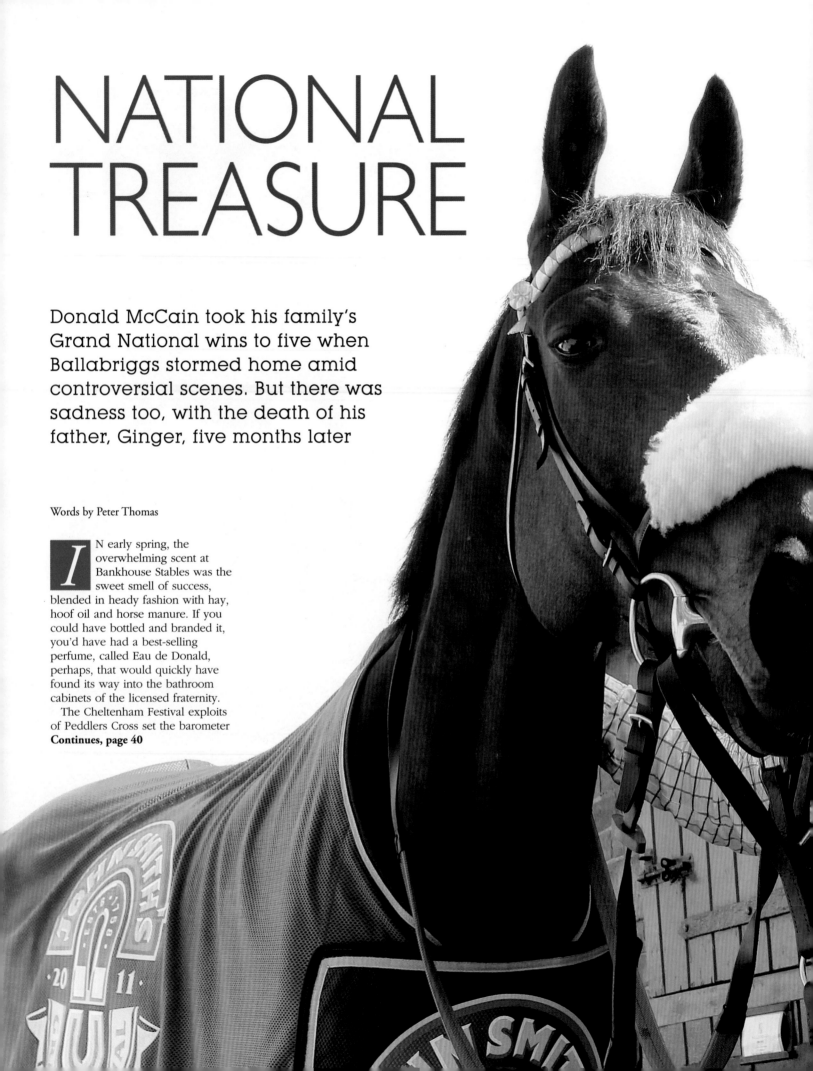

NATIONAL TREASURE

Donald McCain took his family's Grand National wins to five when Ballabriggs stormed home amid controversial scenes. But there was sadness too, with the death of his father, Ginger, five months later

Words by Peter Thomas

*I*N early spring, the overwhelming scent at Bankhouse Stables was the sweet smell of success, blended in heady fashion with hay, hoof oil and horse manure. If you could have bottled and branded it, you'd have had a best-selling perfume, called Eau de Donald, perhaps, that would quickly have found its way into the bathroom cabinets of the licensed fraternity.

The Cheltenham Festival exploits of Peddlers Cross set the barometer

Continues, page 40

To The Memory Of
RED RUM
From All The Lads
Who Will Miss You Most
18th October 1995

AMBERLEIGH
HOUSE
Winner Grand National 2004

needle twitching furiously in the quiet Cholmondeley parkland that insulates Donald McCain's stables from the outside world, but it was the John Smith's Grand National win of Ballabriggs that ensured a full month was spent in the eye of a perfect storm, fomented by history and success, set spinning by public outrage and unleashed with venom by a hungry media.

The racing world will remember the driving finish up the Liverpool run-in, the besuited trainer rushing to greet his hero, the familiarly inappropriate tones of Ginger McCain, a National institution himself, now asked to stamp a hallmark on the precious metal of his son's achievement.

Within five months Ginger had died, aged 80, having been at Aintree to see his son join him on the roll of honour. "I hope I made Dad proud," Donald says, "but it's not really a personal thing. It's just that we've been able to make the place something to be proud of, between all of us as a family.

"If it wasn't for the old man, I probably wouldn't have been involved in horses at all and what we've got now is all down to him. There's been no real change on a day-to-day basis [since Ginger died] except that every now and then you're expecting a bollocking you don't get."

McCain jnr remembers everything about Grand National day 2011 – just as he remembers the less complicated days of Red Rum's three triumphs – but he doesn't remember all of it fondly. The performance of Ballabriggs and Jason Maguire was his vision of perfection, but the ill-informed reactions to the race are still, quite plainly, under his skin as he recalls the scenes that followed – fevered news bulletins and front pages, flailing whips, exhausted horses, restorative buckets of water, emergency supplies of oxygen, accusations of abuse and brutality. Scenes that, it transpired later, had been stage-managed by the course executive to ensure, ironically enough, that horses received the best possible care after their exertions.

"It was absolutely roasting down there in that corner, where there's no breeze, and it was

Continues, page 42

An education quite unlike any other

A stint at Headquarters with Luca Cumani and Sir Michael Stoute gave Donald the chance of a fresh outlook, but mostly it confirmed to him that his dad was something of an instinctive genius.

"What I did learn in Newmarket was that it's all about learning how to use the facilities you've got," he explains. "I worked with some great trainers and picked up little details, but the majority of it is doing things that suit your facilities to get horses fit.

"When Dad was in Southport, it was frowned upon to train horses on sand, but what's everybody doing now? And I haven't yet seen a sand gallop as good as that one.

"He'd go down to the beach first thing, before the horses. He'd have his spike harrows hidden in the sand hills because the gypsies would nick 'em and he'd pull them out every morning, stick them behind whatever machine he was driving at the time, and he'd put sleepers or tyres on top of the harrow to make the spikes bite a bit deeper.

"Sometimes people would set up their deckchairs on the gallop and refuse to move, but when Dad told them there'd be half a dozen horses coming down there at 30mph in a couple of minutes, they usually saw sense.

"The one thing you really miss, the thing you'd like to bottle and bring with you, is the sea, but you have to work with what you've got. It was mind-blowing going to Newmarket and seeing what we'd been coping without, but what he had worked.

"There were a number of times when things were pretty going badly and Dad'd tell you if it hadn't been for Mum there wouldn't be a business today. I think sometimes it's hardest of all for her to adjust to the size and scale of things now, although she gives me an easier time than she gave Dad.

"[Ginger's death] came at the busiest time of year, when we were ready to get going, which I suppose helped. The place is rolling along quite nicely and that's all we ever wanted. It's not even about being successful. It's a way of life, we're settled, and we've got a grand place. Hopefully we'll be around a long time.

"It's only the odd personal moment you're missing. We've all kept busy, kept things rolling on and it's only every now and then you have a little quiet moment or something happens and you realise he's not about."

unbearable," he recalls. "I ducked under the rails and ran towards him and at first I thought there might be something wrong when I saw Jason get off him, but he was just tired, standard-issue tired, after running four and a half miles.

"As soon as I got there, I knew he was fine, but there was all this talk of him being given oxygen, as if something was wrong. They gave him a tube, not even as wide as a pencil, in one side of his nose. What difference is that going to make?

"The trouble is, the public don't see the horse ten minutes later. They have no concept of how he is, just fine, with not a mark on him. He was in the Isle of Man for the summer with [his owner] Trevor Hemmings and he'll be

Continues, page 44

'We don't abuse horses'

McCain on the media storm after last season's big race

"The problem for racing is that what many people see on television is the only bit they see. They don't see the other God knows how many hours. I could count on one hand the number of times one of my horses is hit behind the saddle at home, I won't let it be done, but at the races they are there to work, it's what they're bred for.

"Take Amberleigh House when he was third to Monty's Pass in the National in 2003. We were getting water on him for the best part of 40 minutes afterwards, because you have to get them to a certain stage before they'll take a drink, and he wouldn't take a drink, he was so tired. It's almost humbling because you know how hard they've tried. It's the sign of a good horse, a genuine horse, and you know what to do to get them back into shape. Does it do them any damage? Well, he came out the next year and won the National.

"All you can do for the public is to say let's use the whip less. Personally, I don't think there was an issue, because we don't abuse horses, but if something had to be done, then the best way was to have a set number of strokes, so nobody could be confused. They can all count and, after that, chuck 'em out, disqualify 'em. After four or five times, they'll learn."

ROSSDALES
VETERINARY SURGEONS

Based in Newmarket, Rossdales is a recognised international brand for equine veterinary excellence, providing personalised high quality veterinary services to the Thoroughbred community for over 50 years.

ROSSDALES
EQUINE PRACTICE

Tel: +44 (0)1638 663150
practice@rossdales.com

- First class routine and emergency (24 hour) local ambulatory services for Thoroughbred racehorse trainers and studs

- Advisory and veterinary services at major international Thoroughbred sales

- Consultancy service to the international equine insurance industry

ROSSDALES EQUINE HOSPITAL
& DIAGNOSTIC CENTRE

Tel: +44 (0)1638 577754
hospital@rossdales.com

- Large, well-respected referral centre offering state of the art facilities and equipment for horses and foals requiring specialist diagnostic procedures, surgery, standing surgery, medicine, treatment and care

- Reproductive medicine and surgery

- Referrals seen from practices throughout the UK and across Europe

BEAUFORT COTTAGE
LABORATORIES

Tel: +44 (0)1638 663017
laboratory@rossdales.com

- Specialist equine clinical pathology laboratories for Rossdales and many other UK and EU practices

- Cost-effective and efficient service with rapid turn-around times

WWW.ROSSDALES.COM

LEADERS IN EQUINE VETERINARY MEDICINE AND HEALTHCARE • NEWMARKET

with him for the rest of his life. Trevor has had that horse since he was a yearling and doted on him for all that time, just to see him do that for ten minutes of his ten-year life."

Criticism of the Grand National was given greater than normal credibility this year by the two equine deaths that marred the race, but the quietly outspoken 42-year-old will have no truck with suggestions that he and the vast majority of his colleagues are anything other than responsible practitioners and that his sport has no place in the modern world.

"Perhaps we should at some stage just stand up and say: 'This is what it is, it's part and parcel of what happens with livestock,'" he suggests. "But people just don't understand livestock any more.

"I can justify my part in racing by the way I treat my horses and by going down to the local cattle market and seeing the way the horses that are sold there are treated and how they end up. The public has to understand the options before it judges racing. By the middle of July, 80 per cent of my horses want to come in from the field. There's no fun for them there. They want to be in and they want to be working."

A traditional stockman McCain may be, but he's no unreconstructed backwoodsman. In his youth, he emigrated to Newmarket to serve his time with Sir Michael Stoute and Luca Cumani, picking up such fine detail as he needed to progress from being simply a chip off Ginger's block. And while he still views his charges as simple livestock, he's certainly not lacking in sentimentality, as you'll find if you ask him about his other star performer over jumps, the Stan James Champion Hurdle runner-up Peddlers Cross.

"At Cheltenham, I was absolutely devastated for him, because I could physically see him look Hurricane Fly in the eye, stick his chin out and try to get back past him," says McCain, turning ever so slightly misty-eyed. "It's humbling to see a horse try that hard and it still gets me a bit now. As he was walking back everybody was

clapping him and it gets to you when people who know what they're watching appreciate what you're doing. I think these are the people we should be looking after, not the people who ring up once a year to complain."

If 'Red' was the horse that put the McCains on the racing map, and Amberleigh House was the one that announced Donald, then a humble assistant to his father, as the coming force on Britain's northern tracks, it was the arrival of passionate yard sponsor Jon Glews, along with Hemmings and Tim Leslie, the yard's other great patron, that

enabled the quantum leap into the big time.

Peddlers Cross, a £100,000 purchase by Leslie, is the best example of the new, top-of-the-range model at McCain's disposal. There's a hint of trepidation in his voice as he charts the horse's future, but an underlying conviction that sending him over fences will show him in his best light.

"We're going novice chasing with a 170-rated hurdler," he says with a nervous laugh, "and when you say it like that it sounds crackers, but that's what he was bought for, pure and

simple, because of the way he jumped a fence in his Irish point-to-point win.

"He's the right age to go jumping and the worst thing I can do for him is to spend too long over hurdles now. I've genuinely never schooled him over fences, because he was a bit careful over hurdles and we were trying to get him quicker, but now he's lightning fast over hurdles we'll move on. I still genuinely don't know what trip he wants. I think he could get three miles, certainly two and a half, so already we've got the Arkle or the new two-and-a-half-

'Jason gave Ballabriggs one of the best rides you've seen round Aintree'

McCain on his stable jockey

As a former jockey who, by what seems now like a minor miracle, used to tip the scales at 10st, Donald McCain is both a sympathiser with jockeys' problems and an admirer of their craft, which is why he can be roused to a mild peak of anger by criticism the like of which was endured by Jason Maguire after his National-winning ride on Ballabriggs.

"Anybody in the sport thinks Jason gave the horse one of the best rides you've seen round Aintree," he declares. "All right, he gave the horse one smack too many after the last, but he was trying to win a Grand National. I get frustrated when we get punished for doing our best, yet you see 'the other stuff' going on every day of the week.

"If there's one better jockey around than Jason, then he's the only one, and although I do worry about things, my jockey is one thing I don't have to worry about any more. I'm very lucky and it's not just a working relationship, we're friends as well.

"He knows how I want horses ridden and sadly he takes the brunt of it with the stewards sometimes because I want them ridden positively, but he's one of those very talented Irishmen who've been doing it all their lives. If you asked him what he was doing, he probably couldn't tell you, but he's hard-working, strong, a tremendous natural horseman and a decision-maker – he's got everything. It's only when he's not here that you realise how much he means to the place."

mile chase at Cheltenham to aim at.

"I'm having to look at different bits of the programme book these days, bits I've never seen before, learning as I go along how to deal with a better type of horse."

With Ballabriggs, McCain will know precisely which page he is on. It's full steam ahead for the National again, with every reason to expect another monumental effort. "He'll get what weight he gets, there's no point moaning about it, and Dad used to say if you've got the topweight in the National every year, then great,

he's the best horse in the race.

"He'll be 11 next year, but he's a wonderful, old-fashioned staying chaser and winning the National at ten shouldn't be his limit – he's not French! He's only just creeping into racing at that level, so I don't see why he couldn't improve a touch, although he'll have to."

The National will always be part of the fabric of family and working life, but McCain has a team built along very different lines to the one managed by Ginger in the glory days of Red Rum. He's a different man, too, his own man, trying to develop

Dad's thick skin, but not his endless line of controversial patter.

The change has come hard to him, in many ways, but controlled ambition is steadily getting the better of set ways and old-fashioned good housekeeping.

"I genuinely don't think it's done me any harm dealing with moderate horses over the years," he says. "That's why I'm not entirely comfortable with the horses I've been selling recently. On the one hand, the ones I'm getting in are better than the

Continues, page 46

A NEW McCAIN RISING

2006-07 McCain takes over from father Ginger and makes an immediate impression, sending out Cloudy Lane to win the Kim Muir at the Cheltenham Festival and ending his debut season 20th in the trainers' table *40 winners*

2007-08 Another Cheltenham Festival winner as Whiteoak lands the inaugural David Nicholson Mares' Hurdle. McCain breaks the £500,000 prize-money mark to finish 11th in the trainers' table *58 winners*

2008-09 A season of consolidation with the number of winners and total prize-money up slightly but a drop of two places to 13th in the trainers' table. Cloudy Lane's win in the Grimthorpe Handicap Chase at Doncaster is the biggest success *62 winners*

2009-10 A major breakthrough as Peddlers Cross wins the Neptune Investment Novices' Hurdle at Cheltenham and follows up in the Mersey Novices' Hurdle at Aintree. Ballabriggs gives the stable a second Kim Muir, while Overturn wins the Scottish Champion Hurdle followed by the Northumberland Plate on the Flat. A first top-ten finish as McCain ends the season eighth in the trainers' table *88 winners*

2010-11 McCain continues the family tradition with Grand National winner Ballabriggs. Peddlers Cross wins the Fighting Fifth Hurdle and pushes Hurricane Fly all the way in the Champion Hurdle. Overturn wins the Galway Hurdle and has another big Flat success in the Chester Cup. The year-on-year improvement continues as the stable hits a first century and McCain jumps to third in the trainers' table *100 winners*

ones I'm getting rid of, but the ones I'm getting rid of are horses I'd have been glad to have a few seasons ago.

"All we've ever wanted to do is be around nice horses, though, and that's what we're doing now. Over the summer there was a field a couple of miles from here where there were eight horses, you'd give your eye teeth for any one of them, and another field a couple of miles the other way that was exactly the same. They all came in for the winter and every now and then I'll sit down and think, 'I forgot he was coming in, or he was coming in', and it makes you smile, makes you shake your head sometimes. It can seem like a long summer, waiting for those good horses."

During that long summer wait, with paintbrushes slapping busily and diggers toiling on a new all-weather strip, Bankhouse had a whiff of creosote and masonry paint, with a hint of disinfectant and gentle overtones of diesel fumes and impatience. The fragrance of champions it was not – rather the natural odour of a successful training yard forced into hibernation by the passing of the seasons.

Now, however, with the smell of creosote blown away on the Cheshire breeze, an even sweeter, stronger smell of success is in the winter air again.

National fallout Racing's path to reform

Aintree announced in August that the Grand National course would be modified, in response to the outcry that followed this year's race

Becher's Brook
6th fence on first circuit, 22nd on second
The landing side will be re-profiled to reduce the current drop by between 10cm and 12.5cm across the width of the fence. This will provide a more level landing area for horses. The new drop will be approximately 25cm on the inside of the course and 15cm on the outside. This difference in drop from the inside to the outside of the fence is being retained to encourage riders to spread out across the width of the fence and to retain the unique characteristics of Becher's Brook. The height of the fence will remain unaltered at 1.47m (4ft 10in)

First fence
17th on second circuit
The landing side will be levelled to reduce the current drop and provide a more level landing. This aims to avoid catching out horses that may over-jump the fence early in the race. The height of the fence will remain unaltered at 1.37m (4ft 6in)

Fourth fence
20th on second circuit
The fence will be reduced in height by 5cm to 1.47m (4ft 10in). The review identified that fences four and six (Becher's) were statistically the most difficult to jump

Toe boards
These are the orange boards at the base of each fence that provide a clear ground line to assist horses in determining the bottom of the fence. Their height will be increased to 36cm

Jason Maguire's winning ride on Ballabriggs aroused considerable criticism after he struck his mount 17 times on the run-in. He was banned for five days but would face a much more severe penalty under new rules brought into force in October following a BHA review

The new whip rules
● Jockeys allowed to use whip no more than seven times in Flat races and eight over jumps

● Only five strikes permitted after the last obstacle or inside the final furlong

● Minimum five-day ban for excessive use

● Banned jockeys to forfeit riding fee and prize-money percentage

● Increased penalties for repeat offenders (ban doubled for second offence)

Under the new rules Maguire would have been suspended for 29 days after the National (five days for the breach, plus two days for every strike of the whip above the permitted maximum of five after the last fence). He would also have forfeited his prize-money percentage, amounting to £35,854, and riding fee of £148.95

The McCains were not the only clan to uphold a National family tradition. The Irish version, at Fairyhouse on April 25, was won by Nina Carberry on Organisedconfusion, trained by her uncle Arthur Moore. The six-year-old's five-length victory was Moore's second success in the Easter highlight but the first for Carberry as she joined her grandfather Dan Moore, father Tommy and brothers Paul and Philip as National winners.

Here's the National roll of honour for Nina and her family

Nina Carberry Rides Organisedconfusion to victory in 2011 Irish National for uncle Arthur Moore

Tommy Carberry (father) Wins Irish National as a jockey on Brown Lad in 1975 and 1976 and as a trainer in 1998 with Bobbyjo. Rides L'Escargot to victory in the 1975 National at Aintree for

father-in-law Dan Moore and scores as a trainer with Bobbyjo in 1999

Paul Carberry (brother) Wins 1998 Irish National on Bobbyjo, trained by father Tommy, and follows up in the National at Aintree on the same horse a year later

Philip Carberry (brother) Wins 2006 Irish National on the Pat Hughes-trained Point Barrow

Arthur Moore (uncle) Rides King's Sprite to win 1971 Irish National and scores as a trainer with Feathered Gale in 1996 and Organisedconfusion in 2011

Dan Moore (grandfather) Wins the Irish National as a jockey on Golden Jack in 1943 and Revelry in 1947 and as a trainer with Tied Cottage in 1979. Wins 1975 National at Aintree with L'Escargot, ridden by son-in-law Tommy Carberry

Thirty years ago racing would have circled the wagons and tried to ignore the furore. But times have changed and, thankfully, racing has too

COMMENT
Alastair Down

The sport has to respect sensible opinion

RACING is less defensive and more honest than of old when confronting the inevitable PR calamities that befall it – and there were too many of those in 2011 – even if we are probably not brutal or frank enough about the sport's realities.

In the days after the John Smith's Grand National racing was under siege from a hostile media following the deaths of two horses, the spectacle of exhausted finishers being desperately sluiced with water in unseasonably warm temperatures and the winning jockey being banned for hitting his horse 17 times on the run-in.

Some of the media coverage was hysterical and 30 years ago racing would have circled the wagons and tried to ignore the furore. But times

have changed and, thankfully, racing has too.

Aintree and the British Horseracing Authority announced an immediate inquiry and in August came modifications to the National course and, a month later, new rules on use of the whip – a longstanding area of public concern.

Racing takes place by the consent of the general public. If they found the sport to be cruel it would wither and die. So it is utterly right that we should respect the sensibilities of the majority, and the changes at Aintree and the new whip rules do just that.

But there is a difference between respecting sensible opinion and cravenly kow-towing to ignorance. Racing should front up a little more plainly to the fact that horses and, more importantly, jockeys are killed in what is an inherently dangerous sport and that nothing, short of banning it, will ever prevent such sad fatalities.

Risk is ever-present when horses race. At Ascot on King George day the 30,000 in the stands witnessed the distressing spectacle of the stricken Rewilding careering on after breaking a leg and then, after the screens had been erected, being put down 50 yards before the line.

Winning trainer John Gosden gave a brilliant interview to the BBC when, with compassion and the authority of a lifetime spent with horses, he put Rewilding's fate into perspective and tried to reassure viewers over the

degree to which the horse suffered.

But, of course, Rewilding did suffer and it would be dishonest to pretend otherwise. And, however much we improve safety on racecourses, fatal injuries will occur. People must make their own choice as to whether that is an acceptable price to pay for their sport and entertainment.

We live in an increasingly risk-averse society and there is a sense in which racing will never fully comply with the new orthodoxy. Indeed for many jumps fans it is the conquering of the dangers that is part of the appeal.

But we should never have any truck with those who, by intention or omission, abuse the horse. Racing made the news for vile reasons when Howard Johnson was banned for running a horse after having its leg de-nerved, thereby exposing horses and humans to indefensible and avoidable risk.

With an additional ban for using steroids bringing the total to four years, Johnson was punished in such a way as to make his reappearance in the sport almost impossible. Racing could do no more than cast him into professional outer darkness.

This was a rough year for racing, with the sport so often ending up on the news bulletins as well as the sports reports. But decisive action was taken over Aintree and the whip and a prominent trainer was shamed for irresponsibility and cruelty. That is an eminently defendable record.

Dream COME TRUE

Words by Nick Pulford

An outstanding season for three-year-old fillies was capped by the Arc one-two of Danedream and Shareta. The first part of a special focus on racing's first ladies tells the remarkable story of the German-trained Arc winner

ndrasch Starke had a dream before the Prix de l'Arc de Triomphe but he didn't dare to share it with anyone. If he was asked about his chances on the filly Danedream, the German jockey would answer that he hoped to finish in the first four. "That would be beautiful," he would say. But in his head he was telling himself something different: "If I have the chance to finish in the first four then maybe, just maybe, I can win."

If Starke had voiced his innermost thoughts out loud, few would have taken him

seriously. Danedream's owners may have thought her worthy of the €100,000 supplementary fee three days before the Arc but she was a 20-1 shot, a mere German Group 1 winner in a stellar field. The nine ahead of her in the betting had won 22 Group 1 races between them in top international company as far afield as Japan, Australia and Hong Kong, as well as on the traditional battlegrounds of Europe. And that's without mentioning the winners of the 2011 Irish Derby and Coronation Cup or the previous year's Arc runner-up.

All were seemingly of a higher standard than Danedream, despite the wide margins of her victories in the Grosser Preis von Berlin and Grosser Preis von Baden. Surely the Arc was a 'grosser preis' that was too big for her. When he assessed the strength of the opposition in the cold light of day, Starke was inclined to agree. "No, I didn't think she could win – not judging on her work, on the other horses in the race. She had never run against such tremendous horses. It was a really competitive race, with so many Group 1 winners. How could you say she'd win?"

But there was the other voice, the one that came to him at night. "I didn't say it to anybody, but in my dreams, when I went to bed, I said 'maybe, this is my chance to win the Arc'."

There was some logic at work too. "The one thing about her was that she was **Continues, page 54** winning by five or six lengths every time. I wasn't having to fight to win by a short head. I thought if Danedream hadn't run in those races and they had been won by a Group 1 horse from England instead, the winning distances wouldn't have been any bigger. It made me think I had a little chance to win."

If Starke had dreamt about the whole Arc from start to finish, it would have gone something like this: "I had a beautiful draw, number two. I thought the Japanese horse [Hiruno D'Amour] would go close and I decided to follow him. There was a lot of speed in the race, with the O'Brien horse [Treasure Beach] making the running. I sat very handy in sixth or seventh and there was no trouble. It wasn't rough, it was a beautiful race and I had a clear run.

"Before the last turn, I saw two or three jockeys were riding strongly on my outside and in front of me. When I arrived in the straight I went to the inside and everybody was pushing hard and I just let her go. I didn't even try to push her. I thought 'this is not real', I couldn't believe what was happening. I thought 'I'll wait, I'll wait', but then when I had only two horses in front of me I knew it was time to kick. I knew another horse wouldn't be able to come from behind and catch me. She was going too good."

The reality was better than any dream. Danedream won by five lengths in race-record time, beating the mark set by Peintre Celebre in 1997. "To win on Danedream was a brilliant moment for me," says Starke, 37. "I'd never felt such emotion before. I've won the German Derby five times and I've won in Hong Kong and Singapore, which was a great feeling, but the Arc is something very special. You really get the feeling this is the biggest race in the world."

ON Arc day 2010 Danedream was nothing like the filly she would become. She lined up a 33-1 outsider in the eight-runner field for the Prix Marcel Boussac and finished sixth, beaten just under six lengths by the Aidan O'Brien-trained Misty For Me, who would go on to Classic success as a three-year-old.

There was another notable in the field in Galikova, who finished half a length in front of Danedream, but at the time the also-rans looked nothing special. That impression appeared to

Money doesn't always talk

Several of this year's Group 1 winners were from racing's bargain basement, having been available at sums that barely, if at all, crept into five figures

Danedream The Arc winner cost Heiko Volz just €9,000 at the 2010 Baden-Baden spring horses in training sale and her owner is sure to have made a big profit when he sold a half-share to Teruya Yoshida shortly before the Arc. The Arc took her earnings to almost £2.5m and she is now valued at more than £2m. "She didn't look particularly impressive and her half-siblings weren't very talented, so we decided to sell," said Julia Baum of Gestut Brummerhof, which bred the filly. "It looks a bad decision now"

Tangerine Trees Having been led out unsold at 8,000gns at the 2006 Doncaster October yearling sale, the six-year-old hit the jackpot in the Prix de l'Abbaye for owners Marie Matthews, who bred him, and Pat Barrell. The Abbaye took his earnings past £250,000 and Barrell, a retired nurse, said: "At least we've now got some money in the bank to keep him going"

Dream Ahead Another cheaply bought Arc day winner, adding the Prix de la Foret to his successes in the July Cup and Haydock Sprint Cup. He cost 36,000gns as a two-year-old at the Doncaster breeze-up sale in April 2010 but had been even cheaper as a yearling, fetching just $11,000 at the Keeneland September sale. After the Foret, which was his fifth Group 1 win, his earnings stood at £810,186

Margot Did In the same month that Dream Ahead was sold at Doncaster, Margot Did was an even cheaper breeze-up purchase for 10,000gns at Tattersalls, having cost €16,000 as a yearling at Goffs six months earlier. Like Dream Ahead she turned into a Group 1-winning sprinter, landing the Nunthorpe at York in August to take her earnings beyond £250,000

be confirmed when Danedream was beaten in a Group 3 at Baden-Baden next time and, when she reappeared as a three-year-old, was sent to Italy for her first three starts.

She was beaten in a Listed race, finished a creditable third in the Italian Derby and then won the Italian Oaks, one of the weakest Classics around. "She won very well, but honestly it wasn't the best field," Starke says. "But she couldn't do any more than win easily and she gave me a really good feeling."

Only fifth next time when upped in class for the Group 2 Prix de Malleret at Saint-Cloud, she was kept at home after that for the Group 1 Grosser Preis von Berlin but still the signs weren't promising. "She's not a strong, big-muscled horse, she doesn't look anything much," Starke says, "and at

home she shows you nothing. If she works with a class four or class five horse she just stays alongside. She never works like a Group 1 horse, never ever."

Danedream was a revelation in Berlin, winning by five lengths. She ran away with the Grosser Preis von Baden too, by six lengths, but it was difficult to measure her against the type of opponents she would face if she went for the Arc. "She had never beaten Group 1 horses from England," Starke says. "If two or three Group 1 horses had come from England to Baden-Baden, then maybe you could say she was at their level, but she had just beaten German horses. I didn't really know how to compare them with the international horses."

Heiko Volz, the filly's owner, was **Continues, page 56**

Continues, page 56

Source an
Ex-racehorse

Source an Ex-racehorse is the UKs only website dedicated to the horse out of training and is solely for the purpose of buying, selling, loaning and rehoming such horses, whether directly out of a training yard or having been out of the racing environment for a period time; whether having undergone any formal re-training or not.

The site is open to any horse that has been in training whether suitable only as a companion or for light hacking through to those which show greater potential or are already proven in the competition sphere. At present, statistically, horses directly from trainers' yards are being sold more quickly than other horses as there is increasing demand for horses that have had no formal retraining as riding horses.

Fully endorsed by the RoR, BHA, NTF, ROA and TBA the site is run by Fred and Rowena Cook of Equine Management & Training who are well-known for their experience and knowledge of retraining racehorses; indeed they also run the RoR's Helpline providing constructive, practical advice to owners of former racehorses.

The RoR of course is the Charity set up by the BHA in 2000. Over the years the Charity has established Classes, Series and Challenges for horses and riders of all abilities and also holds demonstrations and training clinics around the country to provide management and training guidance to those wishing to rehome, or have already rehomed, a racehorse.

The idea of Source an Ex-racehorse was a logical development in association with the retraining work of Equine Management and Training and the activities of the RoR. Following a period of consultation and discussion with the Charitys Trustees and Chairman, Source an Ex-racehorse was born.

Although primarily for the purpose of rehoming, the site is also being developed as a resource for information relating to the management and training of the former racehorse.

For further information please visit www.sourceanexracehorse.co.uk

I'll always remember how lucky I was to have this day and a horse like that. Maybe you ride a horse like that just one time in your life

keen to have an Arc runner, however, and the date with destiny was sealed after he sold a half-share to Japanese owner-breeder Teruya Yoshida. The rest, as they say, is history.

STARKE'S journey to Arc winner had a few bumps along the way too. He has a good pedigree, as the son of an amateur jump jockey and a protégé of Bruno Schutz, renowned for his skill as both a trainer of horses and riders.

Nor was there any doubt about his talent, which was quick to shine through after he was apprenticed to Schutz at 15. By the age of 26 he had been German champion three times and won two German Derbies. Skills honed on the ice at St Moritz meant he was at home on the tight turns of Happy Valley in Hong Kong, where he won the prestigious International Jockeys' Championship in 2000.

Anyone who saw his fearless and tactically astute riding that night would have predicted a bright future, but within days Starke had been suspended following a positive breath test at a

Hong Kong race meeting. It was a major blow for a jockey who had been waiting five years for just such an opportunity on the international stage, but worse was to come two years later when he was banned for six months after testing positive for a major metabolite of cocaine, again in Hong Kong. He was still in great demand at home, but chances of international glory were few and far between. Before the Arc his biggest victory outside Germany was in the 2004 Singapore Airlines International Cup on Epalo, trained by Andreas Schutz, Bruno's son.

That helps to explain his joyous celebrations at the Arc. Truly this felt like a once-in-a-lifetime moment. "I'll always remember how lucky I was to have this day and a horse like that. Maybe you ride a horse like that just one time in your life," he says.

"You see how she kicked in the Arc, it was amazing. From the first to the last horse there were so many lengths, I could hardly believe it. Okay, it wasn't the Arc when she won her Group 1s in Germany, but she did it three times in the same style. This filly is definitely something special, like Zarkava."

Zarkava, the 2008 winner, had been the last filly to land the Arc, but perhaps Danedream is more comparable with Urban Sea, the mare who caused an even bigger upset than her in the 1993 Arc. Like Danedream, Urban Sea left her previous form behind that day but ultimately she made an indelible mark as the dam of Sea The Stars and arguably the best broodmare of recent years.

The new Urban Sea? That's what Yoshida will be hoping, but it's another dream entirely.

Win a VIP trip for four to Chester's historic May Festival

CHESTER RACECOURSE

The *Racing Post Annual* has teamed up with Chester Racecourse to offer you the chance to be part of the historic May Festival in 2012 and to take three friends along for the ride.

This fabulous prize includes:
- Admission for four on Wednesday, May 9
- An exclusive behind-the-scenes racecourse tour
- Private table located in the Final Furlong Restaurant
- A glass of Pimm's on arrival
- Two-course carvery (main course followed by a selection of desserts or cheese)

- Complimentary bar (includes house wines, beers, lagers and soft drinks)

PLUS:
- Overnight stay for four in the Chester Abode which overlooks the racecourse, with a three-course dinner in the Michael Caines restaurant
- First-class train travel to Chester with Virgin Trains

Simply answer this question:

WHO TRAINED THE 2011 CHESTER CUP WINNER OVERTURN?

A) RICHARD FAHEY
B) DONALD McCAIN
C) DAVID PIPE

ABode
CHESTER

Virgin trains

BLUE
IS THE COLOUR

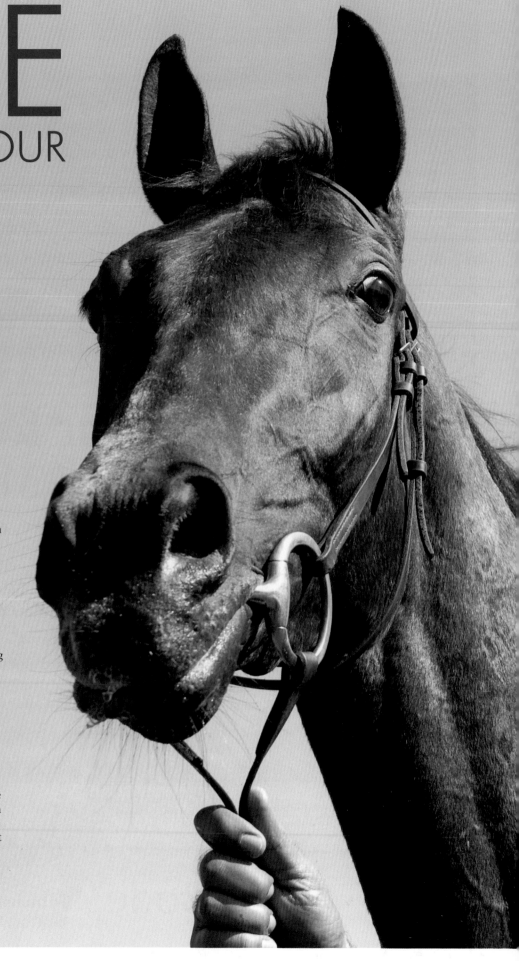

Mahmood Al Zarooni was an unknown two years ago. Now he's a Classic-winning trainer thanks to Sheikh Mohammed's faith in him and a filly called Blue Bunting

Words by Julian Muscat

If Mahmood Al Zarooni continues on the upward trajectory set in his first two years as a Godolphin trainer, Blue Bunting might one day be the answer to a taxing quiz question: who was his first British Classic winner?

The Qipco 1,000 Guineas heroine is surely the first of many for Al Zarooni, given the blue-blooded talent at his disposal and the careful skill he has shown already in bringing the best out of his string. Blue Bunting herself could not add another British Classic, failing for different reasons in the Investec Oaks and the Ladbrokes St Leger, but she also gave Al Zarooni a first Irish Classic success in the Darley Irish Oaks.

Her Guineas triumph may have been a watershed, not just for Al Zarooni but for Godolphin too, as it was their first success in a Newmarket Classic in nine years. The same amount of time had elapsed since Godolphin had won two British or Irish Classics in the same season and again Blue Bunting put that right with her Irish Oaks success.

Just for good measure, and to cement her high status among Europe's fillies and mares, she added the Darley Yorkshire Oaks against her elders, albeit in a sub-standard renewal.

Continues, page 60

Flying high Mahmood Al Zarooni with Blue Bunting, who gave him a first Classic win in the Qipco 1,000 Guineas that was celebrated in trademark style by Frankie Dettori

"For her to win three Group 1 races in the summer was very special," Al Zarooni says. "To me, she is the best horse I have trained so far."

The first is the sweetest, they say, and that helps to explain why Blue Bunting is close to her trainer's heart. But there was always something about her, despite a somewhat troubled start. "She was never quite 100 per cent as a two-year-old," Al Zarooni says, "and she had to have a bone chip removed from one of her legs."

A winner twice from three juvenile starts, she missed the annual migration of horses to Dubai and spent the winter in Newmarket. "William [Balding, a key Godolphin employee] followed the winter programme His Highness set out for her and when we came back [in April] we were delighted with how she looked," the trainer says.

Her wellbeing was apparent before the 1,000 Guineas, when she had flecks of

I still can't believe how lucky I've been. I was very happy but it was also a shock to me. I didn't know how to thank His Highness

roan hairs down one side of her neck that glinted in the sun. Otherwise bay all over, it turned out Blue Bunting was changing colour much later than is common in thoroughbreds.

Those roan flecks dimmed the glow usually associated with healthy bay horses. "When she was young everyone said she never looked that well," Al Zarooni says, "but that was because of the grey hairs in her coat. I have never seen another horse like that."

After her Newmarket triumph Blue Bunting strove to emulate Godolphin's 2002 Guineas winner Kazzia by adding the Oaks, but a troubled passage saw her find racing room all too late and her misfortune was compounded when Frankie Dettori eased her prematurely to forfeit third place.

It was a different story when she travelled to the Curragh for the Irish Oaks. Opposed by Dancing Rain and Wonder Of

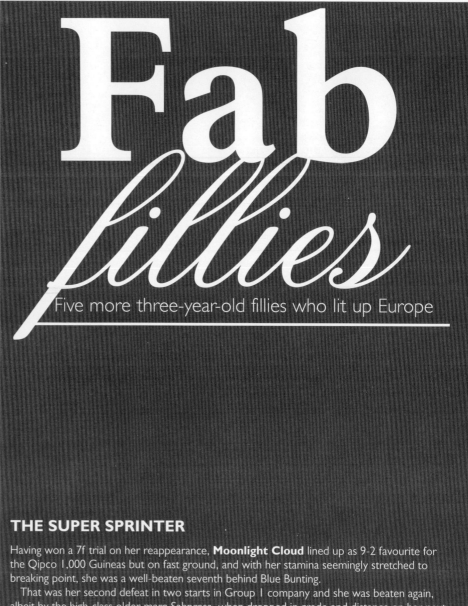

Fab fillies

Five more three-year-old fillies who lit up Europe

THE SUPER SPRINTER

Having won a 7f trial on her reappearance, **Moonlight Cloud** lined up as 9-2 favourite for the Qipco 1,000 Guineas but on fast ground, and with her stamina seemingly stretched to breaking point, she was a well-beaten seventh behind Blue Bunting.

That was her second defeat in two starts in Group 1 company and she was beaten again, albeit by the high-class older mare Sahpresa, when dropped in grade and distance on her next start in the Group 3 Prix du Palais-Royal over 7f. A less exacting Group 3 brought her back to winning ways and then it was time for another crack at a Group 1.

This time Moonlight Cloud was stunning as she stormed home by 4l in the Prix Maurice de Gheest over 6½f at Deauville, with four Group 1 winners among the next six home. Her RPR jumped 11lb to 122, putting her firmly in the big league even if she was disappointing in the British Champions Sprint at Ascot in October.

And she was not the only three-year-old filly to shine in the top sprints, with Margot Did going from Listed class to victory in the Coolmore Nunthorpe Stakes.

Wonders, who had finished first and second at Epsom, Blue Bunting reversed the form with a late thrust that nailed Banimpire in the final stride. Banimpire and Wonder Of Wonders were again among her victims in the Yorkshire Oaks, when she wore down Vita Nova close home.

Defeat in the St Leger did nothing to dim her lustre. "I had a feeling she wouldn't run so well there," says Al

Zarooni. "She had gone in her coat and she'd had a hard season."

Sheikh Mohammed plucked Al Zarooni from anonymity in 2009 by installing him as assistant to Saeed Bin Suroor. He oversaw Godolphin's horses at Moulton Paddocks for one season and returned there in 2010 with a trainer's licence. He has not looked back.

"I still can't believe how lucky I've been. I was very happy but it was also a

THE LATE BLOOMER

Immortal Verse blossomed in midsummer and conjured a majestic display in the Prix Jacques le Marois. Confronted by a stellar field, she burst from the rear to overhaul Goldikova, who had not been beaten by a filly in almost two years.

Three months earlier that level of performance seemed most unlikely. She was withdrawn from the Qipco 1,000 Guineas after playing up in the stalls and was well beaten behind Golden Lilac in the French 1,000. In truth nothing much had been expected of her in either Classic (she was sent off at 66-1 and 25-1 respectively) after managing only one win in her three previous starts, in a minor conditions race at Deauville on her debut as a two-year-old.

The first real hint of ability came three weeks after the French Guineas when she won the Group 2 Prix de Sandringham at Chantilly and by now she was progressing fast. Just 12 days later she was at Royal Ascot for the Group 1 Coronation Stakes and charged from last in the 12-runner field to mow down Nova Hawk.

She earned an RPR of 122 after doing the same to Goldikova, a remarkable rise from the personal-best 97 she had recorded in the French 1,000.

THE LADY IN WAITING

Galikova, as well as being one of an uncommonly talented French crop of three-year-old fillies, is half-sister to the remarkable Goldikova. Disappointment often waits in store for the younger siblings of equine luminaries, but Galikova has risen to the challenge.

She was runner-up to Golden Lilac in the Prix de Diane – a race in which Goldikova was third as a three-year-old – and turned the tables to beat that filly

THE GIANT KILLER

Surprisingly, for a filly who was a dual Group 1 winner at two, **Misty For Me** was sent off favourite just once as a three-year-old and on that occasion was only third behind Emulous in the Group 1 Coolmore Fusaichi Pegasus Matron Stakes.

By then, however, Aidan O'Brien's filly had proved herself again at the top level with a Classic victory over better-fancied stablemate Together in the Etihad Airways Irish 1,000 Guineas and, most impressively, a front-running success that left Midday trailing six lengths behind in the Stobart Ireland Pretty Polly Stakes.

An RPR of 120 for the Pretty Polly was one of the standout performances by a three-year-old filly in a season when internationally proven mares such as Midday and Goldikova at times found it tough going against the juniors.

handsomely in the Prix Guillaume d'Ornano. She followed up by winning her first Group 1 prize in the Prix Vermeille before finishing ninth in the Arc. That run may not have been indicative of her talent, as she had beaten Arc runner-up Shareta, her fellow three-year-old filly, in three previous meetings.

This daughter of Galileo stays better than Goldikova – and stays in training in 2012. Her rate of improvement was such that her four-year-old campaign is anticipated with bated breath.

THE FRONT-RUNNER

When **Dancing Rain** made all to land the Investec Oaks in June, much of the credit went to Johnny Murtagh for stealing the race on the 20-1 shot. But after the William Haggas-trained filly won two more major races in similar fashion, she should be given her due too. After all, she won two Classics, beat her elders on British Champions Day at Ascot and earned almost £550,000.

After winning the Oaks by three-quarters of a length Dancing Rain was only fifth of nine in the Darley Irish Oaks behind Blue Bunting, the Epsom fourth, after being denied the lead.

But she was back in her preferred role in the Preis der Diana (German Oaks) at Dusseldorf and scored an easy three-length win.

Haggas prepared her carefully for the valuable autumn races and she did not run again until Champions Day, when she was one of a trio of three-year-olds in a ten-runner field for the Qipco British Champions Fillies' and Mares' Stakes. And there was a continuation of two familiar themes – the juniors beating the elders and Dancing Rain making all – as she held Bible Belt by two lengths in a one-two for the three-year-olds.

shock to me [to get the job]. I didn't know how to thank His Highness. It was not enough to say thank you, so I said to myself: 'Mahmood, you must try your hardest to pay him back with good results'."

Blue Bunting is the kind of early repayment that comes with no penalty and then there was Rewilding, who promised so much with his victories in the Sheema Classic and Prince of Wales's

Stakes before his untimely end.

Finding another Rewilding won't be easy, but there are promising Group-winning juveniles in Gamilati, Lyric Of Light and Discourse, and Al Zarooni hopes Blue Bunting will stay in training in 2012.

After this year's successes and his surge up the trainers' table, what Al Zarooni does from now on will be watched with great interest.

Godolphin's three-year-old filly Deraasa
exercises at Al Quoz stables, Dubai, in March
against the backdrop of the Burj Khalifa, at 828m
the world's tallest building **Edward Whitaker**

LONG
LIVE THE
KING

The old regime was swept aside as the six-year-old Long Run captured the biggest prizes in jump racing, the Cheltenham Gold Cup and King George VI Chase. Owner Robert Waley-Cohen and his son Sam recount their glorious campaign and look forward to a lasting reign

Words by Peter Thomas

*I*F Robert Waley-Cohen has a weakness as a racehorse owner and breeder, it's his enthusiasm. Not that it's such a bad thing to be wildly and eternally optimistic in a game that crushes dreams like eggshells, but there are times when a little restraint can come in handy.

When Long Run stretched out of the home turn in the Totesport Cheltenham Gold Cup, with former champions Kauto Star and Denman at his mercy, the unstoppable 62-year-old simply couldn't control his vast reserves of vocal positivity. He began shouting as his son Sam unleashed the mighty bay up the Cheltenham hill and didn't stop until the last roars of a feverish crowd had floated away on the March breeze – and rest assured this was no ordinary shouting, rather the full-throttle bellow of a man whose lifetime's ambition was being realised on jump racing's most hallowed strip of turf.

"I'm told the volume of noise was quite amazing," he recalls with a smile. "I shouted him home from the last bend and finished utterly hoarse. I've never known a race take so long from the last fence to the winning line.

"Luckily, my brother Stephen is chairman of RADA and he called me later to say the Head of Voice had offered me an hour's tuition on how to shout without losing your voice, which I took up gladly. I went to the Gielgud Theatre and practised addressing people in the rafters. I didn't lose my

Continues, page 66

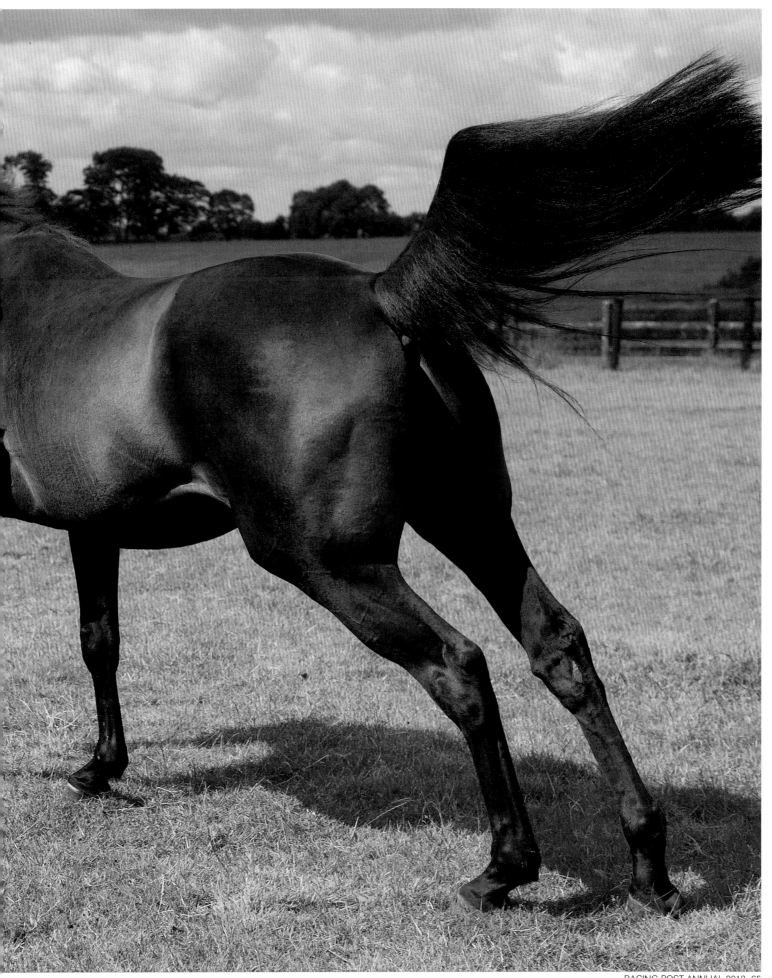

All my geese are swans and every new horse is a possible Gold Cup winner. The trouble is, if you tell people that, some of them take it literally

voice in the Grand National, cheering Oscar Time into second place, so clearly she was a good tutor."

With friends in such high places, it's plainly easier to recover from the after-effects of high excitement, just as a family fortune, a country estate in Oxfordshire and a thriving business will always ease the pain of dashed hope, but for Waley-Cohen his love of racing is about anything but financial gain. His optimism covers every equine purchase he makes and every mating for each of his precious broodmares, and it is the lifeblood of his passion for the Turf.

When he bought Long Run, he paid a small fortune, not in the hope of making a large fortune, but in the expectation of making a heavy loss and the fantasy that he would end up with a champion on his hands. This was the fourth horse he'd had out of the mare Libertina, the third full-brother, and the others had proved not especially sound and not gifted enough to be remembered, so it was a leap of faith for both Sam, ever the realist, and Robert, the self-confessed romantic.

"My expectations are always sky high," the owner laughs, with just a hint of self-deprecation. "All my geese are swans and every new horse is a possible Gold Cup winner. The trouble is, if you tell people that, some of them take it literally.

"After he won his Grade 1

hurdle as a three-year-old in France, nobody wanted to enjoy the moment, they all asked me what next. I said: 'Look at him, in five years' time, when he's eight and he's won three Gold Cups, he'll go and win the National,' and they all scribbled it down. I said, 'If you seriously think I know what this horse will be doing in five years' time, if he or the rest of us are even alive by then, you must be bigger fools than I think you are.' But at least we're on target!"

The first of Long Run's bullseyes came when he turned the long-delayed King George into a procession at Kempton, the second on that gloriously noisy afternoon at Cheltenham, and anybody who saw the handsome dark bay loping up

the hill that day wouldn't bet heavily against his owner's pipe dreams of multiple championships becoming reality.

In a race that contained the winners of the previous four Gold Cups, all of them still in the front line as the fight reached its fiercest heat, the raw recruit surpassed all expectations at Cheltenham with an effort worthy of a battle-hardened campaigner. If they'd been giving out medals, he'd have been handed a chestful, for valour, bravery, devotion beyond the call and simply for being the best long-distance steeplechaser in training. As it was, Waley-Cohen received a small, shiny trophy for his mantelpiece and Long Run was rewarded with a **Continues, page 68**

When we were young

How Long Run measures up to some of the all-time great chasers at the same age

Long Run's British career in pictures

1 Feltham Novices' Chase, Kempton, December 26, 2009. Won

2 Kingmaker Novices' Chase, Warwick, February 13, 2010. Won

3 RSA Chase, Cheltenham, March 17, 2010. Third

4 Paddy Power Gold Cup, Cheltenham, November 13, 2010. Third

5 William Hill King George VI Chase, Kempton, January 15, 2011. Won

6 Totesport Cheltenham Gold Cup, March 18, 2011. Won

Long Run Started chasing in France just a month after his actual fourth birthday and seven months later he won the Grade 1 Feltham Novices' Chase on his British debut. Won the King George shortly after his official sixth birthday and his Cheltenham Gold Cup win came 18 days before his actual sixth birthday. Career record: 1 Gold Cup, 1 King George

Arkle Won the Broadway Chase (the equivalent of the RSA Chase) in 1963 as a novice at the age of six and was beaten by Mill House later that year in the Hennessy. The first of his three Cheltenham Gold Cups came in March 1964, just over a month shy of his seventh birthday, as he asserted his supremacy over Mill House. Career record: 3 Gold Cups, 1 King George

Desert Orchid Was pulled up in the 1985 Champion Hurdle and by the time of his last run that season, two days after his actual sixth birthday, his race record stood at seven wins from 20 starts. Won his first King George just before officially turning eight and had to wait until the age of ten for his sole Gold Cup. Career record: 1 Gold Cup, 4 King Georges

Kauto Star Became a Grade 1 winner in the Tingle Creek Chase a month before he officially turned six but fell in the 2006 Champion Chase four days shy of his actual sixth birthday. Won his first King George later that year and won his first Cheltenham Gold Cup three days before his seventh birthday. Career record: 2 Gold Cups, 4 King Georges

Sam Waley-Cohen
The strange life of an amateur

I've always competed, in show jumping and eventing, then in point-to-points, and I always wanted to race, but it was always about fun. When you start riding and you're going to Mollington point-to-point for a ride in the members' race, you don't think of winning a Gold Cup. It's about the lifestyle and the long-term outlook, it happens organically, racing carries you into places rather than you having a mission.

Nothing dramatic happened until I won the Mildmay of Flete on Liberthine in 2005, but I didn't go into it with that as an ambition. You're aware there's a lot of responsibility, that you're carrying a lot of people's money, and I take it seriously and I'm devastated when things don't go right, after all the months of blood, sweat and tears. But racing has to be fun for an amateur, because you're not making money out of it and you're taking as much flak as you're getting praise. Professional jockeys ride a bad race and go on to the next one, and I've had to learn that from them – that's racing, things don't always go to plan.

Obviously it's different for me, though. I have a full-time job buying and running dental practices, with 200 staff, and it's not something you can drift in and out of. You have to fit your sport in around your work.

So I'm in a regime where I can manage my weight, because wasting is very hard when you've got a job. I don't care what anybody says, your brain doesn't function properly if you're not eating – you're not sharp, either riding or working. You have to build it into your life, decide if the sacrifice is worth it or not, and then be cautious all the time. My friends would say I don't eat normally, but it's not a big deal and Dad wouldn't ask me to starve myself unless it was really worth it. He's a big investor in the business and he wants that to succeed too.

What I can manage is my fitness. I do lots of running, boxing, riding quite a lot, working on the Equicizer, and if I cycle or run to a meeting instead of taking the tube or a cab, that's 20 minutes each way, which is 40 minutes of exercise you've fitted in to your day, even if you do turn up in a sweaty mess.

For me, it's about enjoying it and doing justice to the horses. If I couldn't have done that for Long Run, or if I'd found work getting in the way, I'd have got off him. And if all he'd ended up doing was winning a point-to-point, then that would have been fine. This is just what Dad and I do together and the horse will carry us where we go.

summer out at grass, maturing into an even more impressive beast than he had already proved himself to be.

Watching him from the ground has been the newly-wed Sam, who lined up at Cheltenham with his more vociferous critics suggesting the 29-year-old amateur, who spends most other days in the business of running dental practices, might prove the final straw that broke the back of his mount's big-race challenge. Luckily, those doubts were shared neither by owner, nor rider, nor horse.

"I've had horses since 1974 and Sam wasn't born until 1982," explains Robert, "and he wasn't in any position to ride them until a good long time after that, so it was about a quarter of a century before he sat on one of mine, but it's been hugely more fun with him riding them. If he wasn't up to it, I wouldn't have embarrassed him or thwarted the potential of the horse by allowing him to ride it. But he had his first winner at the festival in 2005 and I've always known he had that talent and skill, as well as the huge self-discipline and the determination, and I'd have to say my confidence in him was well placed."

Sam, likewise, wasn't fazed by the prospect of riding the 7-2 Gold Cup favourite, who attracted a flood of public money as off time drew near.

"If I ride the right race, in a point-to-point or a Gold Cup, and the horse is good enough, he'll probably win and the rest is irrelevant," he states baldly. "Also, it's about faith in the horse. The one advantage I have over the professionals is that I have a relationship with the horse and can do a lot with him over the months, work out in a lot of detail a game plan that will suit him, the questions we want to ask him. A regular jockey wouldn't have the time or the opportunity to do that, or the chance to change their style to suit one horse."

When push came to shove, horse and rider proved a good fit, with Sam urging and Long Run, sharpened up by some one-to-one coaching from jumping guru Yogi Breisner, standing off assuredly, aware of the responses required from him. Nonetheless, Gold Cups aren't given away in cereal packets and even a great horse doesn't win one without having to stare into the abyss for a few furlongs. The

Continues, page 70

Fairyhouse
LEADING THE FIELD

Fairyhouse Fixtures 2012

Sunday 1st January
Wednesday 11th January
Sunday 22nd January

Saturday 4th February
Wednesday 15th February
Saturday 25th February

Easter Festival 2012
Sunday 8th April NH
Monday 9th April NH
Tuesday 18th April NH

Wednesday 6th June (E)

Wednesday 13th June (E)
Wednesday 4th July (E)
Sunday 15th July

Monday 24th September (E)
Saturday 13th October

Wednesday 7th November
Wednesday 21st November

Premier Festival 2012
Saturday 1st December NH
Sunday 2nd December NH

Saturday 15th December

Fairyhouse Membership 2012
Adult €160, OAP €110, Couple rate €280, Joint Fairyhouse & Navan €240
Groups of 10+ €140 plus one free membership

Membership includes:
• Admission to 20 race meetings including the Ladbrokes Irish Grand National •
• Reciprocal days with other racecourses in Ireland and the UK • Access to our New Members Lounge in the Powers Stand •
• Members Car Park • Members trips throughout the year •

www.fairyhouse.ie
Ferryhouse Racecourse Ratoath County Meath Ireland
Tel: 00353 (0)18256 167 Email: info@fairyhouse.ie

six-year-old had been crabbed for his poor record at the track, for his lack of years and for his partnership with an unpaid, overworked, underfed toff; now he would have to answer all those doubts and a hundred more besides, the biggest of them being his ability to stand alongside Kauto Star, Denman and Imperial Commander and not be dwarfed by their awesome presence.

"The start was calm, the nerves were gone and it was like any other race: concentrating on jumping the first fence, keeping the horse calm," recalls Sam, who went to post with the initials stitched into his saddle of his late brother Thomas, who died in 2004 from a rare form of cancer.

"These are races in which you have to dig deep from flagfall, not just cruise into them. It's an out-and-out war, a test of whose will breaks first, and there was definitely a stage in the race where I thought we weren't travelling as well as we wanted to be. They turn on the tap and you're under pressure, and quite early on there's a feeling that it's shit or bust, he's got to pick up for me – and he did.

"Then you start travelling again. You're flat out but they're not getting away from you and you're just hoping your courage and resolve don't give out. The plan was always to try and get a lead off the bend, which was what happened, and when I asked him to go he picked them up very quickly and all I needed was a good jump at the last."

And there it is. Get a lead from three of the best chasers of the modern era and kick on up the hill. What could be simpler? It's testament to Sam's straightforward mental attitude and positive, uncomplicated style that the plan was formulated and executed with such a lack of fuss, but it's a tribute to Long Run that the race was won in a style that thrilled and delighted in equal measure and suggested such great things for the future.

None of this was lost on Robert Waley-Cohen, who spent much of the summer wondering how much higher his pride and

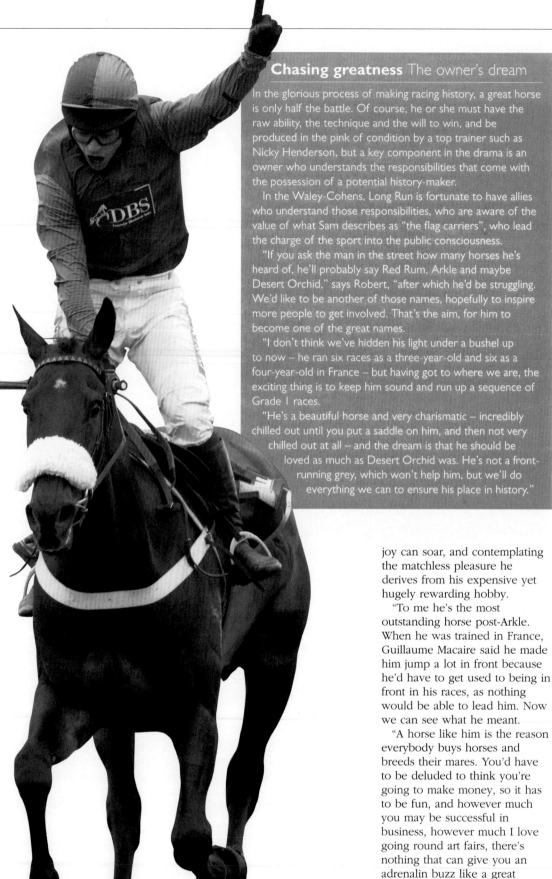

Chasing greatness The owner's dream

In the glorious process of making racing history, a great horse is only half the battle. Of course, he or she must have the raw ability, the technique and the will to win, and be produced in the pink of condition by a top trainer such as Nicky Henderson, but a key component in the drama is an owner who understands the responsibilities that come with the possession of a potential history-maker.

In the Waley-Cohens, Long Run is fortunate to have allies who understand those responsibilities, who are aware of the value of what Sam describes as "the flag carriers", who lead the charge of the sport into the public consciousness.

"If you ask the man in the street how many horses he's heard of, he'll probably say Red Rum, Arkle and maybe Desert Orchid," says Robert, "after which he'd be struggling. We'd like to be another of those names, hopefully to inspire more people to get involved. That's the aim, for him to become one of the great names.

"I don't think we've hidden his light under a bushel up to now – he ran six races as a three-year-old and six as a four-year-old in France – but having got to where we are, the exciting thing is to keep him sound and run up a sequence of Grade 1 races.

"He's a beautiful horse and very charismatic – incredibly chilled out until you put a saddle on him, and then not very chilled out at all – and the dream is that he should be loved as much as Desert Orchid was. He's not a front-running grey, which won't help him, but we'll do everything we can to ensure his place in history."

joy can soar, and contemplating the matchless pleasure he derives from his expensive yet hugely rewarding hobby.

"To me he's the most outstanding horse post-Arkle. When he was trained in France, Guillaume Macaire said he made him jump a lot in front because he'd have to get used to being in front in his races, as nothing would be able to lead him. Now we can see what he meant.

"A horse like him is the reason everybody buys horses and breeds their mares. You'd have to be deluded to think you're going to make money, so it has to be fun, and however much you may be successful in business, however much I love going round art fairs, there's nothing that can give you an adrenalin buzz like a great racehorse. Here we are already marking off in our diaries the days that really matter for the new season."

The next campaign has already been boldly pencilled in by

"Everybody will be plotting how to beat us"
Why keeping the crown won't be easy

Left to right: Master Minded, Captain Chris, Noble Prince, Wishfull Thinking, Time For Rupert

Glory is the target for Long Run, a string of titles to go with the one he grabbed as last season's young pretender. Robert Waley-Cohen, however, has been in the game too long to believe that the new campaign will be anything other than a string of brutal wars against ferocious opponents.

"Everybody fears the youthful prince who comes to seize the crown, as we found last year," he says. "The trouble is, there are more youthful princes born every year who want to seize your crown. On our side is the fact that the young pretenders will actually be older than Long Run and we believe he's still getting better, but nothing will come easy.

"Paul Nicholls will have accepted that Kauto Star isn't going to bowl us over in the King George, so he'll be aiming to bowl us over with Master Minded instead and I'd be deeply disappointed if every trainer wasn't thinking the same way.

"Everybody will be plotting how to beat us, the same way we plotted to beat Kauto Star last season. And that's the way it should be for a champion. There's no glory in walkovers."

Master Minded Yet to race beyond 2m4f but a step up to 3m for the King George became a live option after his brilliant win in the John Smith's Melling Chase at Aintree in April. Former 2m champion chaser is still only eight and recorded three of last season's top 11 performances on RPR, more than any other jumper Pre-season King George odds: 6-1

Captain Chris Shrugged off seconditis to finish last season with three Graded wins, including the Arkle at Cheltenham and the Ryanair Novice Chase at Punchestown. Unproven at 3m but connections confident the trip will suit him at Kempton in the King George Pre-season King George odds: 9-1

Noble Prince Beat Wishfull Thinking 4l in Jewson Novices' Chase at the Cheltenham Festival and arguably had the measure of Realt Dubh when falling two out at Punchestown in April. Yet to win a Grade 1 Pre-season King George odds: 16-1

Wishfull Thinking Runs in the same colours as Captain Chris and marginally better than his stablemate on RPR last season, making him the top novice chaser. Another who has to prove himself at 3m Pre-season King George odds: 14-1

Time For Rupert Long-time RSA Chase favourite last season but finished only fifth to Bostons Angel after an interrupted preparation. Loves Cheltenham and no stamina concerns for Gold Cup Pre-season Gold Cup odds: 16-1

connections. The mid-season target again is the King George; the choice of Aon Chase or Ascot Chase should a prep be needed (although Sam favours a point-to-point outing) for the Gold Cup, with anything further not yet ruled out, at least by his owner, who will return to the Cheltenham Festival as the new course chairman. All that remains is for Henderson to have Long Run spot-on for this handful of runs and for the horse to retain his eagerness for the quest.

Sam remains hopeful yet accepting of all the possibilities. "When you've won a Gold Cup, all you can do is go and win another one," he says. "But all

horses have only a certain mileage in them. It's like an elastic band – you can stretch it so far and then no more. With that in mind, he's probably got five more Gold Cups and five King Georges in him and you can only ask so many of those questions, physically and psychologically.

"I haven't sat on him since Cheltenham, but he's definitely bigger this season, looking at him in the field, bigger and stronger, although whether that makes him quicker isn't certain. A lot depends on his mentality. He's a handful in the yard, he bucks and squeals, so what's he going to be like now he's a year

older? Will he still want to do it for us? Will he be more grown up, more mature as a seven-year-old, settle into a race, or will he get worse? But he'll be what he'll be, not what I want him to be.

"And it doesn't really matter if his Gold Cup was one of the greatest races or if he becomes one of the greatest horses. Captured in its time, that day has its own legacy for us, as a reminder of what a privilege it's been to have him."

Long Run is a horse in whom wild dreams and empirical reality have already merged into one. With a little luck, he could become one of the greats.

BACK FROM THE BRINK

Two vets said Monet's Garden should be put down when he developed a serious foot infection. But he pulled through, thanks to the dedication of the people around him and his own will to live

Words by Steve Dennis

THE white horse in the field lifts his head, pricks his ears. From this distance he looks like statuary. Then he puts his head back down, worries away at the last of the summer grass. Summer's all but over, but there'll be another one, and another one.

At the beginning of 2011, Monet's Garden's life was being measured in days, every turn of the hourglass a little victory in a battle that was turning steadily against him. What you are reading now might easily have been his obituary. Now he stands in a paddock at home in Greystoke, near Penrith, basking in the thin autumn sunshine without a care in the world.

"He's fine," says Nicky Richards, two

Continues, page 74

words that must roll off his tongue with an extra relish, words he must have thought he'd never say again when the darkest clouds gathered at the turn of the year. "He's had a good summer at grass, put a bit of beef on. It's a big weight off our minds, a big relief. He has his New Zealand rug on during the day and comes in at night now that the evenings are drawing in. Don't worry, [my daughter] Joey keeps him wrapped up in cotton wool."

Turn back the pages of the calendar to the first week of January, when the headlines read 'Monet's Garden fights for life'. The news prompted a vast outpouring of support from the racing public, but hope was all anyone had to hang on to with the thread of life fraying by the day.

There was such a contrast between the news of the beleaguered grey and his last public appearance that it seemed hard to believe that such a change could have been so swiftly wrought. Monet's Garden had produced a trademark display of strength and class – "He was like a lion," Richards told the Racing Post in March – when winning the Old Roan Chase at Aintree at the end of October, his third victory in the race.

But the worm was already within the apple, the clock ticking on a time-bomb in the gallant grey's off-fore (right) foot. The courage Monet's Garden showed at Aintree would be needed a thousandfold in the days and weeks to come.

"About a week after Aintree he was still very quiet, the race took a lot out of him," said Joey, who has looked after Monet's Garden for more than ten years, in that March interview. "I was walking him and could see he wasn't 100 per cent sound, so he went off to Graham Russ at the Oaklands vet practice in Yarm."

The general consensus was that Monet's Garden had bruised the sole of his foot, and when a little bit of poison emerged from the coronet band on that hoof all seemed straightforward.

"Grand, we thought, whatever is in there is coming out and he'll be fine," said Nicky. "He came back and two days later he wasn't improving at all. He went back to Graham and gradually got worse. It was doom and gloom from one week to the next.

"He stayed at Graham's for three months and had four operations, scans and everything. For the first two months we thought the next phone call would be the one telling us we'd lost him. They were dark times."

The navicular bone had become infected and because Monet's Garden

Hell and back: the toughest year in the life of Monet's Garden

One day I got a text saying 'get well Monet's, all of Ireland's praying for you'. What a wonderful thing to send, it gave everyone at the yard a big boost

had given his all at Aintree he lacked the residual strength to fight off the initial stages of infection. The poison took hold, a death grip. Another vet recommended the horse be put down; a second opinion mirrored the first. People who own horses – own any animal – know that sometimes they must be cruel on themselves to be kind to an animal in extremis.

Everyone at Greystoke believed the end was near. No-one else was aware of it, though, and whenever he went racing Richards found himself the target of friendly enquiries about when the old grey might be back on a racecourse. He knew the horse would never run again and the strain of keeping a straight face was too much to bear.

After consulting the grey's owner David Wesley Yates, Richards made an announcement in the first days of 2011. Then came the headlines, the messages from the public, the anguish shared and reduced by that sharing.

The Richards family was overwhelmed by goodwill, the burden no longer borne alone. The horse was still dangerously ill but hope was renewed with every kind word. "After the news came out it was unbelievable," said Nicky. "The telephone calls, the emails, the cards, the letters, some with a fiver in, or a cheque for a tenner and a note saying 'get him a bag of carrots' or whatever. You

October 13, 2010
Treated for suspected arthritis by Graham Russ of Oaklands veterinary centre, Yarm

October 23 Monet's Garden wins the Old Roan Chase at Aintree, his final race

November 1 'Not quite right' and returned to Yarm

Early November Returns to Greystoke

Two days later 'Not improving'; back to Yarm

December Condition gradually deteriorates

January 4, 2011 Announcement of horse's condition in Racing Post

Late January Condition begins to take turn for better

Early February Monet's Garden comes off antibiotics

February 17 Returns to Greystoke

May/June Turned out in field

September Wedge removed from shoe and normal shoe affixed

Road to recovery 1 Monet's Garden at Oaklands Veterinary Centre on January 13; 2 Getting ready to leave Oaklands on February 17, with vet Caroline Blakiston (left) and Joey Richards; 3 Out for a walk with Joey Richards on February 20; 4 In his stable at Greystoke on March 22

wouldn't believe the depth of feeling for the old horse.

"When I went racing, I'm not kidding you, if one person asked me how he was there were 20 or 30 asking every day. There was goodwill offered everywhere we went. One day I got a text saying 'get well Monet's, all of Ireland's praying for you'. What a wonderful thing to send, it gave everyone at the yard a big boost."

Another message gave Monet's Garden a bigger boost. An anonymous well-wisher (the cliché cloaking a million good intentions) suggested homoeopathy. Richards and vet Caroline Blakiston, who considered every suggestion for its merits, gave it a try alongside the ongoing treatment.

And somewhere along the line, in some quiet corner of a straw-strewn stable, the tide turned. Death stepped back into the shadows and the sun began to peep through the gloom.

"Caroline phoned and said, 'I'm not sure, but this thing might be starting to slow down'," remembered Richards. "She was still cautious, worried that as soon as he began to come off the antibiotics it would start running away with him again. But a few days later, she talked about getting him home in a fortnight."

On February 17, a horsebox pulled up at Greystoke and a tottery Monet's Garden stepped gingerly down the ramp. In the duel between life and death, life had won. Monet's Garden, so often a winner, had emerged victorious once again.

"He's still improving quietly," says Richards. "The farrier Hugh Dyer initially put a four-inch wedge in his shoe to support his foot, but he's only on the thinnest of wedges now and next time he's shod it might be with a normal shoe.

"He still gets the odd letter or card, I still get the odd phone call about him, and whenever I go racing someone always stops me to ask how the old horse is.

"At Christmas we were just praying he'd be able to hang on and enjoy a few warm days of summer, but now look at him. We'd like to take him to parade at the races, he'd love it and it would be a thank-you to the public for all their support."

He's a public favourite and Wesley Yates is happy to share him. "At the beginning, all I ever wanted was to get him into a field so he could enjoy his retirement," he says. "But he had the right attitude, he wanted to live, and it encouraged everyone to do their best for him. In the darkest days I remember thinking about where we'd bury him. Oh, it doesn't bear thinking about now."

Wesley Yates would like Monet's Garden to have an active retirement if he's able, citing the showing classes and competitions run by Retraining of Racehorses as ideal outlets for his energies. And for anyone wanting Christmas present ideas, the Injured Jockeys' Fund is selling a 1,000-piece jigsaw of this most photogenic of horses.

The greatest thanks, of course, go to those who put the real jigsaw – the one of Monet's Garden's off-fore foot – back together: Russ, Blakiston, all those at Oaklands. But Richards also wants to thank all those who couldn't help the horse but helped lift the atmosphere around him with their support.

"The old horse is happy and we're just so glad we've got what we've got," says Richards, his words echoed by Joey, who still sprays a homoeopathic solution on the grey's carrots each morning.

"What we did for him was payback, because he's been such a good horse for us and given a great many people so much pleasure," adds Wesley Yates. "I was up at Greystoke recently to see him and when I got out of the car there he was in the next field, larking about with a pal."

If you cry at happy endings, now is the time for your tears. But there were plenty shed in the dark days of last winter, so let's not have any more. Anyway, all it takes is one look at the white horse in the field and you can't help but smile.

MAGNIFIQUE!

Mickael Barzalona's breathtaking Derby-winning ride on Pour Moi owed more to Frank Sinatra than Lester Piggott as he did it his way

Words by Scott Burton

'Nobody wants to be parked deep on the track. The wider you are the more Epsom's camber works against you. Unless they've gone a million miles an hour you don't want to be any further back than fourth or fifth on the run to Tattenham Corner' – Richard Hughes

A MINUTE AND A HALF into the Investec Derby and Mickael Barzalona seems to have got it all wrong on Pour Moi. As the 13 runners hurtle downhill towards Tattenham Corner, Pour Moi is stone last and already Barzalona is having to manoeuvre to the outer to stand any chance of making up ground once they straighten for home.

This is not how it's supposed to be done at Epsom, as Richard Hughes had explained in his Racing Post column that morning. Hughes is a believer in the model established by the greatest Derby jockey of them all: get a good position from the off, stay as close as possible to the rail, aim to be in fourth or fifth place on the run to Tattenham Corner, then go to win your race in the straight. "I know how the jockeys will want to ride the race, which is pretty much how Lester Piggott rode it year in, year out," Hughes wrote.

That belief system, which has held good for half a century or more, is about to be shaken to its core. As the runners take their final strides around Tattenham Corner, Barzalona is still in last place and he's wide out on the track. To many eyes the latest French catastrophe in the Derby is unfolding and no wonder: Barzalona is only 19 and has virtually no experience of

Continues, page 78

Back to front Barzalona rewrites the Derby textbook

Tattenham Corner
Pour Moi is stone last of the 13 runners as Memphis Tennessee, the leader from the start, holds a clear advantage over Treasure Beach. Carlton House, the 5-2 favourite, is a couple of lengths in front of Pour Moi on the outer

Key

- ● Memphis Tennessee
- ■ Carlton House
- ▬ Treasure Beach
- ■ Pour Moi

Two furlongs out
Memphis Tennessee is coming back to the field as Treasure Beach winds up to challenge his stablemate and Carlton House moves smoothly into third. Pour Moi is still only ninth and has an awful lot to do

②

Epsom's twists and turns.

But it's not the disaster it seems: Barzalona, you see, has a plan. He knows he's on a colt with lightning acceleration, having come from last to first on Pour Moi to land his Derby trial, the Prix Greffulhe at Longchamp. Andre Fabre, the master French trainer who has guided the nascent careers of Pour Moi and Barzalona, sees no reason to change at Epsom. The plan is to wait and wait, and Barzalona is sticking to it.

Pour Moi has nine in front of him at the three-furlong pole and is still only eighth at the two-furlong pole. The momentum is building, but now Barzalona faces another problem. Just as Hughes had warned, being wide out on the track means the camber is working against his mount. Pour Moi lugs to the left, down towards the rail, but Barzalona – with a deftness that becomes more apparent on the race replays – straightens him quickly and keeps him running.

As the leaders bunch up, Pour Moi flies into the picture in the space of a furlong. He is really motoring now, although he is only sixth as they pass the furlong pole. There is still hope of a first Derby victory for the Queen with Carlton House but today's triumphal tune is going to be La Marseillaise, not God Save the Queen.

Pour Moi, finishing fastest of all, tears down the outside and gets his head in front 50 yards from the line. At the same moment Barzalona, realising victory is his, stands bolt upright and celebrates before he has passed the post. It's a cardinal sin most of the time, but surely he can be forgiven. He has, after all, just broken virtually all the cardinal rules about how to win the Derby.

'I had no interest in racing when I was young. I never went to the course or watched on television. I much preferred rugby. I played when I was a kid, but I was too small to go on with it' – Barzalona

BARZALONA was born in Avignon but grew up on Corsica, Napoleon's island. His first love may have been rugby, but he was given a white Camargue as an eighth birthday present and horses were in his blood too: his grandfather, Christian, is a trainer on the island. At 5ft 3in and 8st, the youngster was built to be a jockey rather than a scrum-half and he joined the jockeys' academy, first in Marseille and then in Paris.

At 16 he was apprenticed to Fabre, the first key moment in his racing career. "In the early years I was riding out, gallops and canters, and I rode Mosaic – a champion in his own small way. At Monsieur Fabre's stable, they are all champions. The most important horse for me was Simon De Montfort. He gave me my first Group 1 ride and my first Group win at Longchamp. I've been very lucky. Monsieur Fabre decided to send me to Godolphin to spend the winter and I've been there twice now."

Barzalona first made the world sit up and take notice of him on 2011 World Cup night at Meydan, winning the UAE Derby for Godolphin on Khawlah, and it was a sign of things to come. He waited off the pace before challenging in the final quarter-mile and, seemingly always confident he'd win, put the filly's nose in front on the line. Perhaps unwisely, in an exuberant gesture,

he waved his whip in celebration as he flashed past the post. Sound familiar?

"I can only be thankful I've had the opportunity to ride such good horses for Godolphin," Barzalona says. "I found riding at Meydan easier than in France, where the races are very tactical. Abroad in places like Dubai you get some faster races, some slower races. The tactics suit my style. To even have a ride on World Cup night was magnifique, then to win a race like the UAE Derby, a Group 2, that was magical. And then to finish third in the World Cup [on Monterosso] was the cherry on the cake."

More success was to follow, with Barzalona riding his first Group 1 winner as he conjured another late surge aboard Wavering in the Prix Saint-Alary, just a fortnight before the Derby. Already it was a good year, but it was about to become a vintage one.

'It's a good idea to come here, both for the horse and the jockey. [Mickael] has shown a lot of ability. He seems to know exactly where the winning post is, which is very important for a jockey' – Andre Fabre

NINE DAYS to go until the Derby and Barzalona, Fabre and Pour Moi are at Epsom for the Breakfast with the Stars event, which allows connections to test their horses on the Downs before the big race.

Fabre is one of four trainers to take up the invitation and it's an important stepping

One furlong out
Treasure Beach moves into a narrow lead from Memphis Tennessee with Carlton House just behind. In the space of a furlong Pour Moi has made up a tremendous amount of ground but still has five in front of him

①

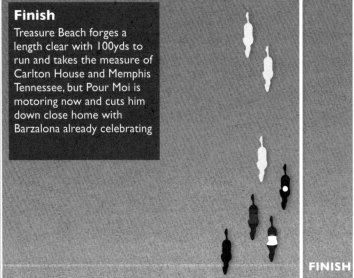

Finish
Treasure Beach forges a length clear with 100yds to run and takes the measure of Carlton House and Memphis Tennessee, but Pour Moi is motoring now and cuts him down close home with Barzalona already celebrating

FINISH

stone as it gives Barzalona and Pour Moi their first taste of Epsom. Galloping over a mile and a quarter of the track, with stablemate O'Kelly Hammer for company, Pour Moi has no problem with the bend and the downhill run. It will be different under race conditions, but Fabre is pleased.

"It was a good occasion to get him more racecourse experience and show him the track," the trainer says. "He's a very good horse. We don't have many occasions on which to judge these horses, so it's a matter of feeling: his conformation, his pedigree, the way he won last time. All those are indications. I am in love with him. All of my Derby runners have been a disaster so far, but Pour Moi is the best chance I've had. I accept it would be unpopular beating Her Majesty's horse, but I wouldn't feel guilty."

Barzalona is happy too. "We had a good chance to look around and get a feel of the track and he worked well. The track is not flat, but if you've got a good horse it doesn't really matter. After each run he has matured and hopefully he has matured since last time."

A week later he is back at Epsom and has his first race ride on the track in the Investec Oaks, finishing 12th on Why. By the time he gets into the saddle on Pour Moi his race experience around Epsom extends to three rides, with a best finishing position of fourth.

The colt seems more nervous than his young jockey in the preliminaries. "He always used to sweat freely before his races, so when he did it before the Derby I wasn't worried. That's just the way he was," Barzalona says.

'I didn't have the experience to know whether he was a Derby horse, but it was clear he was very good. When he won the Prix Greffuhle it confirmed he was improving and growing in maturity' – Barzalona

And so to the two and a half minutes that would change Barzalona's life. Even now, months later, he can recall the details of the race, the moments that made the difference.

Fabre had said he believed the stronger pace of British racing would help Pour Moi relax and, as the stalls opened, it quickly became apparent that the plan was to test the theory to the full.

"We were at the back, but he had grown more mature and he settled beautifully," Barzalona says. "It was a bonus that the good horses were all just ahead of me and they went a good even pace early on. The race didn't really begin until we were coming down the hill and it all began to unfold perfectly. Carlton House had a bit of trouble just in front of us, but Pour Moi remained well balanced throughout. He was able to quicken and then quicken again.

"As we straightened up he was breathing well and we were ready to go. He drifted a little into another horse, but I only needed to give him a couple of cracks to encourage him to run straight."

With a furlong to run, with the principals crowding at the front, Carlton House still looked the one to beat and the excited commentator on French television, yet to

Continues, page 80

spot Pour Moi's effort, urged the favourite on with a full-throated, and slightly unpatriotic, "Allez la Reine!"

But it was not to be for Ryan Moore, nor for the textbook ride of Colm O'Donoghue on Treasure Beach. Not now the textbook was being frantically rewritten as Barzalona bore down on the leaders.

"I thought I'd get there maybe 50 metres from the post. And on the line I was sure I'd won. I don't know how I felt exactly when I stood up, I had all these emotions, and that's just what happened. It was the Derby."

Pour Moi's amazing Derby run was his last, more's the pity, but Barzalona looks sure to be competing in the top races for years to come. He has resisted the temptation to cash in on his sudden fame and stature, content to sign an extension to his contract as number two jockey to Alain and Gerard Wertheimer, rather than become number one elsewhere. "I just want to keep progressing, to keep learning, and I hope to find another great horse."

Maybe he will be lucky enough to find another. But it'll never be like the first time. That will always be special.

Leave 'em wanting more Pour Moi exits the stage

The previous four Derby winners had gone on to further glory with at least one more Group 1 victory but Pour Moi never got the chance as he became the first Epsom hero to be retired without racing again since Secreto in 1984.

Pour Moi reached the pinnacle on only the fifth start of a racing career that lasted barely eight months. He started inauspiciously as a two-year-old with eighth place on his debut in a 1m contest at Fontainebleau on September 23.

A month later, with Mickael Barzalona in the saddle for the first time, he had improved enough to take the Prix des Feuillants, a conditions race over 1m1f at Longchamp on soft ground.

He was beaten again when he reappeared as a three-year-old in the Group 3 Prix La Force over 1m3f at Longchamp in April, finishing third of five, but once again he improved for the outing. On his next start, dropped to 1m2f in the Group 2 Prix Greffulhe at Saint-Cloud on May 7, he was held up last of the nine runners until the straight and then burst through to score impressively by a length and a half.

The Derby was his first start at 1m4f and his first on good to firm ground, but the same waiting tactics thrillingly made him the first French-trained winner of the Epsom Classic since Empery in 1976.

Nobody knew it at the time, but Pour Moi had saved the best until last. His retirement, owing to an injury to his near-fore fetlock sustained on the gallops, was announced on August 27 and he will stand his first season at Coolmore in 2012.

Eight months was not long, but it was enough for one of the stars of 2011 to emerge.

RPR view While it's impossible to know what Pour Moi might have gone on to achieve, it can be stated with some certainty that we didn't see the best of him, *writes Paul Curtis*. His Derby-winning RPR of 123+ doesn't rate among the great Epsom performances and, while Treasure Beach and Memphis Tennessee went on to frank the form at the Curragh, the Epsom form is more solid than spectacular.

Pour Moi's Derby form falls short of the best recent winners, Workforce (2010, 129), Authorized (2007, 130) and Motivator (2005, 129), the latter pair arriving at Epsom more exposed, having won the Racing Post Trophy at two. But a non-vintage Derby is no barrier to future greatness as evidenced by Sea The Stars' Derby-winning mark of 124+, fully a stone shy of his subsequent peak figure.

Given his lightly raced and rapidly progressive profile, Pour Moi's Derby win looked very much another step forward rather than revealing the true extent of his ability. It is conjecture to say how much more there might have been to come, but given everything we knew of him there was clear potential for Pour Moi to develop into a top-class colt with a big part to play in the championship middle-distance races.

20 12

HORSES AND PEOPLE TO WATCH

The London Olympics will dominate the headlines but here's our pick of the rising stars who could be pure gold in racing

CHARLIE HILLS

The new master of Faringdon Place stables has a lot to live up to, and many will judge him on what he achieves in his first full season in 2012. Hills, 33, started well after his father Barry handed over the reins in August, winning with his first runner and quickly adding a first black-type winner (Sajwah) and first Group winner (Ransom Note).

But 2012 will be a proving ground and the standards are high. In his 42-year career, Barry trained ten Classic winners in Britain and Ireland and became only the fifth British trainer to send out 3,000 winners. After his first bedding-in season at Faringdon Place, the £3m state-of-the-art training facility that is his legacy, he never had a season with fewer than 70 winners and nearly always topped the £1m mark in prize-money, sometimes pushing £2m.

Fortunately, Hills snr is still on hand, along with a core of long-standing staff and brother Michael as stable jockey. "It's hard for Dad having done it for 40 years; he can't walk away overnight," Charlie says. "He's a positive influence and it's still early days for me, so it's good to have him there. It's been good having the staff – you need experience around you. You can fall back on that when challenges come to you."

The first big challenge will come in the 2012 Flat season, when Hills hopes to make the breakthrough at Group 1 level. "I'd like to think I could do it, I have every chance to. Hopefully some of the two-year-olds will make up into nice horses and we'll be able to stock up at the yearling sales, which should give us a good few to run in the good races."

Among his three year-olds for 2012, he identifies a couple of promising fillies. "I really like Cockney Dancer. When she strengthens up, she'll be a really fun horse to go racing with. Hazel Lazery is a lovely filly too. She won a conditions race at Newbury and was second in the Tattersalls Millions. She's one I'm looking forward to."

For Khalid Abdullah he trains Perennial, an impressive Doncaster maiden winner and runner-up in the Group 3 Autumn Stakes. "I'd like to think he could contest the good races. He's the sort who should be there with his breeding and how he won first time out."

The older team will be led by proven Group performers Ransom Note and Red Jazz. "It's good to have a core of older horses to rely on. Another one is White Frost, who is going to be the type for all those big handicaps like the Victoria Cup and the Hunt Cup, which should be exciting."

Like a football manager taking over in mid-season, Hills feels he'll have more of his own stamp on the yard by the start of the new campaign. "I'm looking forward to it. Winners are the most important thing and to keep the number of winners up. Keeping the horses healthy and getting the yard full are the things I need to do. Do that and everybody will be happy."

Words by Peter Scargill

TIM VAUGHAN

There are two voices in Tim Vaughan's head. One is telling him that anything is possible, even, at some point down the line, champion trainer honours. The other voice is urging him to be realistic and resist getting carried away. You sense Vaughan listens to the first voice much the most.

Who can blame him? Like his horses, Vaughan is a trainer going places fast. The former chartered surveyor, who embarked on a training career in 2005, moved to his present base in the Vale of Glamorgan as recently as March 2008. Since then his progress has been spectacular. The first campaign at what is now home yielded 55 winners, the second 88 and the third 91. Yet it was what happened in the final month of that most recent season that matters most.

In April Vaughan enjoyed his first Grade 1 success with Saint Are at Aintree. Eight days later Beshabar won him a Scottish National. To cap it all, Spirit Of Adjisa then bagged his trainer a second Grade 1 at the Punchestown festival.

"We had an unbelievable time," he says. "I had been training lots of winners of lower-grade races but kept hitting the crossbar in the bigger races. Winning the Grade 1 with Saint Are provided mental relief as much as anything else. It showed that with the right ammunition we can do it. Now I just need more of that ammunition."

He thinks he might have it. Having made his name improving bad horses, Vaughan now prefers to work his magic on better raw material, either in the form of proven performers – such as the former Paul Nicholls inmate Beshabar – or untapped talent, increasingly from the point-to-point field.

Among that number he pinpoints King's Sunset and Minella For Party as two worth watching, while easy bumper winner Allan Islands – Vaughan's first J P McManus-owned inmate – is thought capable of big things. Of the big-race winners he describes as his "three pinnacle horses", Beshabar stands out and impresses as a genuine John Smith's Grand National candidate. "He's still open to plenty of improvement," says Vaughan, who reckons Saint Are will be "far better over fences than hurdles". Spirit Of Adjisa, on the other hand, could find life tougher in handicap hurdles.

Even if he does, Vaughan will not be fretting. His stable will increasingly be known for quality as much as quantity, which is exactly how he wants it.

"I have endless ambition and a desire to succeed," he admits. "We've made giant strides already but I want to continue climbing the ladder. I'm not daft enough to think it's going to come easily but, dare I say it, I would love to be champion trainer."

Vaughan will try hard to make it happen. There might be two voices in his head, but one of them does by far the most talking.

Words by Lee Mottershead

SAMAIN

Trainer Willie Mullins
Form 2/111-

The story so far As short as 8-1 for the Champion Bumper at Cheltenham after two wins early in the year but was not entered, with owner Michael O'Leary not a fan of exposing young horses to the hurly-burly of the festival. Trained by Eddie Hales when a close second on bumper debut in April 2010 but then bought by O'Leary for £165,000 and sent to Mullins, who recorded a hat-trick with him from January to April without testing him too highly.

The next chapter Should make a cracking novice hurdler and looks ready for the step into Graded company. Travelled strongly in his wins and, although he has raced on nothing better than soft, Mullins believes that the German-bred is a good-ground horse.

What they say "He's probably the best bumper horse in Ireland. He had a bit more in the tank [on his final start]" – rider Patrick Mullins

If he were an Olympian he'd be Kirani James (Grenada's 400m world champion). Prodigious talent with star quality

BORN TO SEA
Trainer John Oxx ● Form 1

The story so far Final foal of the outstanding broodmare Urban Sea, making him a half-brother to Sea The Stars as well as 2001 Derby winner Galileo and a host of other high-class performers. Thrown straight into Listed company on September debut at the Curragh in 6f Blenheim Stakes and won by 1½l. Quoted as short as 6-1 for 2,000 Guineas and generally 16-1 for Derby after opening win.

The next chapter Seven of his half-siblings have run in Classics, winning four and being placed in another three, and he's in good hands for his attempt to add to the family's illustrious record. Sea The Stars came to hand early enough to go for the Guineas and this one might too.

What they say "He's a lot more precocious than his brother [Sea The Stars]. The plan was to run in July but he got sore shins. He did very well to come off the pace and quicken up the way he did as he was quite green. I'm not expecting him to be his brother again but if we win something nice that's great" – Oxx

 If he were an Olympian he'd be Ben Ainslie (GB sailor). Backed by long record of success on the sea

QUITO DE LA ROQUE
Trainer Colm Murphy
Form 122141/12111-1

The story so far Brought along steadily since winning maiden point-to-point in November 2009 and had a low-key campaign as a novice hurdler, reaching RPR high of 144 after winning 3m novice handicap hurdle at Fairyhouse on final start of the 2009-10 season. As expected, much improved when sent chasing last season and only defeat was in Grade 1 Fort Leney at Leopardstown Christmas meeting, beaten three-quarters of a length by subsequent RSA Chase winner Bostons Angel. Won four straight Graded chases after that, culminating in victories at Aintree and Punchestown festivals.

The next chapter Stamina clearly his strong suit and could step up to fill the gap at the top of Ireland's staying chase ranks. Aintree and Punchestown wins came on the best ground he has raced on and, while he is effective in a bog, better conditions may bring more out of him. Missed Cheltenham last year, with the undulations thought to be against him, but has other options.

What they say "Physically there is still more to come, but we won't get carried away. Time will tell if he can make it. He would have to improve for us to start talking about Gold Cups" – Murphy

If he were an Olympian he'd be Mo Farah (GB 5,000m world champion). Talent was always there and now proving it over long distances

HENRY BROOKE
Brooke, 21, is from Middleham, North Yorkshire, and comes from a racing family: mother Julia is a point-to-point trainer and father Glenn is a blacksmith who worked at Michael Dickinson's stable during the glory years. He rode 17 winners in 2010-11, his breakthrough season over jumps, and is attached to the powerful Donald McCain stable

How did you get started? When I was at school I went to Kevin Ryan's. He was really good to me, he let me ride a good bit of work. I went to Jim Bolger's in my six-week holiday and after that I went to Peter Beaumont's and got experience of jumpers. Then I was given a pointer – an ex-racehorse called Pikachu Blue – and Kate Walton helped me with training him. Richie McGrath helped me a lot too, he used to take me to the racing college at Doncaster and he had a word with Donald when I was looking for a job as a conditional. I wouldn't be here now if it wasn't for him.

You had your first winner in May 2010 and by the end of the season you were close to winning the Martin Pipe Conditional Jockeys' Handicap Hurdle at the Cheltenham Festival on Son Of Flicka. What have been the highlights so far? I had a few early winners that put me on the map and Any Given Day won the Silver Trophy at Chepstow. He's the best I've ridden so far, along with Son Of Flicka, who was only just touched off by Willie Mullins's horse [Sir Des Champs] at Cheltenham. I joined Donald not long after my first winner and it has been great from the start. He's good to me, he puts me on good horses, and everyone here has been a big help.

You have ridden on the Flat too and had a big ride on Overturn in the Northumberland Plate. What's the plan from here? My agent thought it would be a good idea to ride on the Flat over the summer, just to tidy me up in the finish, but I've finished with it now. I'm concentrating fully on the jumps. I've got good people around me and I just try to work hard. It's paying off.

What are your hopes for this season? I'm hoping it'll be a great season for me. Donald has got class horses and my agent does a great job getting me outside rides on good horses. The aim is the conditionals' title, or at least to be in the top three. People say you can lose your claim too quick, but when the winners are coming you don't want to turn them away.

HIDDEN CYCLONE

Trainer Shark Hanlon
Form 1/113111-

The story so far Hasn't exactly been hidden but full extent of ability may not be in the open after missing all the big spring festivals. Won bumper and maiden hurdle on first two starts and then ventured into Graded novice hurdles on four occasions, winning three and beaten narrowly by First Lieutenant (the subsequent Neptune winner) and Zaidpour in Grade 1 Future Champions at Leopardstown. Proved stamina with easy win on final start in minor 2m7f race at Navan, in Cheltenham Festival week.

The next chapter Highly rated by Hanlon and a top-class chasing prospect. Sole defeat came in a muddling contest and he looks up to Grade 1 class. Has won easily at 2m and almost 3m and, while bumper win was on good ground, has done best on soft to heavy.

What they say "I thought he was a good horse the day he won his bumper and I think he'll be a top-class chaser" – Hanlon

If he were an Olympian he'd be David Rudisha (Kenya's 800m world champion). Talented runner with underrated Irish trainer on his team

TOM SYMONDS

Symonds, 26, is in his first season as a trainer, having been Nicky Henderson's assistant for five years, and is based at Dason Court Stables, near Ross-on-Wye, Herefordshire. Dason Court, which has been in his family since 1992, was part of John Edwards's training operation at Caradoc that produced a stream of top chasers including Pearlyman, Yahoo and Monsieur Le Cure

What's your background in racing? I rode out for Venetia Williams in the school holidays, at the time when she had Teeton Mill and Lady Rebecca, and that was when I became obsessed with racing. I left school at 18 and worked for Michael and Peter Scudamore, then for James Fanshawe in Newmarket, where I went for three months and stayed for three years. Then at the age of 21 I moved on to Nicky Henderson's.

What was behind the decision to start up on your own? The five years at Nicky's were fantastic, but there's a point at which it becomes a bit unfulfilling because it's not yours. I've been very lucky to be entrusted with this place. It was always in the back of my mind to come back here one day and restore what was already here. I've got about 30 boxes and I started with 25 horses, but there are lots of empty barns and the aim is to expand slowly but surely. The gallops here are defunct, but over at Caradoc they are in full working order and I have use of them in the mornings.

What did you learn from working at the Henderson yard? He's probably the most hands-on trainer I know, he's everywhere. He never stops working and he's still hungry. You have to work very hard to do what he does, to try to find the horses to fill the gaps – a Triumph Hurdle horse or whatever. He's got the energy of a 12-year-old, he's an example to us all, and he was a great guy to work with.

What's your aim this season? It's a difficult one to answer. I could say ten winners, or 20 winners, but really what I want is for every horse to do what it can to fulfil its potential for the season.

Which of your horses might do well? Duc De Regniere is a great horse to have, but he's so hard to place to win a race. He will become a veteran chaser after Christmas, which will help him. Mirific, owned by Michael Buckley, is a nice horse if I can keep him in one piece. He was at Nicky's and we thought very highly of him there. Scholastica is a four-year-old filly who won on her only start last season when she was with Charlie Longsdon. She'll go over hurdles. First Act is a half-sister to Darlan, who is with Nicky and could be an absolute monster. She's a nice filly and she's won a point-to-point, which gives her a bit of experience.

EX CIT ING

Speed, power, balance...
The emotion of the best derby
captured in all its intensity
in the perfect anatomy of these purebred,
that seem to be suspended in mid-air.
An artistic and technical challenge
for the most talented artists.
A porcelain handcrafted
at the Lladró workshops
in Valencia - Spain.

At the derby
35 x 100 cm
Limited edition

BRYAN COOPER

Cooper, 19, is the son of Forpadydeplasterer's trainer Tom Cooper and last season was Irish champion conditional jockey over jumps with a record 37 winners, having been attached to Dessie Hughes's stable. He lost his claim at the end of August and this is his first season as a professional. Originally from Tralee in County Kerry, he now lives in Kildare

Winning the conditional title last season was a great achievement, only 18 months after your first winner, but the first season without a claim can be difficult. How do you see it going? It's a big help to have two good stables behind me with Dessie and my dad. They'll support me. This is my second full season and I'll have to improve on my riding as I go on and work extra hard now I'm a professional. The aim at the start of last season was to have ten or 12 winners and I fairly hammered that. I never thought I would be champion. It was only after Christmas that I started to think about it.

You've come a long way in a short time. What have been the highlights? Winning a Listed race on Coscorrig at Fairyhouse and having a winner at the last two Galway festivals was great, as well as getting the opportunity to ride at the Cheltenham and Aintree festivals.

Most of your wins have been over hurdles – is your riding over fences something you're looking to improve? I was restricted to riding over hurdles for quite a time and Dessie didn't want me riding over fences. I was never in any rush to do it either. But I've done well over fences this year. I had a chase winner at the Galway festival and the Listed win on Coscorrig was over fences.

Which horses are you looking forward to riding this season and will we see you on Forpadydeplasterer? Dessie has a lovely bunch of young horses. Rick and Canaly will be going for the good hurdle races and there are good handicappers like Western Charmer. The deal with the owners of Forpadydeplasterer is that if Barry Geraghty isn't available I'll be the next choice. It would be a dream come true to ride him in a race because it was only three years ago that I led him up at the Cheltenham Festival.

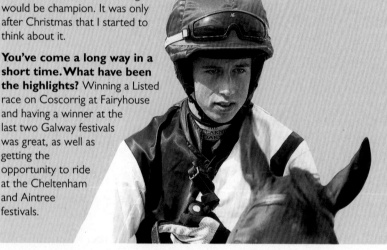

MAYBE

Trainer Aidan O'Brien ● *Form 11111*

The story so far Started her juvenile campaign early with a 4½l cruise in a 6f Naas maiden on May 11 and was a successful 5-2 favourite in the Chesham Stakes at Royal Ascot, despite concern about the rain-softened ground, After that Listed win, she progressed to win a Group 3, a Group 2 and finally the Group 1 Moyglare Stud Stakes from Fire Lily (later runner-up in the Prix Marcel Boussac) and Group 1 winner La Collina.

The next chapter First target is the Qipco 1,000 Guineas, for which she ranged from 3-1 to 5-1 favourite when it was announced in October that she had been put away for the year. O'Brien has other promising fillies in Wading and Kissed but Maybe – bred on the Galileo-Danehill cross that produced 2011 Guineas winners Frankel, Roderic O'Connor and Golden Lilac – was top of the pile.

What they say "With a filly of her class you have to think about the Guineas. She's an uncomplicated filly and has the gears" – O'Brien

If she were an Olympian she'd be Rebecca Adlington (GB swimmer). The proven golden girl in a strong team

GEORGE BAKER

Baker, 46, was a City trader, assistant to Paul Webber and journalist for The Sportsman before setting up as a trainer in March 2008. Originally based in Warwickshire, he moved to the historic Whitsbury Manor Stables, Hampshire, and 2011 was his first year there

You always said the move to Whitsbury would take you to the next level. Has that been the case? "Definitely. I looked upon this year as a bedding-in year, so to have trained more than 40 winners by October was a dream come true. I'm still learning my way around the gallops. Whitsbury is a magical place and I have every hope we can push on again next year."

Did you always want to be a trainer? "I always had a copy of the Racing Post tucked into the Financial Times when I worked in the City, but if Barings hadn't collapsed I'd probably still be there. My involvement in racing would have been purely as a hobby. When I worked for The Sportsman I loved the fact that I was being paid to go racing – that was the second-best job I could have hoped for. Now I've got the best."

How difficult is it to attract owners in the current economic climate? "My time at The Sportsman taught me that I had to be open and transparent with the media. If people aren't writing about you, things aren't going well. I'm more open than many and that gets my name in the frame. You've got to be imaginative, go down the line of syndicates and ensure you make ownership jolly good fun. You've got to make it more attractive than having a boat on the south coast or a season ticket at Chelsea."

Do you have a 'killer horse' who is going to make headlines in 2012? "Belgian Bill, who was second in a Group 2 in Turkey, could take us to big races in Dubai and Hong Kong. I don't think he's Group 1 material, but there's more to come from him. Place In My Heart is pretty special and Sweet Ophelia, a big, backward filly who ran well on her debut, is one to watch out for."

ansarinô™

CAPTAIN CHRIS
Trainer Philip Hobbs ● Form 4111/222211-1

The story so far Fourth in a bumper on his debut and then won his first three starts over hurdles before finding Silviniaco Conti 10l too good in Grade 2 Persian War at Chepstow on reappearance last season. Seconditis continued when switched to novice chases, finishing runner-up three times before finally getting off the mark at 2-5 in three-runner Pendil at Kempton. No stopping him after that, with Grade 1 wins in the Arkle at Cheltenham and the Ryanair at Punchestown.

The next chapter Pipped to champion novice chaser title by stablemate Wishfull Thinking but could turn out to be the stable star this season. Only win in five attempts beyond 2m1f came in the Pendil but connections believe his future lies over longer trips, with the King George touted as the big mid-season aim. How he fares there will decide future targets, but plenty of options given the speed he showed to win at the festivals.

What they say "He's a gorgeous horse. He really needs two and a half miles, but they always say you want a two-and-a-half-mile horse for the Arkle and he proved that. My thought is that his race will be the King George. He loves Kempton and three miles around there would be just the job" – Hobbs

If he were an Olympian he'd be Fran Halsall (GB swimmer). Took time to click as teammates won titles but could become the big star

HARBOUR WATCH
Trainer Richard Hannon ● Form 111

The story so far Was not seen after July but did enough in three runs in the space of seven weeks to mark himself out as a serious 2,000 Guineas contender. Showed good turn of foot on soft ground to win 6f Salisbury maiden by 3¾l on debut, won just as easily next time in conditions race at Newmarket July meeting and then recorded RPR of 117 with 2¼l victory over Bannock in Group 2 Richmond Stakes at Glorious Goodwood. Had been due to face Group 1 test in Dewhurst but was put away after "a little setback".

The next chapter Guineas the clear target, although yet to be tested beyond 6f and in Group 1 company. Has been talked about in the same breath as the stable's former star miler Canford Cliffs, described by jockey Richard Hughes as "the only other two-year-old to work like him"

What they say "He's a very good horse. He worked with [useful three-year-old] Casual Glimpse and went right past him. He has kept improving and he will get even better. He will get seven furlongs easily and, while the Guineas is another furlong, he is a big, strong horse and there is no reason he won't get a mile next year" – Richard Hannon

If he were an Olympian he'd be Sir Chris Hoy (GB track cyclist). Speed and class in abundance.

DARYL JACOB

Jacob, 28, from Enniscorthy, County Wexford, moved to Britain at the age of 19 and his big-race successes include The Listener and Diamond Harry, last year's Hennessy winner. Last season he had his first Cheltenham Festival winner on Zarkandar in the Triumph Hurdle and passed the half-century of winners for the first time. This is his first season as No.2 to stable jockey Ruby Walsh for British champion jumps trainer Paul Nicholls

You had a big winner for Paul Nicholls on Zarkandar, but how did the job as No.2 come about? And how long did it take to say yes? I was chatting to Paul one day towards the end of the season and it went from there. I wasn't expecting to be asked that question and there was an awful lot to think about, it wasn't as easy as saying 'yes' straight away. I had to think about it for a good month or six weeks. I had a great job with Nick Williams, we had won the Hennessy last year and we

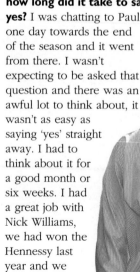

had a great association. There was also David Arbuthnot, we had a great season too with Topolski winning at Aintree.

As a No.2 you don't know which horses you'll be riding. Is that a difficult change to make from being stable jockey for Nick Williams? That's just the way it is, it's the job you take on board. Ruby's over in Ireland quite a bit and there's plenty of horses to ride when he's not around or he's riding at another meeting on a Saturday. It's a team effort and hopefully I can slot into that team.

And what about outside rides? Nick's got his stable jockey with James Reveley, but I'm hoping to ride the majority of David Arbuthnot's horses. He's been a good supporter and he's got a lot of exciting horses this season.

Last season you had a personal-best of 56 winners, but you were already halfway to that total by the end of August this time. What are your aims for the season? No real targets, I just want to settle into the role and help the team as much as I can. The quality is very good here, very strong all year round. It's an exciting time for me.

ALL YEAR ROUND RACING!

UTTOXETER RACING & EVENTS

THE **BIG ONE**

BETFRED

MIDLANDS GRAND NATIONAL
SATURDAY 17 MARCH

www.uttoxeter-racecourse.co.uk

NEWCASTLE RACING & EVENTS

Three days of prestigious racing...

THE NORTHUMBERLAND **PLATE** FESTIVAL

SEATON DELAVAL RACEDAY
GOSFORTH PARK CUP NIGHT
JOHN SMITH'S NORTHUMBERLAND PLATE DAY
28 - 30 JUNE

www.newcastle-racecourse.co.uk

FONTWELL PARK RACING & EVENTS

FONTWELL PARK **FESTIVAL**
Two days of first class jump racing!

FULLERS LONDON PRIDE RACEDAY
SOUTHERN WATER CHARITY RACEDAY
5 - 6 OCTOBER

www.fontwellpark.co.uk

CHEPSTOW RACING & EVENTS

THE **PRIDE**
THE **PASSION**

CORAL

WELSH NATIONAL **2012**

WELSH NATIONAL
THURSDAY 27 DECEMBER

www.chepstow-racecourse.co.uk

NORTHERN RACING & EVENTS

Northern Racing Ltd includes; Bath, Brighton, Chepstow, Fontwell Park, Great Yarmouth, Hereford, Newcastle, Sedgefield and Uttoxeter racecourses

TOM EAVES

Eaves, 30, a graduate of the British Racing School, has long been considered one of the best jockeys on Britain's northern circuit. The Wigan-born rider crowned another successful campaign in 2011 with a first Group 1 win in the Prix de l'Abbaye on Tangerine Trees, trained by his principal employer Bryan Smart.

You've enjoyed a fabulous year. What was the target at the start? "Things have gone even better than I could have wished for. As the year progressed the target was to reach 100 winners in a season for the first time. By early October I was close to my personal-best of 87, so I've got to be delighted. I'm not going away in the winter. I'll be sticking around and riding on the all-weather again."

What have been the highlights of 2011? "Tangerine Trees has been an absolute star for me. I've won three races on him this year and it was an amazing day when he won the Prix de l'Abbaye. I'm still on a high from it and I'll never forget it. Bryan Smart has given me plenty of winners and I've ridden plenty for Michael Dods too. People have supported me and I appreciate it."

Which horses are you most looking forward to riding in 2012? "Tangerine Trees is the best I've ridden and I hope he can win a few more Group races next season. Move In Time is another I'm excited about. He progressed really well this year and held his own in Group and Listed races before winning the Rous Stakes at Ascot. He stays in training and should have another good season. I'd like to ride a few more Group winners, enjoy some success in a big handicap or two and ride 100 winners. Those would be my targets."

GRANDS CRUS

Trainer David Pipe
Form 97212/11122-6

The story so far Nothing special in his first season, with just a Plumpton novice hurdle to his credit from five starts, but was second to a couple of high-class performers (Wishfull Thinking and Sanctuaire). Transformed in second season and plans to go novice chasing were shelved when he scored easy wins in handicap hurdles at Cheltenham and Haydock before running away with Grade 2 Cleeve Hurdle. Would have been champion staying hurdler but for a certain Big Buck's, who put him

in his place at Cheltenham and Aintree (Grands Crus respectively 1¾l and 7l clear of the others). Sixth in French Champion Hurdle behind Thousand Stars in June, when the early pace was slow and he pulled hard.

The next chapter One of the best hurdlers to go chasing in recent years (peak RPR of 171) and Pipe is excited about his potential over fences. Started the season as ante-post favourite for the RSA Chase and has the right credentials as long as he takes to fences, being proven at 3m in top company over hurdles and at Cheltenham (two wins and second in World Hurdle from three starts).

Biggest worry at Cheltenham is whether the going will come up too fast for this soft-ground lover.

What they say "I've always held him in the highest regard. He's unique in that he is very quiet in the box and he walks down to the gallops with his head on the floor, but when you get him on the gallops you can't stop him, hence we hold him up and try to preserve as much energy for the end as possible" – Pipe

If he were an Olympian he'd be Phillips Idowu (GB triple jumper). Only good enough for silver last time but widely expected to be on the top step this time

LAWNEY HILL

Hill trains from her husband Alan's 1,000-acre family farm at Aston Rowant, Oxfordshire, and was a successful point-to-point trainer before taking out a full licence in 2005. Last season was her best yet, with 26 winners, including smart handicap hurdler Ski Sunday

You made a big jump with 18 winners in 2009-10 and took another step up last season. Where do you go from here? The aim is to improve every year. We said we'd give it five years to see if it worked, but you have to bear in mind that the first year we had only three horses. After three years we were struggling, but then we turned the corner.

You had a good summer, with 14 winners by the end of August, and look well on target for another personal-best total. What are your aims for the season? I'm nervous of setting targets, but that's not to say we're not optimistic and forward-thinking. What we'd really like is to improve the quality of the string and I think we've done that. You want horses good enough to go to the bigger meetings and we'd love to have a winner at one of them.

Alan has a point-to-point yard at the farm. How do the two operations fit together? They work well together. The young horses can go point-to-pointing, which gives them the chance to get racing experience before they come into my yard, and it works the other way too – for example, Sarahs Gift, who has been brilliant for us and won six handicap chases, is in the handicapper's grip now and he'll go point-to-pointing out of Alan's yard. I probably have 30 to 50 horses in throughout the season, but only 23 on my books at any one time.

Ski Sunday was your flagbearer last season. Which horses are you most hopeful about this time? Ski Sunday is not with us anymore – the rugby guys who own him wanted to have him nearer home in Wales and he's back with Tim Vaughan – but we've got a nice bunch of horses. Universal Soldier is a very good horse who was with Nicky Henderson and won well at Chepstow on his only run over hurdles for us. He's on a mark of 143 over hurdles and he'll go chasing now. He needs every inch of three miles and a staying course like Chepstow is his cup of tea. Doctor David has come to us from Caroline Bailey, again because the owners want to be closer to him. He's a high-class chaser, suited by flatter tracks and between two and two and a half miles. Brough Academy is a nice young horse we bought in Ireland, where he won a bumper on his last run. He has schooled well and, although he's not very big, he looks an exciting prospect.

TOP OFFER
Trainer Roger Charlton ● *Form 1*

The story so far Arrived at Newbury for his debut in August with such a big reputation that he started 6-4 favourite and he didn't disappoint, winning his 7f maiden by 3½l. He was a little slowly into stride and took a keen hold, but showed a willing attitude and stretched clear in great style to leave his 14 rivals well strung out. Was entered in the Dewhurst and Racing Post Trophy and Charlton initially said there was no point putting him away but, after a slight setback, that was exactly what happened.

The next chapter Richard Hannon was among those "very impressed" by Top Offer and was keen to avoid taking him on with Harbour Watch, which is some compliment. Top Offer is by Dansili, the sire of top-class 1m4f performers Harbinger and Rail Link, and entries as a two-year-old suggest connections will be looking beyond 1m for him in 2012. Quoted at 20-1 for the Derby after debut success and looks another excellent prospect for owner-breeder Khalid Abdullah.

What they say "I've always thought he was my best two-year-old. If I could keep only one of my two-year-olds, it would be him. He looks the part and has always been a nice mover" – Charlton

 If he were an Olympian he'd be Bradley Wiggins (GB cyclist). A leader on his team and inspires respect from his rivals

QUEST FOR PEACE
Trainer Luca Cumani ● *Form 3-31115*

The story so far Galileo colt who had four starts for Aidan O'Brien and won the last two, including a Listed 1m4f contest at Roscommon in July after which he was described as "a big baby" by jockey Colm O'Donoghue. Bought by a partnership including US owner Earle Mack and former Australian cricketer Simon O'Donnell and transferred to Luca Cumani, winning the Group 3 Cumberland Lodge at Ascot on his first start in Britain and then finishing fifth in the Grade 1 Canadian International.

The next chapter Looks set to excel as a four-year-old in Group races at 1m4f and Melbourne Cup a long-term target (owners and trainer had seventh-placed Manighar in 2010). Improved RPR to 116 at Ascot (from 108 at Roscommon) and has "a big future" according to jockey Kieren Fallon. Cumani clearly looking towards 2012 as his big year.

What they say "I knew he'd run well [at Ascot] because he'd been working well and improving each time in his work. He's a got a very good action and is well balanced" – Cumani

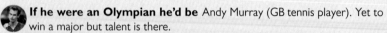 **If he were an Olympian he'd be** Andy Murray (GB tennis player). Yet to win a major but talent is there.

FIRST LIEUTENANT
Trainer Mouse Morris
Form 11/41311-312

The story so far The €255,000 top lot at the 2008 Derby Sale lived up to the price tag with Grade 1 wins at Leopardstown and the Cheltenham Festival last season. Won a maiden point-to-point and a bumper on his first two runs for Gigginstown House Stud but then lost two of his first three starts over hurdles, both on soft ground he reportedly did not handle. In that case, winning the Grade 1 Future Champions at Leopardstown on heavy ground was an excellent effort. Kept back for Cheltenham after that, he was the narrow winner of a Neptune thriller in which he benefited from Oscars Well's blunder at the last. Morris said that race was "plan A, B, C and D" and put Punchestown defeat down to First Lieutenant being over the top.

The next chapter Has made a good enough start as a chaser, which was always expected to be his forte, and the hope is that he'll thrive in top-level company, as he did last season. Ireland's Grade 1 novice chases, along with a return to Cheltenham for the RSA Chase, are on the agenda. Not surprising that this son of Presenting (also sire of Morris's Gold Cup winner War Of Attrition) showed his best form on good ground at Cheltenham and the future looks bright.

What they say "The Neptune was very slow and wasn't a real stayers' race. It turned into a bit of a sprint, which would not suit him as he has a high cruising speed rather than a turn of foot. Chasing will be his game" – Morris

If he were an Olympian he'd be Paddy Barnes (Irish boxer). Fighting Irish with a strong track record

DENIS HOGAN
Hogan, 24, from Cloughjordan, County Tipperary, is one of the most intriguing personalities in Irish racing. He is attached to Charlie Swan's yard as a jockey, riding 13 winners in 2010-11, and the past year has seen him break through as a trainer in his own right, with ten winners from a small dual-purpose string

How did you get started? Although my family are into farming none of them is into horses. When Charlie Swan, who is a neighbour of ours, retired from race-riding, he opened a riding school near where I live and I went along for a look. I learnt to ride there and drifted into the racing yard from that. It didn't take me long to be caught by the bug. It's safe to say the whole family are big into horses now.

Combining the role of jockey and trainer can't be easy. What does your typical day involve? I'm usually down at Charlie's to ride out a couple of lots and then head back to my place for breakfast around 9am before getting stuck in to our own horses. It's busy, especially during the summer when you're travelling to ride at meetings that evening, but there's an incredible buzz from it when things are going well. It takes a bit of juggling but I'm lucky to have good help at home.

How do you think riding horses helps your other role as a trainer? Knowing a horse from his work at home in the mornings means you're always looking for an angle, thinking about what track could suit the horse and where it should go next. For me the most interesting part of training horses is placing them and riding them on the track can only help with that.

What are your hopes for this season? The plan is to have good-quality horses in training and keep riding away. I would love to become a bigger trainer but for the moment I love what I'm doing and I hope I have time on my side to progress as a jockey first. You have the rest of your life to train horses.

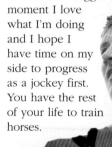

ZARKANDAR
Trainer Paul Nicholls ● *Form 111*

The story so far Half-brother to Arc winner Zarkava out of multiple Group 1 winner Azamour but failed to live up to regal breeding for the Aga Khan. Only success in three Flat starts came on his debut in minor 1m4f race at Clairefontaine but was a revelation over hurdles after being bought by Nicholls for owners Chris Giles and Jared O'Sullivan. Immediately sent into Graded juvenile hurdles, he impressed in the Adonis at Kempton and just 20 days later landed the Triumph at Cheltenham. After another 20 days, he added a second Grade 1 in the Anniversary at Aintree.

The next chapter The Champion Hurdle – the one big Cheltenham race missing from Nicholls's roll of honour – is the target. Has never won by far and has some way to go from an RPR of 147, but the Aintree win in particular may be better than it looked as he had been suffering with a mouth abscess in the days before the race. With the Cheltenham form franked in different ways by Unaccompanied and Grandouet, connections are justified in aiming high.

What they say "When I bought him I loved him, but he was coltish and badly behaved. He would have killed you if he could, but since we had him gelded he is like your best mate. He'll be a great horse. He's our little Hurricane Fly" – Nicholls

If he were an Olympian he'd be Mark Cavendish (GB road cyclist). A little devil at times but unbeatable in the right mood

OSCARS WELL
Trainer Jessica Harrington
Form 270/21114-

The story so far 'Unlucky' only begins to describe how he was beaten in the Neptune at Cheltenham, where he jumped the last in front but skewed on landing and finished fourth. Everything had gone so smoothly until that 'OMG' moment, with two Grade 1 wins – including the Deloitte at Leopardstown – among his three successes from four starts over hurdles before Cheltenham. All his wins have been on soft or heavy, although good ground did not seem to inconvenience him in the Neptune.

The next chapter It's never a good idea to chase your losses and the Oscars Well team were level-headed enough to put him away after Cheltenham rather than try for the big win at Aintree or Punchestown. The Neptune form was looking weaker by the end of the season, but he is highly progressive and should do well in whichever sphere Harrington chooses.

What they say "He travelled so well at Cheltenham, almost too well really. He jumped the last fine and just knuckled on landing. Robbie [Power] said he would have won. He said he hadn't even gone for him" – Harrington

If he were an Olympian he'd be Dayron Robles (Cuban 110m hurdler). Chance of revenge after victory was taken away in dramatic hurdles race.

MON PARRAIN
Trainer Paul Nicholls
Form P1P1316112/5312-

The story so far Already has plenty of experience, having started his career over hurdles in France shortly after his actual third birthday. Progressed steadily in 12 French runs, winning three of his seven chase starts, but possibly not best suited by having to race mainly on very soft and heavy ground. Reported to have had a problem in the autumn of 2010 but joined Nicholls and hugely impressive on first start in Britain (his first in nine months) when winning 3m1/2f handicap chse at Sandown by 22 lengths. Favourite for Topham at Aintree next time and looked set to win until fading late on.

The next chapter Superb jumper who was exhilarating over the Aintree fences and looks a Grade 1 chaser (Nicholls considered the Totesport Bowl at Aintree before settling on the Topham). Aintree defeat was hard to explain but, that nagging worry aside, the champion trainer has high hopes for him. Youth not a barrier for French-breds, as Long Run proved, and could go all the way to the Gold Cup, possibly even this season.

What they say "I was astounded by the way he won on his first run for me. He'd only been with me a few weeks and hadn't done that much work. You will not see a better exhibition from a five-year-old" – Nicholls

If he were an Olympian he'd be Dai Greene (GB 400m hurdles world champion). A fast, slick jumper who oozes class.

HARRY BENTLEY
Bentley, 19, honed his riding skills with hunting and pony club action before jumping at the chance of an offer to join Sussex trainer Gary Moore as an apprentice. After 13 winners in 2010, he more than trebled his total in 2011 to mount a strong challenge for the apprentices' title

You've firmly established yourself as a young rider going places. You must be thrilled with how the year has gone. "Absolutely. It all started off so well, riding winners at the Dubai Carnival, and there have been some high-profile wins this summer, particularly Navajo Chief at York's Ebor meeting for Alan Jarvis and a win in a Class 2 handicap at Newmarket's July course."

How aware are you of the difficulties most apprentices face when their claim runs out? "I've got to prove to trainers that I'm as good as the top lads. It's definitely in the back of my mind, but I'm confident in my ability. Gary Moore has held my licence this season, but he has allowed me to ride for lots of other trainers. In some respects, I've been a freelance. He's been great to me."

Are you going back to Dubai again this winter? "Yes, that's the plan. It's great out there. There are only three meetings a week and the trainers seem to like apprentices. I've still got my 3lb claim and hopefully I'll be in demand again. Last year I was getting a full book of rides against the top jockeys in the world. I learnt a lot from my spell there and it has served me well in England this summer."

Plenty of people are tipping you for stardom. What's your biggest ambition in racing? "I'd love to win an English Classic or a Group race and to be considered a top jockey. Ryan Moore has helped me immensely. He came in one morning about a year ago to ride out for his dad and it was just me and him on the gallops. He promised he'd sort Dubai out for me and, along with his mum Jane, he was as good as his word."

CARLTON HOUSE
Trainer Sir Michael Stoute ● *Form 21-134*

The story so far A brief recap for anyone who's been on a desert island for the past six months: the Queen is given gift horse by Sheikh Mohammed; the colt wins Dante and goes off 5-2 favourite for Derby; nation's hopes dashed as Carlton House finishes third to Pour Moi at Epsom; more disappointment when fourth in Irish Derby, again as favourite.

The next chapter Sense of anti-climax with his Classic season but reached RPR of 121 and still lightly raced. Hard to say lost shoe in closing stages made a difference in the Derby but there was the mitigating factor that Stoute had a poor season by his standards. If the trainer is back to his usual form in 2012 and shows his customary skill with high-class older horses, Carlton House could still bring joy to the royal household.

What they say "He had a hold-up close to the Derby and during it he got too far back and then had to run wide into the straight. He's a high-class horse and he will have a big day" – jockey Ryan Moore

 If he were an Olympian he'd be Zara Phillips (GB three-day eventer). Hopes of royal success after a year that could have gone better

IMPERIAL MONARCH
Trainer Aidan O'Brien ● *Form 1*

The story so far Fourth in betting on debut in 1m Curragh maiden in September, with stablemate Wimpole Street favourite, but won smoothly by 3½l on yielding to soft ground. Ranged from 16-1 to 25-1 for Derby after that.

The next chapter Well-related colt by Derby winner Galileo out of 1m4f Listed-winning half-sister to Derby runner-up Blue Stag, making him a

half-brother to another Derby runner-up in The Great Gatsby. No prizes for guessing what the ultimate aim is with this colt.

What they say "He has a lovely pedigree and worked like he was ready to run. Usually some of ours can be a bit green but he wasn't" – jockey Seamie Heffernan

If he were an Olympian he'd be Jason Kenny (GB track cyclist). First, not another second, is the aim

DISCOURSE
Trainer Mahmood Al Zarooni ● *Form 11*

The story so far Winning debut in 6f Newmarket maiden in June came at expense of odds-on stablemate Gamilati, by a short head at 16-1, but soon became clear she was held in high regard by Godolphin. Six weeks later she won the Group 3 Sweet Solera over 7f by 4½l, earning RPR of 112, and looked likely to play major role in late-season Group 1 races. Reported in mid-September to have suffered a minor setback, however, and did not appear again.

The next chapter Blue Bunting was a dual Classic-winning filly for Al Zarooni in 2011 and he has high hopes again with Discourse, Fillies' Mile winner Lyric Of Light and Pimpernel. Stable vibes and running plans – Discourse seemed first choice for the Fillies' Mile, with Lyric Of Light earmarked for the Prix Marcel Boussac – suggest she is their No1 for the Guineas going into the winter. Shortest-priced of the Godolphin fillies in the Guineas betting at general 8-1.

What they say "She should get a mile no problem. Before her first run we thought she was a nice filly but then she improved physically. She has three-year-old written all over her" – Charlie Appleby, assistant trainer

If she were an Olympian she'd be Jessica Ennis (GB heptathlete). Could be a flagbearer if she gets over 2011 setback

KISSED
Trainer Aidan O'Brien ● *Form 1*

The story so far All about the pedigree as Kissed is a half-sister to 2011 Derby winner Pour Moi and Gagnoa, who achieved an RPR of 115 when 3l runner-up to Zarkava in the French Oaks and again when third to Moonstone in the Irish Oaks. More than satisfactory racecourse debut on soft ground in 1m maiden at Navan in October, winning by 1½l and 9l clear of the third.

The next chapter Generally shorter for the Oaks (16-1) than the Guineas after maiden success, not surprisingly as her debut was over 1m and she has the pedigree to go further. Pour Moi improved once he got fast ground in the Derby and this filly looks set to blossom next summer.

What they say "She's a very nice filly. It was very testing [at Navan] and there should be plenty of improvement in her" – jockey Joseph O'Brien

If she were an Olympian she'd be Katie Taylor (Irish boxer). Big hopes that this Irish girl can pack a punch

BRED IN AUSTRALIA AND WINNING AROUND THE WORLD

Rocket Man   Black Caviar   Sacred Kingdom   Anabandana   Kinshasa No Kiseki

Australian-breds have demonstrated their unrivalled versatility, durability and quality by winning a total of 66 Group 1 races in 7 different countries in both the Northern and Southern Hemispheres over the 2010-11 racing season.

This success was highlighted by Australian-bred **Black Caviar** topping the official World Thoroughbred Rankings at 130, the first time ever a runner from the Southern Hemisphere has achieved this honour.

From Australia to New Zealand, around the Middle East, South Africa and throughout Asia, Australian-bred Thoroughbreds are setting new standards for international success.

Winners last season include: **Black Caviar** (Australia), **Anabandana** (New Zealand), **Rocket Man** (Dubai and Singapore), **Better Than Ever** (Singapore), **Igugu** (South Africa), **Delago Deluxe** (South Africa), **Sacred Kingdom** (Hong Kong), **Kinshasa No Kiseki** (Japan) and **Ultra Fantasy** (Japan).

Australian-breds are renowned for being tough, versatile and fast in any environment and are sought after by the world's best judges.

Wherever you reside, wherever you want to race your horses, you can share in the thrill of winning like so many other owners of Australian-bred horses.

www.aushorse.com.au   *Igugu*

DAVID O'MEARA

O'Meara, 34, from Fermoy in County Cork, was a jump jockey in Britain for ten years until retiring from the saddle in 2008. He has been training since June 2010 at Nawton, North Yorkshire, at the Arthington Barn Stables owned by Roger Fell, his business partner

You had 25 winners in 2010 but look set to double that total this year. What have been the highlights of 2011? Plenty of them – Pepper Lane winning the Great St Wilfrid, Blue Bajan winning a Group 2 and running really well in the Goodwood Cup, Smarty Socks winning a big handicap at Ascot, Viva Colonia winning a Listed hurdle at Market Rasen.

Several of your handicappers have run up sequences this year after being bought cheaply. What do you look for? In a yard that's just starting out, you have to work on a budget. If a horse has shown a level of form, but perhaps not for a while, you know it's in there somewhere and it might be worth a go. But I have to like the horse. Count Bertoni, for instance, had hardly beaten a horse in his last four races before he joined us, but his best mark was nearly a stone better. He was only £2,000 and he's won three times this year. We don't expect that kind of improvement but we do our best.

What's the next step for you? We've done well at some of the big meetings at York, Ascot and Goodwood and we'd like to keep doing that. We've bought some yearlings and paid a bit more for them, so hopefully we'll have some nice two-year-olds. We had 65 horses at the height of the season this year and we'll have 75 boxes next year, so if we can fill them we'll be happy.

Are there any horses we should watch out for? War Poet is a lovely horse to go jumping. He won twice for us on the Flat this summer. Mont Ras won three times for us this year and then was fourth at York. We put him away after that and I think he'll be very useful next year. Blue Bajan will be back for some Cup races – if he can be as competitive again at ten years of age we'll be delighted. Smarty Socks could have a crack at a Listed race and maybe Pepper Lane will get some black type.

PEDDLERS CROSS
Trainer Donald McCain ● *Form 1/111111/1127*

The story so far A brilliant novice hurdler in 2009-10, rounding off an unbeaten season with impressive victories in Grade 1 Neptune at Cheltenham and Grade 2 Mersey at Aintree. Graduated to the senior ranks just as smoothly last season, defeating Binocular in Grade 1 Fighting Fifth and heading to Cheltenham still unbeaten. Gained more admirers with a never-say-die effort in the Champion Hurdle but found Hurricane Fly just too good, then after that hard race put in his only disappointing run when well beaten by Oscar Whisky at Aintree.

The next chapter Now it's time to go chasing and fences aren't unfamiliar to him, as he won a maiden point-to-point in Ireland before joining McCain. The aim is the Arkle at Cheltenham, rather than the longer RSA, and no doubt he has the speed after his Champion Hurdle display. A most exciting prospect.

What they say "Everything he does scares me to death. The worry for me is not having had a horse like this before and the fear that I could make a mess of the chance we've been given. This is a horse to dream about" – McCain

 If he were an Olympian he'd be Tom Daley (GB diver). A prodigy from an early age who could fulfil his destiny this year

PARISH HALL
Trainer Jim Bolger ● *Form 12821*

The story so far Out early as at two, winning in April, but was then held back until July. Failed to win in first three attempts in Pattern races, most disappointingly finishing eighth of nine in Group 1 Phoenix, but turned his form round with 20-1 victory in driving finish to Group 1 Dewhurst at Newmarket.

The next chapter Bolger's fourth Dewhurst winner in six years merits respect, as the previous three include Derby winner New Approach and unbeaten but subsequently unraced champion juvenile Teofilo (Parish Hall's sire). At 16-1, shorter for the Derby than the Guineas and Epsom is the big target.

What they say "He's very good on top of the ground. He's in their [Bolger's Dewhurst winners] league and is a very solid horse. I'd look on him as an Epsom horse" – Bolger

If he were an Olympian he'd be Louis Smith (GB gymnast). Balance as well as strength needed for big test

Join us at
The Currragh in 2012

featuring a mouth watering menu of some of the world's leading races

THE Curragh RACECOURSE

Sun 25th Mar	**Lodge Park Stud Park Express Stakes & Irish Lincolnshire**
Sun 22nd Apr	**Big Bad Bob Gladness Stakes**
Mon 7th May	**Newbridge Community Race Day (BH)**
Sat 26th May	**Abu Dhabi Irish 2000 Guineas**
Sun 27th May	**Etihad Airways Irish 1000 Guineas & Tattersalls Gold Cup**
Sun 10th June	**Silver Stakes**
Fri 29th June	**Derby Friday (Eve)**
Sat 30th June	**Dubai Duty Free Irish Derby**
Sun 1st July	**Stobart Ireland Pretty Polly Stakes**
Sat 21st July	**Lifetime in Racing Achievement Day**
Sun 22nd July	**Darley Irish Oaks**
Sun 12th Aug	**Keeneland Phoenix Stakes**
Sat 25th Aug	**Galileo Futurity Stakes**
Sun 26th Aug	**Irish Cambridgeshire**
Sun 9th Sept	**Moyglare Stud Stakes**
Sat 15th Sept	**The Irish Field St Leger**
Sun 30th Sept	**Juddmonte Beresford Stakes**
Sun 14th Oct	**Hackett's Bookmakers Irish Cesarewitch**

FOR FURTHER INFORMATION ON our variety of Admission, Dining & Hospitality, Race and Stay Packages, Membership, Advertising Opportunities and Sponsorship PLEASE CALL
045 441205 EMAIL info@curragh.ie or SEE www.curragh.ie

Runners and riders at the start of a 3m
handicap chase at Huntingdon in February.
Honourable Arthur, ridden by Denis O'Regan,
won the race **Edward Whitaker**

BATTERED BRUISED & BRILLIANT

Hurricane Fly, Big Buck's and Quevega dominated the major hurdle races at the big festivals and for Ruby Walsh it was a perfect spring after the winter from hell

Words by Steve Dennis

R UBY WALSH is sitting in the sunshine outside the weighing room at Listowel and every five minutes or so someone comes over to shake his hand. The racegoers speak with one voice: "Good to see you back, Ruby. Best of luck, hope you stay safe and sound this season."

Walsh thanks them, assures them he'll try to stay in one piece. Everyone knows it isn't that simple. Walsh is three days into his second comeback of 2011 and the enforced downtime has lent a sour note to the year. "Of the last 17 months I've missed ten," he says. "That's a hell of a lot of time to be sat at home. I was lucky when I came back last time and hopefully I'll be lucky again, get a clear run."

The long periods of inactivity began on April 10, 2010, when he broke his arm in three places in a fall from Celestial Halo at Aintree. Walsh was back in action in mid-August, only for the inaction to begin again after he broke his right leg when Corrick Bridge fell at Down Royal in early November. Back in the saddle at the beginning of March in time for Cheltenham, Aintree and Punchestown, Walsh then damaged his neck at Killarney in July. Now here we are at Listowel, in the middle of September.

Missing eight weeks of the summer isn't the disadvantage for a jump jockey that missing eight weeks in November and December would be, of

Continues, page 108

course, as Walsh's main employers Paul Nicholls and Willie Mullins are not noted for busy summer campaigns. Sitting out the heart of the jumps season, as Walsh had to do, is a living nightmare.

"Am I a good patient? You'd have to ask my wife Gillian about that," he says. So we did. "He's easier to live with in the summer than the winter when he's injured," she says. "But he's a good patient and he had the two girls and his ride-on lawnmower to keep him busy this summer."

At least Walsh has the consolation of an immaculate lawn, which is almost certainly no consolation at all. The only consolation that counted last season was being back in time for Cheltenham 2011; Walsh never doubted he'd make it. "I'd always have Cheltenham driving me on to recover. To ride any winner at Cheltenham is special. All those long days in the gym, when it's hard work and feeling like it, I just started thinking of Cheltenham and it spurred me to do a bit more.

"I thought I'd be back riding in early February, but I probably didn't accept that the leg was broken as badly as it was. The arm was probably a worse injury but, looking back, the leg was pretty mangled at the time. Realistically, I did well to make Cheltenham, but being a jockey, a bit of a career optimist when it comes to injury, I was sure I'd make it.

"It healed very well. I was lucky, I had a cage around the leg like a halo, which meant I could put all my weight on the leg. It was a bit inconvenient but I could do a lot of gym work and keep up a general level of fitness. Having a toddler around the house [daughter Isabelle] meant I had to be mobile to keep up with her, so it was lucky I had the cage and I could get about. Mentally you might stop yourself putting weight on the damaged leg, but with a toddler disappearing into the distance you just forget about that, you get up and go. I was confident I was more than fit enough when the time came. Match practice was all I needed."

Big Buck's 'An aeroplane, incredibly good'   **Quevega** 'A deadly mare'

By that time, the imperative of returning in time for the biggest meeting of the year was being keenly felt. Given the festival's overarching importance, match practice would be kept to a minimum. Having missed so much, missing a little more wouldn't hurt.

"The surgeon asked me 'do you have to be back in the middle of February?' and I said 'no, I have to be back at the beginning of March'. As soon as I said that he said 'fine, then the cage isn't coming off until then'. I couldn't take it off myself, not like the old plaster casts that you could cut off if you were desperate. The extra two weeks did it good and I had the backing of Willie and Paul that they didn't mind me not coming back until March."

That brought its own problems. The show had been going on without Walsh, other jockeys riding the horses he normally rode. There were certain horses that Walsh could be sure he'd ride at Cheltenham – the holy trinity of Big Buck's, Hurricane Fly and Quevega, for example – but such a prolonged period on the sidelines meant any notion of collateral form, or knowledge of the invisible, ineffable way a horse may have been progressing, was denied him.

During his winter layoff he had ably articulated the feeling, saying: "Nothing beats the interpretation I can get from riding in races against other horses rather than taking someone else's word for it. If my first day back was the first day of Cheltenham and I had choices to make in certain races, I'd be more likely to pick the wrong one than I would with six weeks' race-riding under my belt."

There is the theory; Walsh was **Continues, page 110**

Hurricane Fly 'A very high-class horse'

A queen and a pair of kings
Where Walsh's star hurdlers rank among the best

Big Buck's
*Festival wins in 2011 Ladbrokes World Hurdle (Grade 1, Cheltenham),
BGC Partners Liverpool Hurdle (Grade 1, Aintree)*
Irresistible in the staying hurdle division since switching back from fences at the start of 2009, winning 12 straight races up to the end of the 2010-11 season, and among all hurdlers of the past 20 years only Istabraq has achieved a higher RPR. Seven-time Grade 1 winner and has scored hat-tricks in the World Hurdle and Liverpool Hurdle. Best RPR of 178 (achieved in 2011 Liverpool Hurdle) puts him 2lb clear of Baracouda, Deano's Beeno, Iris's Gift and Limestone Lad in the staying hurdle division and 4lb ahead of Inglis Drever, the only other triple World Hurdle winner

Quevega
*Festival wins in 2011 David Nicholson Mares' Hurdle (Grade 2, Cheltenham),
Ladbrokes.com World Series Hurdle (Grade 1, Punchestown)*
Indisputably the best jumps mare of recent years after three consecutive wins in the Grade 2 David Nicholson Mares' Hurdle at Cheltenham, as well as twice beating the males in the Grade 1 World Series Hurdle at Punchestown. Best RPR of 159 was achieved in latest Punchestown win, putting her joint-seventh on the list of top jumps mares since 1990 alongside Mysilv and Shuil Ar Aghaidh, with Lady Rebecca top on 169

Hurricane Fly
*Festival wins in 2011 Stan James Champion Hurdle (Grade 1, Cheltenham),
Rabobank Champion Hurdle (Grade 1, Punchestown)*
Seven-time Grade 1 winner in Ireland before impressive victory in 2011 Champion Hurdle, on first visit to Cheltenham, erased any doubt about his standing as a top-class 2m hurdler. RPR of 173 in the Champion was the joint-best figure by a 2m hurdler in the past decade, alongside Istabraq and Rooster Booster. Joint-fourth on 2m hurdler list since 1990 – Istabraq (181) is the clear leader but Hurricane Fly is close behind Alderbrook and Dato Star (both 175) and alongside Collier Bay and Rooster Booster

quick to illustrate the practice. Faced with a choice of two Nicholls-trained contenders in the Triumph Hurdle, he got it frustratingly wrong. "I rode Sam Winner instead of Zarkandar in the Triumph, finished fourth instead of first," he says, the wrong choice still a vexation at six months' remove.

"I hadn't ridden either horse but had been impressed by Sam Winner and I often find the form at Kempton in February [where Zarkandar made a winning debut] can be false. That's how I read the situation, maybe if I'd have ridden them both I'd have come to a different decision. Maybe. You don't always get it right when you're riding but you're in a better position, not guessing so much. Because you're always bloody guessing anyway."

Walsh wasn't guessing at all when it came to Big Buck's, Hurricane Fly and Quevega. The opportunity to ride just one of those three would have dragged any jockey off his sickbed and the prospect of spring glory had kept Walsh going through the literal and figurative dark days of winter.

Cheltenham is a hard place on horses, with the parades, the crowds, the atmosphere. It didn't buzz Hurricane Fly up, but it didn't help him

The festival started as well as he could have dreamed with victory aboard Al Ferof in the Supreme Novices' Hurdle. The boost it gave to his confidence was immeasurable. Three races later he was on the Champion Hurdle favourite Hurricane Fly, the pair reunited after the seven-year-old had won four successive Grade 1s in the hands of Paul Townend. It was like Walsh had never been away.

"All I had time to do was hack him out on the Monday and Tuesday mornings before Cheltenham," says Walsh. "I set out with a game plan and thankfully it came off, although he ran a bit freer than I'd have liked him to. Cheltenham is a hard place on horses, with the parades, the crowds, the atmosphere. It's easier for them at Punchestown, say. No, it didn't buzz him up but it didn't help him.

"He's a very high-class horse. I wanted him to jump the first couple of hurdles quick and get in the position I wanted him in, rather than let him just **Continues, page 112**

Looking forward to . . .

I'm very fortunate, Paul's the best trainer in England and Willie's the best in Ireland and they're always getting new talent, which is what you need to keep going forward.

There's a lot to look forward to this season. There's Zarkandar, although it's always tough for a five-year-old in the top hurdles. He's a hugely exciting horse, he had a hard race in the Triumph Hurdle but then went to Aintree and still won – you have to love that.

Obviously there's Hurricane Fly, Quevega and Big Buck's. I'm sure Al Ferof *(right)* and Sam Winner will be great novice chasers, I'm really looking forward to riding them.

There's Kauto Stone *(bottom right)*, he's not over-big but he had great form in France – whether I can see him carrying 11st 10lb I don't know. I hope he can but I'd need to see him do it first. If he can carry that kind of weight he could be anything.

Quel Esprit *(top right)* is well handicapped. He fell when leading in the RSA Chase, then got knocked over at Punchestown. He's never shown his true potential and is on a lenient mark – there's definitely a big race in him.

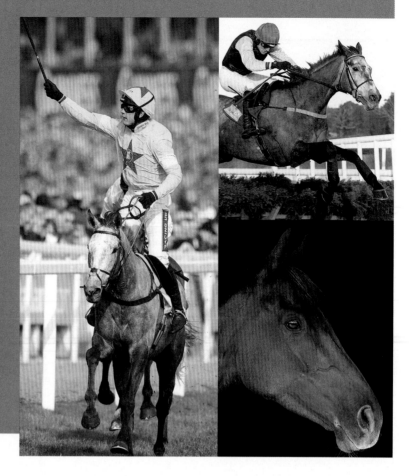

pop the first two and relax. I was prepared to get him on the bridle and going forward rather than sacrifice the position I wanted."

Hurricane Fly was always travelling well and Walsh was able to ride the blueprint race he must have long planned. Smuggled into the race before being driven into the lead at the final flight, Hurricane Fly seemed always to have the measure of Peddlers Cross on the run-in and prevailed by a length and a quarter.

It was Walsh's first Champion Hurdle, making him one of the few jockeys who have won all four of the festival's great races. The day was going well; it got better. An hour later he was lifted aboard Quevega, the banker of the week for so many, in the David Nicholson Mares' Hurdle.

"She's a very good mare and has been exceptionally well trained by Willie," says Walsh. "All I had to do was keep out of trouble and keep it simple. The only one I was worried about was Sparky May and she lined up behind me. I was fairly confident I'd beat all those in front of me and then Sparky May ran a bit free and passed me, so I just slotted in on her tail and followed her.

"I was having some day that day, so my confidence was up, and in that state you try things and they just come off, you get the rub of the green and get lucky, not unlucky. She took a right step at the last, clipped the top, could have turned over. But she didn't."

It was easy. Quevega is the best mare around by a long way, by ten lengths that day. She was still on the bridle at the last, on a tight rein on the run-in. There was punditry afterwards about trying a different angle after completing this hat-trick in the David Nicholson – maybe the Champion Hurdle or the World Hurdle – but not for the first time Walsh adheres to the 'keep it simple' argument.

"I'd listen to Willie, he's dead right. Why, when you can line up a hot favourite for a race at Cheltenham, would you send her for a race that she might not win? The other races are more prestigious but any Cheltenham winner is a great winner. She'd be more likely to go up rather than down in trip anyway. Oh, she's a deadly mare."

Stick not twist, then. It might be wise, for however good Quevega is she'd have a hard time against Big Buck's, the third leg of Walsh's precious patent. Walsh doesn't want to have to make the choice, is pretty sure he won't have to, wouldn't have to think too long about it anyway.

"Big Buck's is an aeroplane," he says, which doesn't really seem fair on the others. "He's not the greatest jumper ever but he's an incredibly good horse, a machine. He's a great horse to ride, he always keeps a bit for himself."

What percentage the preternaturally talented eight-year-old allows himself to expose is always enough. His winning streak stood at 12 by the end of the season, but there were whispers before the World Hurdle that perhaps his match might have been found. It lent the race the prospect of a duel rather than a parade, but then again an aeroplane will beat a mere horse any time.

"Grands Crus would have been an exceptional winner in any other year, but he ran into arguably the best staying hurdler there's ever been," says Walsh, animated now. "I knew they were going to follow me, they had to follow me. That's what I would have done if I'd been riding against Big Buck's, so I just had to ride my own race. I had to judge it so that the horses in front could carry me to a point where I could set sail for home.

"When I went for it they were coming at me from both sides, Mourad and Fiveforthree

Continues, page 114

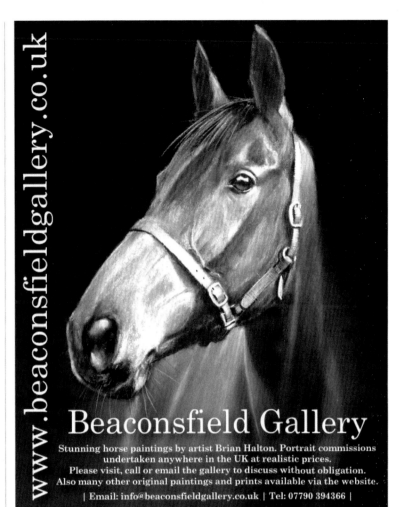
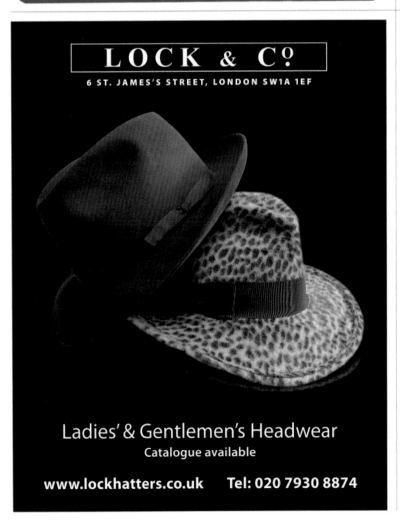

No pressure
Paul Nicholls allowed Walsh to come back in his own time

on my right and Grands Crus on the left, so I had to work out which side to go with, had to wait for them to come to me because I didn't want to go one side and then find them dropping away on me. Thing is, Big Buck's is just a better horse than Grands Crus. I threw everything at him and there was plenty there."

Big Buck's raced with an unaccustomed prominence on his World Hurdle hat-trick bid, chasing the leader Cross Kennon for the final circuit before taking it up between the last two. Walsh dropped his whip at the last and Grands Crus loomed menacingly as they started up the hill, but Big Buck's had more in reserve (not including the bit he was keeping for himself). A length and three-quarters was more than enough.

And then Walsh says, almost as an afterthought, a few words that send a shiver up the spine. "We've never seen Big Buck's flat out. If we ever do, it'll be something all right."

That spring offensive, continued by the victories of Big Buck's at Aintree and Hurricane Fly and Quevega at Punchestown, was rich compensation for the time lost through injury. Winners are one thing, big winners are quite another as far as Walsh is concerned.

"I've ridden 31 winners at the Cheltenham Festival and those 31 would make me far better known and give me a far higher profile than being champion jockey in Ireland [eight titles] would. Don't get me wrong, it's a privilege to be champion, but for me it's about the big

winners, the big days, Grand Nationals, Gold Cups. I get a much bigger kick out of that."

The temptation is to ask whether Walsh would forgo large chunks of the season in exchange for the guarantee of big-race wins at the spring festivals; that temptation is resisted for fear of a scornful answer. Because he's back now, doing what he loves and is best at, better at than most.

The hope is widespread that he gets the clear run he's looking for, stays out of the emergency room. Walsh couldn't be blamed for being more selective about his rides, more circumspect about the risks he faces whenever he leaves the weighing room. But that's not the jump jockey's way.

"Look at it," he says, looking at it. "Celestial Halo, you could never see that happening. Corrick Bridge, I must have ridden him a dozen times. These weren't dodgy rides. The last one [Friendly Society] didn't even fall. The horse in front of me jumped across him and he clipped heels, and I went out over his ears. It's what happens. If you go out half-hearted you may as well stay inside."

With that, he goes out to ride Blazing Tempo in the Kerry National, leaving behind a warm glow engendered by his parting comment. "Anyway, I'll be around for a lot longer yet – I've got to make up for all the time I've missed."

What a prospect that is. On the way to the parade ring someone stops him, shakes his hand. You can't hear what they're saying but you can guess.

'Better than me'
Walsh on Townend

"There's no rivalry between us. It's a big picture. Paul can ring me and ask anything he wants about a horse and I'll tell him honestly, and I'll do the same with him. That's the way we work. It's a team. You want to ride every horse, every day, but that can't happen.

"He's a hell of a jockey and a great lad as well, confident but not cocky, and that's a rare combination. He's clever, he's well-mannered, he has a lot of things going for him.

"A better jockey than me? I'd say he is. He's only 21 and he'll undoubtedly be a better jockey when he's 26 and again at 31, physically stronger, mentally harder – just imagine him in ten years."

GIVE YOURSELF THE BEST CHANCE

Many Happy returns

Five previous Cheltenham Festival winners did the business again in 2011. The people who know them best explain the magic attraction of the Cotswolds in March

Words by Steve Dennis,
Jessica Lamb and Nick Pulford

BUENA VISTA *above and left*
Festival form *6365211*
Festival wins *Pertemps Final (2010, 2011)*

It was deja vu all over again at Cheltenham in 2011, not once but five times. Big Buck's and Quevega completed hat-tricks in the Ladbrokes World Hurdle and the David Nicholson Mares' Hurdle respectively, while Albertas Run won his second Ryanair Chase and Sizing Europe did the Arkle-Champion Chase double.

Those four top-notchers were joined by a true Cheltenham Festival stalwart, not a big name, not a superstar, but one who through the unexpected nature of his feats has become a public favourite among the

festival crowds.

Buena Vista is the sort of horse who makes jump racing special. Now ten, he has run seven times at the festival, competing there in every season of his career. He started out in the Champion Bumper in 2005 (finishing sixth), then tried his luck in the Supreme Novices' Hurdle (third), Arkle Chase (sixth) and Pertemps Final (fifth, runner-up, winner, winner). He comes alive in the spring as though he grew in the ground, feeling the "force that through the green fuse drives the flower" better than any bed of daffodils.

Before he hit the jackpot in the 2010 Pertemps, David Pipe's hardy perennial hadn't won for more than three years. Not too many people imagined he'd win again a year later, a 20-1 chance on a seven-race losing streak partnered by a conditional jockey who had never had a ride at the festival. But he did.

"I wasn't worried about the build-up, didn't have time, because I didn't know I was riding him until the day before the race," says Conor O'Farrell, who claimed a valuable 5lb off the old-stager, some of whose rivals had not been born when he first ran at the festival.

"Mr Pipe told me to jump off handy, be in the first five or six, and if he pulled his way to the front then let him go on, but I'd watched the video from the year before and I decided we were going to make the running.

"It was the best feeling I've ever got from a horse over hurdles. Unbelievable. The first time I thought we might win was when we turned down the back side for the second time. Knockara Beau joined me going to the second hurdle down the back and I said to myself 'I need to wing this' . . . and he came up outside the wings for me, made two lengths in the air. He just took off again. Then we stretched them coming down the hill and I kicked for home.

"He loves Cheltenham, something makes him come alive round there. It was my first Cheltenham winner and to do it on a horse like him and with the reception we got afterwards made it very special. I was overwhelmed, it didn't really sink in until a week later, and everyone was still talking about it."

The previous year Buena Vista had given 3lb claimer Hadden Frost his debut festival victory and chances are he'll have a new rider in 2012 as O'Farrell is likely to have ridden out his claim by then.

"He's looking fantastic at the moment and he'll have another busy season before heading back to the festival in March," says Pipe. "What helped him most in the last two seasons was the ground drying out and hopefully he'll get conditions to suit him again. We'll look after him and he'll tell us whether he can do it again – he's been at the yard so long it's like he owns the place."

He has a proprietorial air when it comes to Cheltenham too and, if he turns up for a scarcely credible eighth time, if he comes down the hill on the final circuit in front with the hat-trick in his grasp, there'll be another twang of deja vu to reckon with.

A generation ago, Willie Wumpkins completed a hat-trick in the race (1979-81) when it was known as the Coral Golden Hurdle. Like Buena Vista, he was no superstar, but he loved Cheltenham and peaked in the spring. He is the sort of horse grandfathers tell their grandsons about and perhaps we have another from the same mould in Buena Vista – never the favourite but the public's favourite.

'We leave everything to Willie, all we do is party and enjoy'

QUEVEGA *above left*
Festival form 1 1 1
Festival wins David Nicholson Mares' Hurdle (2009, 2010, 2011)

The Hammer and Trowel Syndicate, a group of friends in the building trade who have known each other for 25 years, have really struck lucky since they went into racehorse ownership five years ago. Over fences they have had J'y Vole, who beat Big Zeb by five lengths in a Grade 1 novice chase, and they have the fast-
Continues, page 118

developing Thousand Stars, winner of the French Champion Hurdle in 2011. But, above all, they have Quevega, the queen of Cheltenham after three consecutive victories in the David Nicholson Mares' Hurdle.

They don't see much of the Willie Mullins-trained mare on the racecourse, but it's worth waiting for. As well as her three Cheltenham wins, she has also beaten the boys in the Grade 1 Ladbrokes.com World Series Hurdle at Punchestown for the past two years.

"She's been trained specifically for those two races," says a spokesman for the syndicate. "We run strictly on Willie Mullins's advice and guidance. We leave everything to Willie, all we do is party and enjoy."

All eight syndicate members were at Cheltenham last season and they enjoyed that all right. "It was a dream come true to do the treble and we're still partying on the back of it. The ambition is to go back and defend her title in 2012. I don't think any horse has ever won the same race four years in a row at the Cheltenham Festival. That would be the great goal for the lads. It would be just unreal."

If she wins again, the party will continue all the way from Cheltenham back to their "headquarters", Manzor's pub in Clane,

County Kildare. "We do nothing but talk about racing from one end of the week to the other. It's our whole life."

It's quite a life with Quevega around.

'That slog uphill from the last suits him so well'

BIG BUCK'S *below*
Festival form 7111
Festival wins *Ladbrokes World Hurdle*
(2009, 2010, 2011)

Few horses have dominated their specialist field as completely as the great staying hurdler Big Buck's, who completed a memorable hat-trick in the Ladbrokes World Hurdle last March.

"He just loves coming up the hill at Cheltenham," says owner Andy Stewart. "It's far and away the best track for him, whereas at Ascot, say, I always feel there's the possibility he may get caught out.

"As he's grown older he hasn't been hitting the flat spot that used to trouble him and that slog uphill from the last suits him so well.
Continues, page 120

Every year he's won at Cheltenham he's been upsides good horses but has had the natural strength and ability to take the initiative when it counts.

"On the evening before his first World Hurdle I was staring at my laptop, looking at Kasbah Bliss's Flat form, and in the end I phoned Paul [Nicholls] and said, 'Look, we're just wasting our time here.' And he said, 'You know, I think you might be surprised.'

"Last season, when he became the only horse to win the race three years on the trot, was very special and so was the party afterwards. The plan stays the same this season – Newbury, the Long Walk Hurdle, Cheltenham and Aintree."

'To see a horse you are with every day winning there is an amazing feeling'

SIZING EUROPE *above left*
Festival form 011
Festival wins Irish Independent Arkle Chase (2010), Sportingbet.com Queen Mother Champion Chase (2011)

In the past two years Sizing Europe has banished his Cheltenham demons with victories in the Arkle and Champion Chase, with trainer Henry de Bromhead's head man Tommy Maher guiding him all the way at home.

Why Sizing Europe is so good at Cheltenham is chiefly down to the time of year, but that's not all there is to it. "He loves the speed of the races there," Maher says, "and the competition. He seems to love the battle up the hill, as he proved by winning the Arkle and the Queen Mother. And, of course, he was going very well in the Champion Hurdle in 2009 before he got injured.

"To see one of the horses you are with every day winning a race at the best National Hunt meeting of the year is fantastic, it's an amazing feeling. It's one of the reasons why we work in the industry."

At home Sizing Europe is relaxed and easy to deal with. "He's self-assured and confident," says Maher, "and he loves his own space. He's an absolute gem to ride and gives you a great feel. I wish all the horses I ride gave me that feeling but then that's what makes him so special."

With a full team at home needing his attention, Maher can't go to Cheltenham but he's looking forward to watching another bold show when Sizing Europe tries for a festival hat-trick. "Before Cheltenham he seems to enjoy his work more, it's as if he knows he's getting ready for something big. I've no hesitation in saying that if we get him there in the same frame of mind and condition he was in this year, he'll be the one to beat in 2012."

'Last season was the best, it was just great'

ALBERTAS RUN *above right*
Festival form 01911
Festival wins Royal & SunAlliance Chase (2008), Ryanair Chase (2010, 2011)

"He's a spring horse, that time of year seems to see the best of him," says trainer Jonjo O'Neill. "And he likes Cheltenham as well, which is a plus."

Albertas Run has won at three of the past four festivals, following his victory in the 2008 Royal & SunAlliance Chase by taking the past two runnings of the Ryanair Chase. For such a talented horse, his chances on the big stage are often underestimated by punters and pundits alike.

"It's all about getting there on the day and often his form in the build-up hasn't looked great because he's had to contend with physical problems. It's nothing serious – his joints, his back, general wear and tear – but when he feels the sun on his back in the spring it makes a difference," O'Neill says.

"Last season was the best, it was just great. I'd been really struggling with him and he'd had a bad fall at Ascot in November, but he turned in a fantastic performance on the day. It was a great achievement and wonderful to have [owner] Trevor Hemmings there to watch him come back to his best. The target is a third Ryanair Chase."

Bet anywhere

Read, decide, bet – in a flash

RACING POST MOBILE APP

Download FREE now
RACINGPOST.com/mobile

The finest information *RACING POST*   The easiest way to bet

Gigginstown
GIANTS

Ireland had a record-breaking Cheltenham Festival and the charge was led by Michael O'Leary's team. But the Ryanair boss's success in 2011 didn't stop there and the trainers who handle his high-quality string are gunning for more glory in 2012

Words by Jessica Lamb

Run of success Davy Russell flies the flag for Ireland at the Cheltenham Festival on Coral Cup winner Carlito Brigante (opposite page) and (clockwise from left) there are more festival successes for Gigginstown with First Lieutenant at Cheltenham and Quito De La Roque and Lovethehigherlaw at Punchestown

A ll the money I waste on horses and all the money I waste on training bills is worth it for moments like this," said Michael O'Leary after watching First Lieutenant gallop to victory in the Neptune Investment Management Novices' Hurdle, the first leg of a memorable treble for the Ryanair chief executive at the 2011 Cheltenham Festival. With that line he summed up what Gigginstown House

Stud means to him. It goes against every business rule he applies to his airline, but it doesn't matter because it is his hobby and his passion.

Despite being the opposite to his job, Gigginstown is growing just as rapidly and has risen to the top at a similar rate. Before this year Gigginstown's maroon and white had been carried by six winners at the big three jumps festivals of Cheltenham, Aintree and Punchestown, but in 2011

that figure more than doubled. Alongside JP McManus, O'Leary's operation is now one of the twin powerhouses of Irish jump racing and this year's festival successes are likely to be only a taste of things to come.

Wherever Irish jump horses did well last season, Gigginstown was there in the forefront: three of Ireland's record haul of 13 winners at Cheltenham, including a Grade 1 with First **Continues, page 124**

Lieutenant; two more at Aintree, headed by Grade 2 novice chase scorer Quito De La Roque; another two at Punchestown, both Grade 1s with Quito De La Roque and Lovethehigherlaw.

Money is important in the Gigginstown success story, of course, but it is not the whole story. The festivals and the Grade 1 chases are the targets and the quantity is the means to the ultimate end: quality. That's what O'Leary meant when he referred to his spending. The reward, for him, is the big days, the big chases.

The people who run the conveyor belt of talent are crucial to the success of the operation. O'Leary is helped at the top by his brother Eddie, who works as racing manager alongside their main bloodstock agent, Mags O'Toole. Dot Love and Ciaran Murphy at Charlestown Stud break and pre-train the horses and Pat Doyle takes them to the point-to-point field, where multiple champion jockey Derek O'Connor is usually in the saddle. After a season in the point-to-point field they are assigned trainers and Davy Russell takes over in the saddle. Repeat this

process 100 times over and you too might have a Cheltenham Festival treble.

FIVE trainers contributed to Gigginstown's festival successes in 2011 and the only one who did it with two different horses was Willie Mullins. Not bad, even for the champion trainer, when you consider he was sent his first three horses last season. He ran them eight times in Britain and Ireland and won seven of those races. It's little wonder he has been sent two more horses for the new season.

Mullins was patient with each of his three Gigginstown horses and didn't send one to the racecourse until January. First up was Samain, bought from Eddie Hales the previous spring. Eight days after Samain won a Punchestown bumper, point-to-point winner Lovethehigherlaw did likewise at Fairyhouse and nine days after that French recruit Sir Des Champs won a conditions hurdle race at Navan.

Considering O'Leary is no fan of bumpers, nor even much of hurdle races, it augurs well that the Mullins trio – and indeed the two Cheltenham

Festival winners from other stables – all excelled in what Gigginstown treat as the nursery slopes before heading for higher peaks.

The team hope the patience will pay off with Sir Des Champs, whose only other run last season saw a remarkable late charge to victory in the Martin Pipe Conditional Jockeys' Handicap Hurdle at Cheltenham, under Mullins's nephew Emmet.

"Sir Des Champs looks a proper sort," Mullins says. "I was prepared to go over fences with him last season, but they said to wait a year over hurdles. I was delighted they did because it's probably going to crown him having had a nice easy season over hurdles.

"He seemed to improve from run to run and that culminated in a nice win at Cheltenham. It was terrific that Emmet was able to get the ride on him. You could see he had plenty in hand coming down to the last and you could see him thinking, 'if I can just jump this I'll win'. He jumped it very conservatively, got his horse right for it. You could see he was confident he **Continues, page 126**

Gigginstown's 2011 festival winners

CHELTENHAM
First Lieutenant (*trained by Mouse Morris*) Neptune Novices' Hurdle (Grade 1)
Carlito Brigante (*Gordon Elliott*) Coral Cup (Grade 3)
Sir Des Champs (*Willie Mullins*) Martin Pipe Handicap Hurdle

AINTREE
Quito De La Roque (*Colm Murphy*) Mildmay Novices' Chase (Grade 2)
Far Away So Close (*Paul Nolan*) John Smith's Handicap Hurdle

PUNCHESTOWN
Quito De La Roque (*Murphy*) Champion Novice Chase (Grade 1)
Lovethehigherlaw (*Mullins*) Champion Bumper (Grade 1)

V for victory Michael O'Leary celebrates in the Cheltenham winner's enclosure after First Lieutenant, ridden by Davy Russell and trained by Mouse Morris, left, took the Neptune

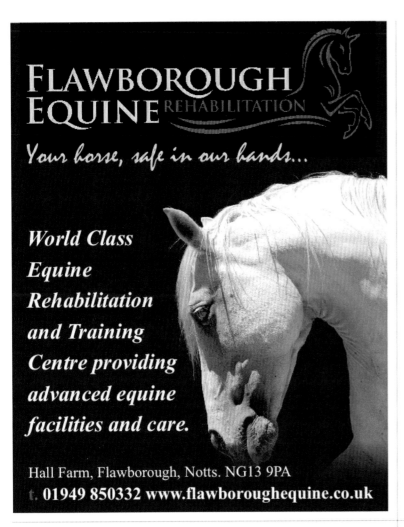

had enough in hand to win it after the last. He played the percentages and got over the last and won the race."

Samain's campaign was kept more low-key and he was unbeaten in three runs. Mullins's only defeat with a Gigginstown runner came in a Limerick bumper with Lovethehigherlaw, who later achieved the most prestigious win of the trio when landing the Betchronicle.com Champion Bumper at the Punchestown festival. It's a long way from there to the chasing arena loved by O'Leary, but they're ready for the next step.

"We decided to wait for the Curragh and Punchestown with Samain and Lovethehigherlaw rather than go to Cheltenham," Mullins says. "That paid off and they're two real nice sorts to go novice hurdling this season. They have a lot of ability. Both of them showed huge stamina and they're not slow either. It's early days but I'd say they're both Neptune horses.

"The way Sir Des Champs stayed on up the hill in the Martin Pipe would give you the impression an extra few furlongs wouldn't make any difference. That would give him the potential to become an RSA Chase horse."

RSA Chase? Now that's more to O'Leary's liking.

MULLINS may have been the top man for Gigginstown at the festivals, but Gordon Elliott got on the Cheltenham scoreboard too and overall he was the operation's leading trainer last season. He also has the biggest team numerically, into double figures at any one time, and his total of winners last season came to a round dozen in Britain and Ireland.

The highlight was Carlito Brigante's Coral Cup victory, on the same afternoon Elliott had opened his Cheltenham Festival account with Chicago Grey in the National Hunt Chase. "Yeah, it was pretty special," he says. "We've had Carlito Brigante since he was a juvenile hurdler. He won the Grade 2 for juveniles at Leopardstown's Christmas meeting on his first run for us and he was one of our first runners in a Grade 1 at Cheltenham."

A return to Cheltenham is on the cards for the promising youngster, who finished last term with fourth place at Aintree and third at Punchestown in Grade 1s. Once again, Gigginstown have been patient and Elliott appreciates that. "He's only five and we felt he needed another year over

Fight to the end

Gigginstown, with three winners, was at the forefront as Ireland pushed Britain all the way at the Cheltenham Festival

Tuesday British trainers take the first three races but Ireland come back strong with victory in the next three, including Hurricane Fly in the Stan James Champion Hurdle. The Ferdy Murphy-trained Divers wins the last, the Centenary Novices' Handicap Chase, to put Britain back in front
Running total: Britain 4 Ireland 3

Wednesday A great day for the Irish as they mop up the first six races on the card, including the Sportingbet.com Queen Mother Champion Chase with Sizing Europe and two more Grade 1s with the novices First Lieutenant and Bostons Angel. Britain stop the rot when Cheltenian wins the last, the Weatherbys Champion Bumper
Running total: Ireland 9 Britain 5

Thursday Ireland pick up the winning thread again when Noble Prince strikes in the opener, the Jewson Novices' Chase, but it's all Britain in the other five races, spearheaded by the Grade 1 victories of Big Buck's in the Ladbrokes World Hurdle and Albertas Run in the Ryanair Chase
Running total: Ireland 10 Britain 10

Friday Britain take the main honours with three Grade 1 wins, led by Long Run's stunning victory in the Totesport Cheltenham Gold Cup. Ireland hit back with three more winners, but the last-race decider, the Grand Annual, sees Britain edge in front after the victory of the Colin Tizzard-trained Oiseau De Nuit
Final score: Britain 14 Ireland 13

hurdles before going over fences, so we'll aim him at the big staying hurdle races and maybe work towards the World Hurdle. It's luck more than anything that you end up in this position and it's great to have that kind of team behind you. They are great men to work with, very easy."

The conveyor keeps turning and Elliott believes he has an ace among his youngsters. "We don't know how they're all going to fit in just yet, but Dom Cassock is one we're excited about. He's a four-year-old who works really well at home and could be very good over hurdles this season."

SOME wait a lifetime for a horse like War Of Attrition. Gigginstown found the 2006 Cheltenham Gold Cup hero in its second season on the scene and this term O'Leary has another rising star with a shot at chasing's big prize.

Quito De La Roque, based in Wexford with Colm Murphy, has never been to Cheltenham. He left Ireland for the first time last April and returned with a Grade 2 Aintree novice chase win before stepping up to Grade 1 class to land the Growise Champion Novice Chase at the Punchestown festival. "That's what you get when you send a great trainer rubbish material," O'Leary famously said after that win.

The ever cautious Murphy was quick to reply that his first top-class stayer would have to improve 20lb to be considered for the Gold Cup. Things changed over the summer. Murphy did his dreaming and now he's ready to go to war.

"He did nothing but improve time after time last year," he says. "We thought he was just a big mudlark because he had run only on heavy ground since winning his point-to-point and he'd handled it so well. I took a chance sending him to Aintree on the nice ground, but I knew he was good enough to win if he handled the ground. I genuinely had no idea whether he would. None of us did. At Punchestown he was just as good.

"I'd like to get two runs into him before Christmas. The Lexus Chase is the obvious race for him then, but there's no panic. You'd like to think he could prove by Christmas that he's good enough to go to Cheltenham for the Gold Cup."

That's the plan. As we found out at the big festivals this year, Gigginstown's plans have a habit of coming off.

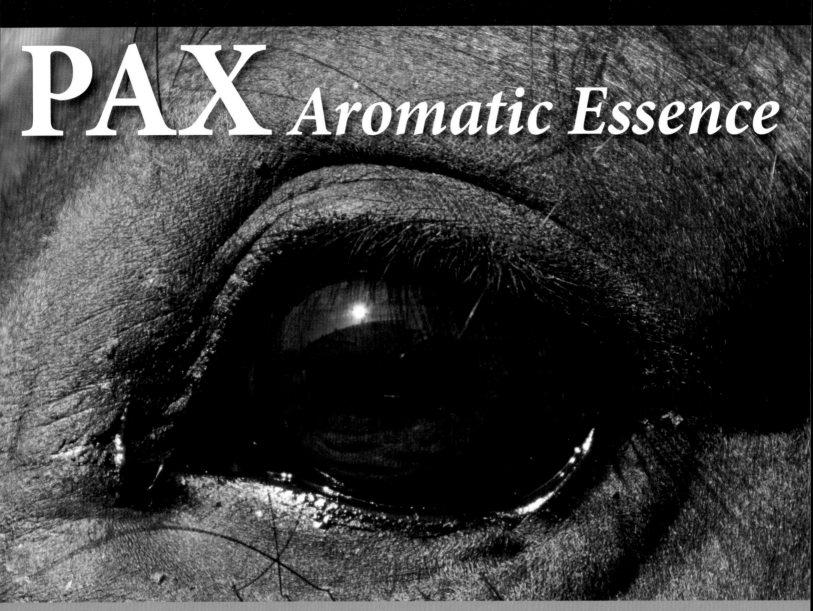

THE BIGGER PICTURE

Fun and fashion on day two of Royal Ascot in June. Despite the recession overall attendance at the five-day meeting was up 3.6 per cent
Edward Whitaker

O'Brien shuffles his pack

No stable jockey was no problem for Ballydoyle in 2011 as the master trainer played his aces and always seemed to have a joker up his sleeve

Words by Johnny Ward

NOVEMBER 6, 2010. At Churchill Downs, as the clock ticked down to the main Breeders' Cup day, Lee Mottershead of the Racing Post surprised Johnny Murtagh by asking for his reaction to the intensifying rumours that he was considering leaving Ballydoyle – the most coveted stable jockey's job in Europe.

Never has a "no comment" retort said so much in so little. Two days later, Murtagh confirmed the end of a glittering three-year period as first jockey that seemed to have given him everything except job satisfaction. His reasons for leaving were not crystal clear – even now that remains the case – and where it left Ballydoyle was anybody's guess.

Guessing and speculation abounded: the names of Ryan Moore, Pat Smullen and Christophe Soumillon – champions all – were soon thrown into the ring. This was to be a winter dominated not by the Classic prospects in O'Brien's stable, nor even by the recruitment of the Australian champion So You Think, but rather by rumour and debate about who would replace Murtagh.

Finally came the announcement that there would be no replacement but that O'Brien would use the best available. After nearly a decade and a half of consecutive years with a stable jockey – from Mick Kinane to Murtagh via Jamie Spencer and Kieren Fallon – the master of Ballydoyle was going to try something new. It seemed that, for him, it was the best option to take – at least for a season.

APRIL 10, 2011. Having had all those brilliant Irish-born riders to guide his horses in the past, O'Brien made a seemingly significant move by sending for an Englishman, Ryan Moore, on Ballysax day at Leopardstown. Moore rode Derby fancy Recital in the Ballysax but came third and was not even the best Ballydoyle finisher, with Colm O'Donoghue runner-up on Regent Street. But, with O'Brien's regard for Moore no secret, O'Donoghue and fellow Ballydoyle stalwart Seamie Heffernan might have wondered that day what scraps they would be left with on the big days.

When the first Classics rolled around three weeks later, Moore was again on board O'Brien's best chance of Guineas weekend at Newmarket when he rode Roderic O'Connor in what turned out to be a hopeless task against Frankel, finishing 11th. The next day, with Moore riding for Sir Michael Stoute, Smullen was on Misty For Me, Ballydoyle's shortest-priced contender for the Qipco 1,000 Guineas. But O'Donoghue produced the stable's best result again with second place on 33-1 shot Together, while Misty For Me came home 11th.

MAY 21, 2011. With Moore unavailable, O'Brien was left to divide his Abu Dhabi Irish 2,000 Guineas contenders among his home-based riders. The best

Continues, page 132

Riding high Clockwise from right, O'Brien with Ryan Moore; Colm O'Donoghue; Joseph O'Brien; Seamie Heffernan; and Moore strikes up a winning partnership with 2012 Classic hope Wading in the Rockfel at Newmarket

PROFIT SHARING

How O'Brien's Group I successes in Britain and Ireland were divided up

So You Think O'Brien's latest high-class Aussie import proved himself at Group I level in Europe with wins in the Tattersalls Gold Cup, Eclipse and Irish Champion, although there were disappointing defeats in the Prince of Wales's and Arc, and another narrow one in the Champion Stakes.
Jockeys who won Group Is on him
Seamie Heffernan (2), Ryan Moore (I)

Misty For Me Produced memorable front-running performance to rout Midday in the Pretty Polly, having got up to beat stablemate Together in the Irish 1,000 Guineas before that. Not disgraced in third when dropped back to 1m in the Matron.
GI wins Heffernan (2)

Treasure Beach Went from nursery defeat last year to Derby success. A game second at Epsom, he beat Seville in the Irish Derby before

enhancing his reputation with Grade I success at Arlington. Limitations exposed when pace-setting in the Arc.
GI wins Colm O'Donoghue (I, plus US GI)

Maybe Went from strength to strength following debut win at Naas in May, making it five from five when easily winning Moyglare in August. That copper-fastened her position at the head of the 1,000 Guineas market.
GI wins Joseph O'Brien (I)

Power Tough son of Oasis Dream whose only defeats came in Phoenix Stakes and when a little unlucky in the Dewhurst. Won his other four races and was particularly good when slamming Dragon Pulse in the National Stakes.
GI wins Heffernan (I)

St Nicholas Abbey The great hope who never really fulfilled the hype but did show

his reserves of stamina when winning the Coronation Cup at Midday's expense. Ran a fine race when fifth in the Arc.
GI wins Moore (I)

Roderic O'Connor Must go down as one of the most limited winners of the Irish 2,000 Guineas, owing victory mainly to the brilliance of his rider. Struggled thereafter.
GI wins O'Brien (I)

Fame And Glory Quelled stamina doubts with resounding success in Gold Cup at Royal Ascot, only to blot his copybook with two odds-on defeats at the Curragh before bouncing back in the Long Distance Cup at Ascot.
GI wins Jamie Spencer (I)

Crusade Had shown little in three starts before causing 25-1 upset in Middle Park.
GI wins Heffernan (I)

Coming of age
The party starts early as Joseph O'Brien, two days short of his 18th birthday, celebrates victory on Roderic O'Connor in the Irish 2,000 Guineas

chance, on 7-2 third favourite Roderic O'Connor, was given to Joseph O'Brien, the trainer's 17-year-old son, with Heffernan on Oracle at 25-1 and O'Donoghue on 40-1 shot High Ruler. The finishing order reflected the betting as the young O'Brien collected a first Classic on Roderic O'Connor.

Heffernan and O'Donoghue are long accustomed to a role mainly outside the spotlight and only occasionally in it, and even the rapid emergence of O'Brien seems not to have rankled with these two exceptionally loyal men. The rise and rise of the teenager had surprised many in 2010, particularly when he was given Listed-race rides ahead of Murtagh, but by the time he was handed his Classic opportunity on Roderic O'Connor it did not send the shockwaves that would usually greet an apprentice getting such a high-profile ride.

Perhaps, in the bigger picture, Roderic O'Connor's relevance to Coolmore should be seen for what it is, but what should not have escaped anyone's notice throughout the developing story of O'Brien's oldest son is that, while he is no doubt privileged, he is also a talented young rider. He is strong and rarely makes mistakes, and that day at the Curragh he showed something else too.

The Irish 2,000 Guineas was far from a remarkable race on the face of it, with a limited horse in Roderic O'Connor beating Dubawi Gold, who had been trounced by Frankel when runner-up in the Newmarket Guineas. But it will long be recalled because of the poise and panache of O'Brien in basically outriding Richard Hughes, who partnered the favourite and came with a run that was all too late. True, O'Brien was riding a less complicated colt, but one could not get away from his guile. His rise in stature was mirrored in physique, however, meaning that his days riding on the Flat are already numbered.

The impression that Moore was seen as the de facto Ballydoyle No.1 was reinforced the following day, when he rode 4-1 favourite Together in the Etihad Airways Irish 1,000 Guineas. But she was only just ahead of Misty For Me in the betting and, in what must have been a sweet success for Heffernan, it was the 5-1 second favourite who prevailed by three-quarters of a length from Moore's mount.

The most significant jockey booking of the weekend, though, was Moore's taking over from Heffernan for the steering job on So You Think in the Group 1 Tattersalls Gold Cup. Heffernan could have won on the 1-7 shot, no doubt, but this was clearly forward planning for the bigger Group 1 races to come for So You Think. He was going to be Moore's ride.

JUNE 15, 2011. Some said Moore went too early on So You Think in the Prince of Wales's Stakes at Royal Ascot, others argued that the Aussie champion had every chance. Either way, it was the biggest setback of the season to date for Ballydoyle as Frankie Dettori drove Rewilding past in the final

strides to win by a neck.

In other big races, Moore was more regularly an opponent than an ally by now – something the Coolmore bosses knew would happen eventually. Eleven days earlier, in the Investec Derby, he had been on the Stoute-trained favourite Carlton House, with four Ballydoyle horses against him. It was to be a triumphant day for Coolmore, but with the Andre Fabre-trained Pour Moi rather than the O'Brien runners.

O'Donoghue, with a ground-saving ride, nearly snared the prize on second-placed Treasure Beach, just ahead of Carlton House. Back in fourth, O'Brien had ridden a peach out in front on Memphis Tennessee. Heffernan would have wondered why Seville so disappointed down the field, but all three riders would have returned to Ballydoyle appreciating that many of the yard's Derby horses had disappointed at Epsom in recent years but left that form long behind afterwards.

That point was proved again three weeks later when Ballydoyle attacked the Dubai Duty Free Irish Derby with quality and

Continues, page 134

quantity, with the three riders keeping the same mounts and Carlton House once again the favourite with Moore on board. As O'Brien watched his three horses land a 1-2-3, he must have felt a quiet satisfaction at the way he had shuffled his pack.

There would have been particular pleasure as Treasure Beach led home the trio under O'Donoghue, who has spent half his life at the famous Tipperary yard but was yet to ride a Classic winner. A positive rider and strong in a finish, the Corkonian was accustomed to playing second (and even third) fiddle in the top races, but he was on the best Ballydoyle runner this time and he made the most of the opportunity with a faultless ride. Typically, he celebrated with humility and no great swagger.

By now, O'Brien's strategy was not just about using the best available, especially with Moore so often unavailable owing to other commitments and injury. What was becoming clear was that the riders at his disposal were being kept on certain horses once they had forged a partnership. Here was loyalty working the other way. O'Donoghue's work with Treasure Beach was to be rewarded again in August when, under a stern drive, the colt won the Grade 1

Secretariat Stakes at Arlington by a neck.

O'Donoghue was keen to thank his boss. "Aidan doesn't get the recognition he deserves for giving us this opportunity," he said. "From a trainer's point of view, it's easier to be able to say to owners that I've got this top jockey and we're going to retain him for the year. Aidan has taken it on board to pick the jockey who is going to suit each horse. He took a lot on his shoulders doing that, so it's great to see so many of the horses winning the big races."

Misty For Me, meanwhile, had become Heffernan's ride after her Guineas win. Even better was to come for the pairing when Heffernan rode a peach from the front to floor Midday in the Pretty Polly. Heffernan, an uncomplicated rider who has moulded a career out of reliability, was never praised as much for his tactical acumen as he was that day.

JULY 2, 2011. This was the day Heffernan really found out about the pressure that comes with riding the big horses in the big races, and it was the day he proved he could handle it. He had got the ride back on So You Think in the Coral-Eclipse but was going head to head against Moore, now on

Workforce. So You Think had been backed into 4-6, but a tactical race was possible with a small field and Moore knew his opponent well. Heffernan, though, was riding the crest of a wave after Misty For Me and his timing was faultless as he unleashed So You Think's turn of foot to beat Workforce by half a length.

Heffernan was just as good when So You Think gamely repelled subsequent Arc third Snow Fairy in the Red Mills Irish Champion Stakes; this time he had come out on top against Frankie Dettori. "The horse had loads left," quipped Heffernan, the comment of a man riding with the utmost confidence.

Speaking in mid-summer, Heffernan admitted that having to wait in line behind a stable jockey had sometimes been difficult to take. "It wasn't frustrating, it was very frustrating – to me, anyway," he told the Racing Post. "Now it seems to be working out well. I'm riding some very good horses and really enjoying what I'm doing. I've worked for Ballydoyle and Coolmore since 1996 and have always been looked after. I managed to win Group 1s and Classics on horses who weren't the first string, but this year, when there doesn't seem to be a stable jockey, Aidan seems to be able to use the jockey he thinks will best suit the horse. I'm happy my name is in the hat and that the odd day it comes out."

Not all about Ballydoyle
Five more who burned bright

Ireland had a newcomer to the list of Group 1-winning trainers in 2011 and there was notable success for other more familiar stables

Parish Hall (Jim Bolger): Teofilo colt left previous form behind when beating Ballydoyle favourite Power on favoured good ground in the Dewhurst. Goes into the winter as a leading fancy for the Derby at Epsom

Lightening Pearl (Ger Lyons): First Group 1 winner for her trainer with a brilliant success in the Cheveley Park at Newmarket. Legitimate contender for Classic glory in 2012

Emulous (Dermot Weld): Rapid improver for master trainer, looking as if she still had more to offer when bolting up in Group 1 Matron at expense of classy Ballydoyle three-year-olds

Banimpire (Jim Bolger): Busy all season, winning six races, and unlucky not to have won a Group 1, having being headed on the line in the Irish Oaks by Blue Bunting

La Collina (Kevin Prendergast): Beat the colts in the Group 1 Phoenix in August, with Power second. Well-beaten third behind Maybe in Moyglare next time, having previously run that filly to a neck in a Group 3

OCTOBER 8, 2011. "Just speculation," O'Brien said when asked about persistent rumours that Moore was about to sign for Ballydoyle. But that would not stop the whispering, especially after Moore was reunited with So You Think for the Qipco Champion Stakes – the richest prize in British racing history. Once again the pair were denied victory at Ascot, finishing second to Cirrus Des Aigles, but Moore gave the gigantic colt a perfect ride and there were no excuses.

Moore had been first choice the previous weekend, too, on Future Champions Day at Newmarket, when he rode Ballydoyle's most-fancied in the Dewhurst, Middle Park and Rockfel Stakes. He won just one of the races – the Rockfel on the hugely promising Wading – and in the Middle Park, riding Reply, he was denied by Heffernan on 25-1 stablemate Crusade. But to many this appeared another piece of forward planning by O'Brien, looking ahead to a Classic link-up with Moore, as this year without a stable jockey moved to a denouement.

O'Brien appreciates Moore's talent and the jockey, for his part, can work with Coolmore. It is a tried-and-tested partnership and putting them together in the 2012 Classics is some prospect.

EXPERIENCE MORE
AT LEOPARDSTOWN IN 2012

2012 FIXTURE HIGHLIGHTS

28th & 29th January	MCR Hurdle & BHP Insurance Irish Champion Hurdle
12th February	Hennessy Gold Cup
4th March	Pre-Cheltenham Schooling Day
28th March	Student Day
15th April & 13th May	Family Fun Racedays
June, July, August	Bulmers Live at Leopardstown
8th September	Red Mills Irish Champion Stakes
26th – 29th December	Leopardstown Christmas Festival

MEMBERS' CLUB

Join the Leopardstown Members' Club and be a part of the action with trainers yard visits, social events, the 'Inside Track' newsletter, exclusive discounts and offers and much more.

Find out more about the Leopardstown Members' Club on www.leopardstown.com

Leopardstown Racecourse, Leopardstown, Dublin 18 **Tel:** +353 01 289 0500
Fax: +353 01 289 2634 **Email:** info@leopardstown.com **Website:** www.leopardstown.com
Facebook: www.facebook.com/LeopardstownRacecourse **Twitter:** @LeopardstownRC

 Leopardstown Racecourse

RACE 8 2 m PROVISIONAL RESULTS 2.05.94

1st	6	VICTOIRE PISA		
2nd	9		1/2	
3rd	2		NK	
4th			NK	
5th			3/4	
			1	

Words by Nicholas Godfrey

VICTOIRE PISA

Trained by Katsuhiko Sumii, Japan

Victoire Pisa was the horse who, with a little help from his Japanese-trained compatriot Transcend, managed to put a smile on the face of a beleaguered racing community.

If the 2011 Dubai World Cup will never be thought of as one of the best renewals – in short, it was messy – it was none the less memorable for that, thanks to an incredible one-two for Japanese horses in the world's richest race.

The result was the greatest ever achieved by the nation's much-lauded bloodstock industry and it came just 15 days after the Japanese earthquake and tsunami that left 20,000 people either dead or missing.

Few at home may have been giving much thought to equine matters thousands of miles away, but there were tears of joy and sadness among connections after Victoire Pisa had beaten Transcend by half a length, having benefited from an enterprising ride by his jockey Mirco Demuro in a race where nothing got into contention from off the pace.

"To win the richest race in the world when Japan is going through a tough time is fantastic," said winning trainer Katsuhiko Sumii. "I felt the whole country was backing me."

A Classic winner at home as a three-year-old, Victoire Pisa had finished seventh behind Workforce in the previous year's Arc before landing Japan's end-of-season championship, the Arima Kinen.

His four-year-old campaign was compromised after his emotional victory in Dubai and another Arc bid was abandoned owing to a leg injury sustained soon after he travelled to France. His connections intended to give him one more run, probably in the Japan Cup, before retirement.

SEPOY

Trained by Peter Snowden, Australia

Ever wondered what happened to Sheikh Mohammed's maroon and white silks? They're alive and well, being used to excellent effect by the Sheikh's Darley operation in Australia. Horses carrying the colours had a stranglehold on the nation's top two-year-old contests in 2011, when the Darley team of trainer Peter Snowden and jockey Kerrin McEvoy completed an amazing clean sweep of the nation's five Group 1 juvenile races.

Sepoy and Helmet shared four of them. They were both seriously good horses, but Sepoy was blessed with more obvious star quality right from the outset. The son of Elusive Quality was duly named Australia's champion two-year-old after winning the Blue Diamond Stakes and the Golden Slipper, the biggest juvenile contests in Melbourne and Sydney respectively.

Amid rumours that a switch to Godolphin in Europe may be in the offing in 2012, early indicators for Sepoy's three-year-old campaign could hardly have been more encouraging. Going down the sprint route, Sepoy posted an astounding performance against older horses in the Group 1 Manikato Stakes under the lights at Moonee Valley, where things did not go entirely to plan as he missed the kick a stride and looked in danger of getting cut off from his inside gate.

Sepoy's supporters must have been a tad concerned as he had to work hard to get to the front. Appearances were more than a little deceptive, though, as the blistering colt shot clear off the final turn for a comfortable victory over a field also featuring Gai Waterhouse's five-time Group 1 winner More Joyous.

And Helmet? He won the Caulfield Guineas to put himself in line for the Cox Plate. Looks like they are making good use of those silks down there.

ROCKET MAN

Trained by Patrick Shaw, Singapore

The idea of a horse with a monkey on his back conjures some fairly odd mental images. Fortunately for Singapore sprint superstar Rocket Man, he got rid of his in March when he proved a class apart from his rivals in the Dubai Golden Shaheen.

Unbeatable in domestic company at Kranji, Rocket Man had lost four times in 17 previous career starts; all four defeats had come when he was tried against international Group 1 competition, where losing had become an unwelcome habit.

Any suggestion that he wasn't up to that level could hardly be substantiated by the form book. His biggest losing margin was half a length and if he had been just over a cumulative length faster over all four races, he would have won them all.

Still, his cv lacked that all-important success until Meydan confirmed him as one of the world's best sprinters – and two months later he repeated the dose with a spot of redemption in Singapore's KrisFlyer Sprint.

Rocket Man had suffered the ignominy of defeat in both the previous seasons on his home turf, losing on both occasions by a quarter of a length, to world champion sprinter Sacred Kingdom in 2009 and another Hong Kong star, Green Birdie, a year later.

This time there was to be no mistake as Rocket Man destroyed his opponents, winning by nearly five lengths at odds of 1-5, finally giving his adoring fans the sort of display they were so desperate to see.

A luckless passage in Japan in the Sprinters Stakes in October meant he could finish only fourth as a heavily backed favourite but it didn't really matter. Rocket Man had already shown the world what they've long since known in Singapore. Sprinters rarely come much better than this Australian-bred powerhouse.

BLACK CAVIAR left

Trained by Peter Moody, Australia

Are there any superlatives left to use in connection with the fantastic Black Caviar? As charismatic as they come, 'Miss Invincible' is nothing short of a phenomenon in Australia, where she became a household name after a series of jaw-dropping displays against top-class fields full of male rivals, including six Group 1s on the spin.

Black Caviar was named world champion sprinter during the 2010-11 season as she extended a celebrated unbeaten record to 13. That became 14 after a five-month summer break at Caulfield in October, when she began her five-year-old campaign by sauntering away from a Group 2 field at odds of 1-14, never in any semblance of danger at a 5f trip short of her best.

A straightforward victory was laced with sentimental significance down under as the sport's new superstar matched the sequence achieved by the legendary Phar Lap in 1931. That's the sort of league Black Caviar has been playing in.

Owned by a syndicate put together over a few beers on a houseboat and trained by leading Melbourne handler Peter Moody, Black Caviar has captured the imagination like few racehorses before her.

Possessing every bit of the style and elegance suggested by her name, she is also blessed with an abundance of speed, strength and power – plus that indefinable X factor that turned her into public property. Black Caviar became the people's champion, putting thousands on the gate wherever she appeared on a national tour taking in Melbourne, Sydney and Brisbane.

To nobody's great surprise, she was named Australian horse of the year. Her fame spread well beyond native shores, though, and at one time she led the world rankings overall according to official handicappers, despite her never having appeared on the international stage. The intention is for that to be remedied in 2012, when a trip to Royal Ascot is firmly on the agenda.

HAVRE DE GRACE
Trained by Larry Jones, USA

LET'S hear it for the girls. After the dominance of Zenyatta and Rachel Alexandra, it was once again left to the fillies to spark a largely moribund US season into the occasional fit of life via the rivalry between the four-year-olds Havre De Grace and Blind Luck.

The year started with the 2010 Kentucky Oaks winner Blind Luck clearly on top, having beaten her arch-rival on three of the four occasions they had met as three-year-olds (one pyrrhic victory, as Unrivaled Belle beat them both in the Breeders' Cup Ladies Classic).

Blind Luck was named champion three-year-old filly, but the pecking order was to be revised in 2011, despite the score being one-all on the racetrack as Havre De Grace slammed Blind Luck at Oaklawn only to be touched off in the Delaware Handicap when conceding 2lb.

Elsewhere, though, the markedly improved Havre De Grace was unstoppable, beating the boys in the Woodward Stakes at Saratoga before running away with the Grade 1 Beldame at a muddy Belmont. There, an eight-length victory from top three-year-old filly Royal Delta convinced connections to target the Breeders' Cup Classic – a race won by her sire Saint Liam in 2005.

"I seriously think this is the closest I've ever witnessed to the perfect racehorse," said trainer Larry Jones. "I thought Secretariat was that when he retired. If she has a flaw anywhere, anyhow, I haven't found it."

And what about Blind Luck? She put in an abject performance in her Breeders' Cup trial at Santa Anita, where she finished last of seven in the Lady's Secret. A Grade 1 winner at two, three and four, she had never finished outside the first three in 21 previous starts and she was duly ruled out for the rest of the season, number one no more.

ANIMAL KINGDOM *below*
Trained by Graham Motion, USA

BRITISH-trained horses may not have much of a record in the Kentucky Derby but a native Englishman certainly left his mark in 2011 when Maryland-based Graham Motion saddled Animal Kingdom to win America's most celebrated race.

The colt's prospects were not entirely obvious before the race: a turf-bred son of Brazilian-bred miler Leroidesanimaux, he had never even raced on conventional dirt.

Although Animal Kingdom had won his trial six weeks earlier, it was only the lowly Grade 3 Spiral Stakes at Turfway Park, and that's on the all-weather – which is probably why he was sent off a 21-1 shot for his internationalist syndicate owners, Team Valor.

Animal Kingdom made those odds look decidedly generous as he roared down the stretch under the Twin Spires, claiming the $2m contest by an emphatic two and three-quarter lengths to post the most impressive victory in a confused Triple Crown series.

"The horse was just so powerful," said Cambridge-born Motion, whose father Michael used to be the US representative for sales company Tattersalls. "He's a magnificent animal but I wasn't sure he would handle the switch to dirt. He's an amazing horse."

Amazing he may have been, but he wasn't amazing enough to end the nation's Triple Crown drought, although he came close to winning the Preakness, failing by half a length to catch Shackleford after being given too much to do at a more speed-favouring venue.

Three weeks later, he produced an eyecatching mid-race move before flattening out to finish only sixth in a muddy, muddled Belmont, after which it transpired he had suffered a season-ending slab fracture to his near-hind leg that required surgery.

Bad news, then. But the good news is that he'll be back as a four-year-old, with the Dubai World Cup 2012 as his primary target.

AMBITIOUS DRAGON
Trained by Tony Millard, Hong Kong

Ambitious Dragon did not look an obvious candidate for the Hong Kong horse of the year title when he started the season entrenched in the next-to-lowest division of the territory's handicap system.

However, it was this humble New Zealand-bred son of Australian stallion Pins who ended up equalling the Hong Kong record with seven victories, including three Group 1 events.

Cheaply bought at a slice over £20,000, Ambitious Dragon was a revelation, winning six of his seven starts after taking a Class 4 handicap in October for his South African trainer Tony Millard. He progressed quickly, but it was something of a surprise when he took the HK Classic Cup from a field of top performers at Sha Tin in February. It was no fluke, though, as a three-quarter-length victory over subsequent Group 1 winner Xtension in the Hong Kong Derby was to demonstrate before he showed that he had improved out of all recognition with a fine burst of speed to beat an international field in the Audemars Piguet QEII Cup under 11-time champion Douglas Whyte.

"I can't really single out which one was the most impressive as he really shone each time," said Millard. "But either the Derby or the QEII because he was quietly ridden and ran past two very good fields pretty easily in the straight each time."

The form of both those races certainly worked out well with Xtension, Mighty High, Gitano Hernando and Wigmore Hall all later winning at the highest level in various jurisdictions across the racing globe.

Ambitious Dragon continued where he left off on his return to action at Sha Tin in October, shredding a high-class field under a big weight in a Group 3 handicap with his trademark rush from the rear. "He's probably the best horse I've ever ridden," said Whyte.

Jonjo O'Neill before the Aintree Legends charity race, in aid of the Bob Champion Cancer Trust, at the Grand National meeting in April
Edward Whitaker

THE WRITERS' AWARDS

Horse of the year (Flat)
Frankel. Every time he ran it felt like a chapter was being written in the history of the greats.

Horse of the year (jumps)
Big Buck's. His unbeaten run is a great achievement and the turbo-charged win at Aintree was the closest the jumps got to Frankel's 2,000 Guineas.

Race of the year (Flat)
Zafonic was pretty amazing when he flew out of a storm to win the Guineas in 1993, but Frankel was lightning itself.

Race of the year (jumps)
Long Run's Gold Cup. The best staying chasers of recent years going head to head.

Ride of the year (Flat)
Frankie Dettori on Never Can Tell in the Cesarewitch. A great thinking ride by a jockey whose canniness is one of his undervalued qualities.

Ride of the year (jumps) This year's amazing Tony McCoy show was at Warwick in January on Folie A Deux (below, centre), the 9-4 favourite who hit 1000 on Betfair and got up to win.

Personality of the year Sir Henry Cecil. Had us hanging on every word, just like in the old days, and added

immeasurably to the story of Frankel.

Rising star Charlie Longsdon is a trainer to watch.

Comeback of the year
Bensalem. Unlucky losers at Cheltenham don't always get a second chance but he did, after being close to death, and he took it.

Unluckiest horse
Excelebration, a winner every time he didn't meet Frankel.

Most improved horse
Treasure Beach. Beaten in a nursery and looked hardly Group class at two, but beat Nathaniel at Chester, almost won the Derby and did win the Irish Derby.

Flop of the year Workforce. Well done for trying, but keeping him in training at four didn't come off.

Bargain buy Danedream. The €9,000 filly's Arc win is another performance that will live long in the memory.

Best pundit Matt Chapman. Sometimes annoying, always entertaining. He's got what the Morning Line lacks.

Best day at the races The opening day of York's August meeting is always a great occasion.

NICK PULFORD

Horse of the year (Flat)
Frankel, whose performances electrified the summer.

Horse of the year (jumps) Long Run showed there can be life beyond Kauto Star. He looks capable of one day matching the achievements of the jumping great.

Race of the year (Flat) Frankel's 2,000 Guineas for the colt's explosive speed and Sir Henry Cecil's sheer daring in instructing Tom Queally to kill off his rivals early in the race.

Race of the year (jumps) The Cheltenham Gold Cup was the race of many years, not just this one.

Ride of the year (Flat) William Buick's growing maturity as a big-race jockey was never more evident than on Dream Ahead in the Prix de la Foret. He was alive to the tactics of Goldikova's team and nailed her close home.

Ride of the year (jumps) With Long Run as his mount, Sam Waley-Cohen was the equal of McCoy and Walsh at Cheltenham.

Personality of the year The enduringly popular Sir Henry Cecil, whose outstanding career was recognised by a deserved knighthood.

Rising star If Tom Symonds can marry his encyclopaedic knowledge to the training skills learned under Nicky Henderson and James Fanshawe, he could become a major force in the sport.

Comeback of the year Ruby Walsh missed three months of the campaign through injury but returned to win when it mattered.

Unluckiest horse The glut of big races that fell to three-year-

You'd be hard pressed to turn a bigger profit on a racehorse investment than Heiko Volz, who bought Danedream for €9,000

olds underlined the disappointment of losing Pour Moi to injury before he had the opportunity to add to his Derby success.

Most improved horse Prohibit, no better than Listed class last year, suddenly found a new lease of life to win the Golden Jubilee and back that up with a series of solid efforts in the top sprints.

Flop of the year The record of Derby winners that stay in training is not good and, after an outstanding 2010, Workforce fell short of expectations in 2011.

Bargain buy You'd be hard pressed to turn a bigger profit on a racehorse investment than Heiko Volz, who bought Danedream for €9,000, sold a half-share before the Arc and then saw her win the €2.3m prize.

Best pundit RUK's Graham Cunningham. A consummate professional, at ease in front of the camera and in complete command of his subject.

Best day at the races Royal Ascot Tuesday had everything: a memorable battle between Canford Cliffs and Goldikova, another victory for Frankel and more than a dash of controversy.

JON LEES

Horse of the year (Flat)
Frankel. The sight of him romping away from the field in the 2,000 Guineas was one that will have our grandchildren's grandchildren marvelling in years to come.

Horse of the year (jumps)
Long Run, undeniably the best chaser around. Who knows how good he could become?

Race of the year (Flat) The Chester Vase, in which subsequent Irish Derby and Secretariat Stakes winner Treasure Beach pipped Nathaniel, who went on to land the King George VI and Queen Elizabeth Stakes.

Race of the year (jumps) The Scottish Grand National, Beshabar from Wales outlasting Merigo of Scotland and the English Always Right in a cracking four-miler.

Ride of the year (Flat) Eddie Ahern on Overturn, judging things perfectly from the front and turning the Chester Cup into a one-horse race.

Ride of the year (jumps)
Jason Maguire, in front from before halfway on Ballabriggs in the John Smith's Grand National and kept enough in reserve to hold on at the line.

Personality of the year
Hayley Turner, two Group 1 winners in a breakthrough season.

Rising star David O'Meara's exploits with Blue Bajan, Pepper Lane and the like suggest he is a trainer destined for big things.

Comeback of the year What can beat Dominic Fox's emotional winning return at Ayr after nearly two years out,

during which he had lost his father and come close to death himself?

Unluckiest horse Big Buck's, an awesome staying hurdler who does not get the acclaim he deserves as he races in a Cinderella division.

Most improved horse Hoof It (pictured), from useful handicapper to one of Europe's top sprinters.

Flop of the year Binocular had looked so good in winning the 2010 Champion Hurdle that his 2010-11 campaign was something of an anti-climax.

Bargain buy Belle Royal, the £800 filly who has continued on the up to take her record to seven wins and over £80,000 in prize-money for trainer Mark Brisbourne and owner Peter Mort.

Best pundit Graham Cunningham combines the detective's skill of forensic analysis with the stand-up's gift for comic timing – and also the judgment to know the circumstances when each is appropriate.

Best day at the races The opening day of the Grand National meeting with Big Buck's and Nacarat the star turns and Zarkandar, Baby Run and Wishfull Thinking high-class support acts.

DAVID CARR

Horse of the year (Flat) That's easy: Frankel. He looked a freak at two and confirmed it this year even though he was still growing up mentally through the season.

Horse of the year (jumps)
Long Run became the new jumping star at the tender age of six and could hold the title for a few years.

Race of the year (Flat) I haven't seen a Classic like the 2,000 Guineas and don't expect to again.

Race of the year (jumps) The Cheltenham Gold Cup had it all. Three past winners took on Long Run and, with Denman and Kauto Star not lying down against the young pretender, it was a special race.

Ride of the year (Flat) Frankie Dettori on Blue Bunting in the 1,000 Guineas, persuading a quirky filly to put it in with a perfectly balanced and rhythmical ride into a strong headwind.

Ride of the year (jumps) Sam Waley-Cohen on Long Run in the King George VI Chase. A flawless effort, reward for all the hard work to get rider and horse there in top shape

Personality of the year Lord Grimthorpe, Khalid Abdullah's accident-prone racing manager, added to the enjoyment of the Frankel year with quips and quotes aplenty.

Rising star Roger Varian, cut from the same cloth as his late, lamented mentor Michael Jarvis.

Comeback of the year The Tatling winning at the age of 14. It was more feel-good factor than great comeback as the Group 1 winner added a 17th career victory in Class 6 company.

Unluckiest horse Excelebration (pictured), for being born in the same year as Frankel.

Most improved horse Hoof It. From sprint handicapper to so nearly a Group 1 winner with his Betfred Sprint Cup third after a record-breaking romp in the Stewards' Cup.

Flop of the year Harsh perhaps, as he contested four Group 1s, but last year's unbeaten two-year-old Wootton Bassett was never in at the finish of any race.

Bargain buy Fillies' Mile runner-up Samitar, who banked more than £250,000 and became a valuable broodmare prospect, as well as a Classic hopeful, after being snapped up for 39,000gns as a yearling.

Best pundit Nick Luck may not be ahead of some colleagues on reading of the form book but wins it on delivery and style.

Best day at the races
Newmarket July Cup day. The crowd lapped up Hayley Turner's Group 1 success and we also had a Bunbury Cup winner going solo and some decent maidens.

BRUCE JACKSON

The sight of Frankel romping away from the field in the 2,000 Guineas was one that will have our grandchildren's grandchildren marvelling in years to come

The alternative Awards

The 'I'm so shrewd I make Barney Curley jealous' foolish wager award

Nicky Henderson After a trying week at the Cheltenham Festival, Henderson revealed to readers of his Racing Post column that he had taken out some "insurance" by backing himself to have no winners. Acting on this tip-off, the BHA integrity department leapt into action and informed the trainer they would be taking no action. Luckily, Henderson's revelation proved to be a spur as he saddled a final-day double.

The David Haye v Audley Harrison hype award

Big Buck's v Grands Crus There was hype behind the young pretender, but he was floored in uncompromising fashion at Cheltenham and Aintree. Ruby Walsh even threw his whip away at Cheltenham and still Big Buck's packed his usual winning punch.

Not the Lester Piggott award for getting on the right horse in the Derby

Kieren Fallon If Derby day wasn't enough of an event in itself, Fallon ensured he grabbed a share of the headlines with his now infamous decision to ride Recital at Epsom. Except, of course, he didn't ride Recital, or anything else, after a High Court injunction prevented him taking part because of a previous agreement that he would be on Native Khan.

The Brian and Ben award for cutting-edge innovation

The Filly Factor After plenty of hand rubbing and 'thought showers' came the idea of giving the girls the chance to shine in the commentary box and for racing's decision makers to show they are no chauvinists. Hayley Moore won . . . and her prize? To commentate at Brighton when it was cold and foggy. Yeah, it's all for one in this game.

The Willie Carson award for famous last word

John Francome and Willie Carson are joint winners. Francome is likely to be haunted by his off-putting words about Frankel in the paddock before the Greenham, while Carson suggested to punters to "bet your house" on So You Th . . . five minutes before he was beaten at Royal Ascot.

The Guinness Village sing-a-long at Cheltenham song of the year award

The Festival by Mark Boylan Last year's festival build-up record 'Chelt-numb' was rubbish, let's face it. But we who kept faith in the musical ability of racing fans knew something better would come along – after all, this is the sport that produced Jim Lewis's classic 'Best Mate, Best Mate, Best Mate, Best Mate'. Boylan's catchy tune wasn't half bad – in fact, it was rather good.

The God Save the Queen award for overt patriotism

Matt Chapman ATR's shouter-in-chief gave us a memorable two minutes and 20 seconds with his commentary on the German Oaks. Dancing Rain, winner of the Great British Oaks, the best Oaks in the world, was popped out in front by Kieren Fallon with Chapman getting increasingly loud and manic as she went clear. We braced ourselves for a "Kaiser Wilhelm, Michael Schumacher, Heidi Klum, your boys took a hell of a beating" moment, but luckily the race finished too soon.

The Ryan Moore award for extensive media debriefing after a big televised race

Tom Queally After his saddle had slipped, leading to odds-on favourite Vita Nova being beaten in the Lancashire Oaks at Haydock, Queally took a little time out to tell the world what had happened. Pursued at great pace across the paddock by Channel 4's Derek 'Big Fella' Thompson, Queally offered, "A blind man could see the saddle had slipped," before disappearing hastily. Always good to see the Racing For Change media training at work.

The Danny Cook award for failing to learn by your mistakes

Peterjon Carberry If only life wasn't so confusing, eh? One of eight riders suspended for getting lost around Huntingdon and taking the wrong course, Carberry was in trouble again when he mistook the finishing post at Uttoxeter and lost first place. A 40-day ban was the punishment, giving Carberry plenty of time to study certain things.

The Charlie Sheen award for getting it off your chest

Bart Cummings Not many people can match our friend from Down Under when it comes to a good rant. Showing no signs of bitterness after the sale and export of his stable star So You Think, the legendary trainer claimed he couldn't even be bothered to get up and watch him win the Tattersalls Gold Cup because the racing was "not worth two bob". Strewth Bart, take it easy.

The James Sherwood award for Royal Ascot decorum and style

The massed brawlers in the members' enclosure on Ladies' Day This was no ordinary bar-room scrap, as eight immaculately dressed chaps thrashed each other with £98 bottles of champagne – and took off their top hats! What is the world coming to?

The Murray Walker commentator's curse award

Ian Bartlett Often the voice of French racing for viewers in Britain and Ireland, 'Barty' gave us a tremendous account of Crackerjack King's victory in the Prix du Jockey Club at Chantilly. That was until he realised that Reliable Man had won the race and he'd been calling the wrong horse. C'est la vie.

'It was **fantastic**. It's the **best moment I've had** in racing'

MY BIG MOMENT · *Four tales from the saddle*

Ian Mongan landed the first Group 1 win of his career when the Sir Henry Cecil-trained Twice Over beat stablemate Midday by three-quarters of a length to give race sponsor Khalid Abdullah a one-two in the Juddmonte International Stakes at York in August

"I was very excited to be riding in a Group 1. I knew he had a big chance. I wasn't nervous, just excited. There were only five runners and the race panned out just right. I didn't think the pace was particularly quick and he just travelled so easy. As we crossed the line it was complete elation, a bit of a dream. Tom Queally came and shook my hand straight away and I could hear Henry shouting from the stands. I looked towards him and he put his thumbs up. It was just amazing.

"My father-in-law drove me home from the races straight to The Rubbing House, which is the pub at Epsom racecourse. There was a big banner outside congratulating me and we had a few bottles of champagne. It was just fantastic. It's the best moment I've had in racing, it means so much. It took 15 years of riding and a lot of hard work to achieve it. I'll never forget it."

Eddie Ahern had his first Classic winner when the John Gosden-trained Duncan dead-heated with Jukebox Jury, ridden by Johnny Murtagh, in the Irish Field St Leger at the Curragh

"It felt like a very long time waiting to win a Classic and it was probably my first genuine big chance. I knew he would like the ground and I was just hoping I could get a bit of cover in the race. Luckily I did. A couple of strides from the line I thought I was going to win because I felt my horse go in front, but right on the line I could feel Johnny's horse coming back again. I thought I'd held on and after the race Johnny came over and said 'well done' because he thought I'd won too.

"The longer it went on without the result being announced, the more I started to think I was beaten. I was happy to hear it was a dead-heat. The owners [Philippa Cooper's Normandie Stud] were thrilled as it was their first Classic winner too and we shared in the excitement together. I had big celebrations with my sisters, brothers, nephews, actually my whole family. They were all delighted for me."

Dale Swift landed the biggest win of his career on Moyenne Corniche in the Betfred Ebor at York in August

"On the day I went into the house with a lot of the lads in the yard to watch the Morning Line because the boss [Brian Ellison] was on it. He was also running Saptapadi, who was more fancied, but he said Moyenne Corniche had a brilliant each-way chance and wouldn't be out of the places. That gave me a bit of confidence.

"I'd never ridden him in a race and rode only one piece of work on him the previous week, but I was told he could be tricky and pull up when he hits the front, so I gave him plenty of cover. He loves passing horses and all the gaps opened at the right time. I don't think I'd be as lucky again in a race like the Ebor with that number of runners.

"For a couple of years I struggled with my weight, but last winter I got in touch with a dietician and he was a massive help with the right things to eat and drink. It makes you think what you've put your body through sometimes, but winning a race like is so big it pays off. After the Ebor people kept asking what it was like, but I couldn't describe it. It was such a big buzz, unreal."

John Fahy made the most of his 3lb claim to land the biggest success of his career on 40-1 shot Prince Of Johanne in the Betfred Cambridgeshire at Newmarket in September

"It was a great win for me and it came at the right time, with only a few winners of my claim left. It's a race where you need a lot of luck and the luck was with me. About four out the whole field began to come across to the rail and they were about to swamp me. I didn't want to get stuck there and I moved him forward when I saw them coming. By the time they were all the way across, I was in front and had the rail. I wasn't worried about getting him going too early because he travels strongly and stays further. He was going away again by the line."

Clockwise from right
Ian Mongan celebrates on Twice Over, John Fahy lands the Cambridgeshire on Prince Of Johanne, Dale Swift aboard Ebor winner Moyenne Corniche and Eddie Ahern (left) with Johnny Murtagh after their Irish St Leger dead-heat

British Flat jockeys

March 30-October 1

		Wins-runs	Strike rate	Profit/loss to £1 stake	Win and place prize-money £
1	Paul Hanagan	140-926	15%	−244.81	1,382,008
2	Kieren Fallon	131-774	17%	−79.21	1,714,481
3	Silvestre de Sousa	124-816	15%	−167.64	1,005,117
4	Richard Hughes	114-621	18%	+52.16	2,464,286
5	Jamie Spencer	95-543	17%	−56.71	1,390,967
6	William Buick	90-519	17%	−15.40	2,325,346
7	Ryan Moore	84-436	19%	−124.04	2,110,946
8	Tom Queally	80-548	15%	−89.12	1,823,176
9	Neil Callan	73-584	13%	−93.13	917,681
10	Tom Eaves	70-676	10%	−98.18	439,685
11	Phillip Makin	67-543	12%	−162.02	758,498
12	Robert Winston	65-469	14%	+34.51	512,891
13	Frankie Dettori	62-306	20%	−4.89	1,950,208
	Adam Kirby	62-446	14%	+22.24	543,371
15	Luke Morris	59-668	9%	−237.89	419,436
16	Seb Sanders	57-449	13%	−121.12	415,420
17	Hayley Turner	56-367	15%	+31.19	830,661
18	Dane O'Neill	55-514	11%	−142.56	513,284
	Cathy Gannon	55-584	9%	−202.26	310,416
20	Jim Crowley	54-520	10%	−101.84	621,233
21	Ted Durcan	53-407	13%	−85.96	549,709
22	Frederik Tylicki	51-458	11%	−0.13	358,324
23	George Baker	50-393	13%	+67.04	531,382
24	David Allan	49-442	11%	−79.64	504,013
	P J McDonald	49-472	10%	−99.15	264,687
26	Richard Hills	47-317	15%	−128.72	761,919
	Martin Dwyer	47-420	11%.	−84.30	491,614
	Jimmy Fortune	47-454	10%	−70.21	857,388
	Graham Gibbons	47-466	10%	−93.53	389,612
30	Pat Dobbs	46-302	15%	+14.51	340,996
	James Doyle	46-425	11%	−55.57	197,225

Irish Flat jockeys

January 1-October 1

		Wins-runs	Strike rate	Profit/loss to £1 stake	Win and place prize-money €
1	Johnny Murtagh	69-386	18%	−79.73	1,249,005
2	Pat Smullen	67-520	13%	−205.46	1,554,319
3	Fran Berry	50-402	12%	−58.26	1,218,190
4	Joseph O'Brien	48-287	17%	−8.86	1,249,302
5	Wayne Lordan	46-411	11%	−71.88	1,020,425
6	Kevin Manning	43-393	11%	−60.67	1,098,920
7	Seamie Heffernan	37-375	10%	−102.17	1,911,442
8	Ben Curtis	36-396	9%	−52.06	525,305
	Shane Foley	36-401	9%	−147.40	600,762
	Declan McDonogh	36-423	9%	−180.50	934,763
11	Niall McCullagh	27-270	10%	−44.80	508,416
12	Colm O'Donoghue	26-295	9%	−91.47	1,475,568
13	Gary Carroll	19-327	6%	−152.87	333,909
14	Leigh Roche	18-232	8%	−85.37	249,2820
	Sam James	18-260	7%	−85.00	292,159
	Chris Hayes	18-389	5%	−212.25	370,752
17	Ronan Whelan	17-195	9%	−59.87	241,598
	Billy Lee	17-238	7%	−48.50	246,179
19	Danny Grant	16-181	9%	−54.58	176,613
20	Willie Supple	15-234	6%	−78.17	237,515
21	Keagan Latham	14-210	7%	−98.17	281,705
22	Daniel Benson	9-114	8%	−3.00	88,797
	Conor Hoban	9-162	6%	−64.00	111,645
24	Padraig Beggy	7-108	6%	−39.50	78,492
25	Shane Gray	6-128	5%	−86.75	93,740
26	Ryan Moore	5-17	29%	−0.80	392,040
	Mark Enright	5-49	10%	+13.50	31,845
	Emmet McNamara	5-54	9%	−23.87	38,110
	Danny Mullins	5-63	8%	−10.75	55,865
	Ray Dawson	5-65	8%	−11.00	66,490

Battle at the top

Runaway leaders seem a thing of the past and there was little to choose between the top jockeys. Paul Hanagan has cemented his place among the elite, having built on the maiden championship he won in 2010, but this time it was not Richard Hughes who pushed him hardest. Kieren Fallon, whose period of dominance came to an end with his sixth championship in 2003, was back in the thick of it, albeit with lower numbers than he recorded in his pomp. The surprise name in the top bracket was Silvestre de Sousa, who teamed up effectively with Mark Johnston and was a strong challenger to Hanagan on the northern tracks.

On the up

De Sousa (pictured) was a major player, up from sixth in 2010. Tom Eaves and Phillip Makin (25th and 24th respectively in 2010) were other notable movers.

On the slide

Frankie Dettori's number of winners almost halved as he dropped from fifth and Seb Sanders, another former champion, fell from eighth.

Punters' friend

George Baker had the highest profit among the top 30, with the ever-popular Richard Hughes and Hayley Turner also doing well for their supporters.

High strike-rate

Frankie Dettori may no longer be a title contender but he remains a rider for the big occasion and in 2011 he had the best overall percentage too. He was particularly successful for Mahmood Al Zarooni, with a 27 per cent strike-rate. Another partnership to note was Richard Hills-Roger Varian, who had a 32 per cent strike-rate.

Battle at the top

The top three were unchanged from last year's final standings, although this time Johnny Murtagh and Pat Smullen, the 2010 champion, pushed clear of Fran Berry. Murtagh, with his strike-rate again the best of the top three, had the satisfaction of a successful season after parting company with Ballydoyle at the end of 2010, although Smullen was the leader on prize-money won.

On the up

Joseph O'Brien, seventh as joint-champion apprentice in 2010, did best of the Ballydoyle jockeys in a memorable season that brought a first Classic win on Roderic O'Connor, two days before his 18th birthday, and put him on course for the outright apprentice title. Seamie Heffernan also benefited from greater opportunities at Ballydoyle as he climbed from tenth. Shane Foley rose from 14th and Niall McCullagh from 25th.

On the slide

Gary Carroll (pictured), who shared the apprentice title in 2010 with O'Brien and Ben Curtis, found it tougher going this time (Curtis, by contrast, stayed in the top ten and was on course to better last year's total).

Punters' friend

None of the leading jockeys returned an overall profit, but one partnership that paid dividends was Curtis with Andrew Oliver, who had a 24 per cent strike-rate and a €15 level-stake profit.

High strike-rate

O'Brien had the next-best overall percentage after Murtagh and for Ballydoyle his strike-rate was 28 per cent.

'We were **ecstatic**. The owners were **jumping** up and down'

MY BIG MOMENT   *Four trainers tell their stories*

Walter Swinburn had his first Royal Ascot success as a trainer when Julienas won the Royal Hunt Cup, in the year he announced what he hopes will be a temporary retirement

"He was laid out for the race, but he'd had some problems earlier in the year, so it was great to get the reward for all the hard work from everyone just to get him there. It's a different experience to win there as a trainer. As a jockey I'd go to Royal Ascot with 20 or 30 rides and, whatever happened, I would move on quickly.

"During the stewards' inquiry lots of people were giving me the thumbs-up, but I've been involved in so many inquiries I know they can go either way and I'm never over-confident. It was a relief when we kept it. We've had some tough moments this year and Julienas meant a lot to everyone. To win a race as prestigious as the Hunt Cup was great for all the team."

Clockwise from top left Robert Cowell, Frederick Engels wins the Windsor Castle, Alan McCabe with Caspar Netscher and Julienas lands the Hunt Cup

Alan McCabe had his first Group success when Caspar Netscher took the Irish Thoroughbred Marketing Gimcrack Stakes at York in August, before following up with another Group 2 win in the Dubai Duty Free Mill Reef Stakes at Newbury

"We were feeling good going into the Gimcrack. We thought he had a good chance, especially when the rain came. The bookies had ignored him, which took the pressure off. When he passed the post we were ecstatic. We were all jumping around, the owners were jumping up and down, it was great. I didn't get to celebrate on the night – I went home to bed because I had to get up at 5am the next morning – but we are definitely going to have a big party at the end of the year."

David Brown enjoyed his first Royal Ascot success when Frederick Engels ran out an impressive winner of the Windsor Castle Stakes, before following up in the Group 2 TNT July Stakes at Newmarket

"We're a small yard and it was great for all the staff, everyone involved. We knew he was exceptional from an early stage and he was exciting to train. He'd work so well. We thought he had an outstanding chance at Ascot and he did exactly what we expected. I was always confident during the race. Johnny [Murtagh] had to get the gap, but he really asserted in the last furlong and a half."

Robert Cowell hit the big time with his 25-horse stable when Prohibit won the King's Stand Stakes at Royal Ascot, a first Group 1 success for the Newmarket trainer

"From about ten days before the King's Stand there was a buzz in the yard because we knew our horse was training well. I follow the form of these sprinters and I saw Kingsgate Native was second favourite for the race. I thought we were at least as good as him and we were a 12-1 or 14-1 chance.

"I watched the race on the big screen in the paddock with my wife and the owners. The thrill in the last furlong and a half was amazing. Rishi Persad from the BBC had to pinch me before I knew it was really happening. We've since picked up a few new clients and more horses, and the owners of Prohibit have expanded their interest too."

British Flat trainers

		Wins-runs	Strike rate	Profit/loss to £1 stake	Win and place prize-money £
1	Richard Hannon	185-1240	15%	−61.66	3,338,709
2	John Gosden	90-487	18%	−24.66	2,322,526
3	Aidan O'Brien	12-72	17%	−20.24	2,141,381
4	Sir Henry Cecil	50-248	20%	−52.50	2,062,803
5	Mahmood Al Zarooni	64-328	20%	+106.15	1,702,935
6	Richard Fahey	148-1136	13%	-198.98	1,590,068
7	Sir Michael Stoute	50-330	15%	−119.59	1,511,654
8	Mark Johnston	155-1188	13%	−288.95	1,394,065
9	Kevin Ryan	129-738	17%	+82.05	1,309,897
10	Mick Channon	86-713	12%	−148.39	1,032,285
11	William Haggas	70-375	19%	−81.26	1,012,960
12	Andrew Balding	70-489	14%	−6.59	952,994
13	Tim Easterby	82-816	10%	−52.31	846,646
14	Saeed Bin Suroor	41-305	13%	−117.53	773,369
15	David Simcock	41 328	13%	−87.36	770,812
16	Andre Fabre	1-3	33%	+2.00	749,733
17	David Nicholls	90-874	10%	−150.31	687,785
18	Brian Meehan	56-470	12%	−87.83	677,245
19	Roger Charlton	36-203	18%	−19.30	672,989
20	Luca Cumani	46-294	16%	−83.80	663,814
21	Roger Varian	47-215	22%	+56.36	660,014
22	Michael Bell	42-304	14%	−85.26	570,022
23	Barry Hills	51-336	15%	−80.20	564,787
24	Hughie Morrison	41-287	14%	−25.70	544,142
25	James Fanshawe	28-164	17%	+103.88	542,461
26	Clive Cox	40-327	12%	−78.83	535,653
27	Ed Dunlop	53-357	15%	−116.21	500,176
28	David Barron	51-370	14%	−52.94	478,047
29	David O'Meara	46-366	13%	−93.31	466,775
30	Tom Dascombe	48-400	12%	−65.27	440,078

Irish Flat trainers

		Wins-runs	Strike rate	Profit/loss to £1 stake	Win and place prize-money €
1	Aidan O'Brien	81-420	19%	−82.61	4,615,745
2	Dermot Weld	65-382	17%	−82.46	1,504,757
3	Jim Bolger	45-400	11%	−51.67	1,129,712
4	John Oxx	48-259	19%	−42.76	965,105
5	Jessica Harrington	29-201	14%	−52.76	863,535
6	Kevin Prendergast	26-257	10%	−101.75	713,115
7	David Wachman	28-230	12%	−29.97	604,035
8	Ger Lyons	39-311	13%	−52.69	594,608
9	Michael Halford	20-276	7%	−132.90	326,889
10	Tommy Stack	17-123	14%	−29.42	319,325
11	Andrew Oliver	20-145	14%	+24.88	307,937
12	David Marnane	15-194	8%	−24.50	282,500
13	Ken Condon	21-155	14%	−13.25	277,621
14	Mahmood Al Zarooni	1-1	100%	+2.50	250,750
15	Edward Lynam	13-178	7%	−100.33	225,875
16	Ed Dunlop	1-5	20%	−0.50	222,625
17	Joanna Morgan	12-195	6%	−74.25	203,148
18	Richard Hannon	2-7	29%	−0.50	190,800
19	Paul Deegan	14-157	9%	−16.00	187,725
20	Mark Johnston	4-13	31%	+10.50	174,650
21	Charles O'Brien	11-85	13%	+12.38	171,915
22	Patrick Prendergast	6-69	9%	−20.00	170,055
23	Tracey Collins	9-127	7%	−60.75	166,310
24	John Joseph Murphy	9-148	6%	−31.00	149,535
25	Harry Rogers	7-116	6%	−43.00	137,437
26	Willie McCreery	12-154	8%	−53.37	128,264
27	Pat Flynn	13-166	8%	−67.58	126,510
28	Michael Mulvany	5-84	6%	−30.50	112,280
29	David Nicholls	4-7	57%	+4.16	111,400
30	Thomond O'Mara	4-56	7%	−2.12	105,872

Battle at the top
Four trainers broke the £2m barrier but it was Richard Hannon who forged clear late in the season. Hannon, who became champion for the first time in 2010, also had the highest number of wins and the most Group-race successes. John Gosden was buoyed by the wins of Nathaniel in the King George and Masked Marvel in the St Leger, moving up from eighth. Aidan O'Brien posed his usual threat in the major races and Frankel put Sir Henry Cecil back in the big time.

On the up
Mahmood Al Zarooni, 24th in his first year, made a big mark in his second with his flagship horses Blue Bunting and Rewilding. Kevin Ryan also made a significant move, up from 18th.

On the slide
Saeed Bin Suroor, sixth in 2010, dropped down the standings as Al Zarooni emerged as the leading Godolphin trainer. Sir Michael Stoute, champion in four of the previous eight seasons, had his most disappointing season in years.

Punters' friend
Al Zarooni was a trainer to follow and so too was the resurgent Ryan, while James Fanshawe notably had a 24 per cent strike-rate with first-time-out runners – the highest of any British trainer.

High strike-rate
First-season trainer Roger Varian (pictured) showed he had learnt well from his mentor, the late Michael Jarvis, as he placed his horses astutely at a 22 per cent strike-rate. Among the leading trainers Cecil and Al Zarooni both did well to post a 20 per cent return.

Battle at the top
Aidan O'Brien was in a league of his own again as he quickly set course for a 13th consecutive championship and nor was there much change in the places immediately below him. Dermot Weld was best of the rest with Group 1 winner Emulous and consistent Group performer Famous Name leading the way. The ultra-tough Banimpire was by far Jim Bolger's best performer as he broke the £1m mark and John Oxx was as solid as ever, although his top-rated runner, Saddler's Rock, scored his biggest success in Britain when taking the Doncaster Cup.

On the up
Jessica Harrington's increasingly successful Flat string raised her from last year's eighth place and Ger Lyons moved up from ninth, although his most important success came in Britain with Lightening Pearl in the Group 1 Cheveley Park. Andrew Oliver continued his steady rise, up from 21st in 2010.

On the slide
No major fallers, although Michael Halford (pictured) – with no Casamento this year – could not stay in the group that passed £500,000.

Punters' friend
The underrated Oliver rewarded his supporters with a tidy profit.

High strike-rate
The top trainers had the best percentages, in particular O'Brien and John Oxx, but further down the table there were respectable figures for Lyons, Tommy Stack, Oliver and Ken Condon.

'A **wonderful surprise**. I couldn't **believe my eyes**'

The James Fanshawe-trained Society Rock beat an international field to win the Group 1 Golden Jubilee Stakes at Royal Ascot for owner Simon Gibson, giving him the perfect tonic in his recovery from a fall at home

"I had a nasty accident doing some housework, when I fell downstairs and was knocked unconscious, and seeing him win brightened up my life. With all that had happened I felt a lucky bugger really. I wasn't able to go to Ascot on the day. I watched the race with Janet Anderson, the stable's racing secretary, down at Falmouth Lodge. It was the most wonderful surprise, an absolute thrill. He had been second in the race the year before, but when he won I couldn't believe my eyes.

"Because my health hasn't been good I haven't been able to go racing, but I'm very fortunate to have a horse like him. It is very enjoyable to go with Janet to the stables and to watch him when he does his gallops."

The Hughie Morrison-trained Sagramor won the Britannia Handicap at Royal Ascot to fulfil a long-held dream for the Melksham Craic syndicate, who own and bred him. Mark Taylor, a member of the seven-strong syndicate, tells the story

"Initially the syndicate began as an 'investment club' with myself, my brother and some close schoolfriends. We'd always fancied owning a horse of our own and we ended up buying Jasmick, who took us to Glorious

From top Dancing Rain wins the Oaks, Society Rock is led in after the Golden Jubilee and Sagramor (nearside) lands the Britannia

Goodwood, Ascot and the Ebor. The plan had been to knock it on the head with her then, but my brother was really enthusiastic to give the breeding route a go. At the fourth attempt we got Sagramor and after he won his maiden as a two-year-old at Kempton, Hughie said we could think about aiming for the Britannia. That thought certainly

kept us warm throughout the winter.

"With Jasmick we thought it was great just to have a 'Saturday horse' and to be able to go to the festivals. To win at Royal Ascot with Sagramor was absolutely unbelievable. We took my son off sick from school and of course he ended up on TV and in all the photos. We didn't

think that through!

"Nicky Mackay did a brilliant job on him but I also want to highlight Steve Drowne, who did so much work with the horse but had to stand himself down at Ascot because of injury. The whole team at Hughie's have done a great job."

Brothers Martin and Lee Taylor, both corporate lawyers, ventured into ownership three years ago with aspirations of building a breeding operation. With two mares and three fillies in training, they got off to the best possible start when the William Haggas-trained Dancing Rain won the Investec Oaks, as Martin relates

"We bought her as a yearling. Liam Norris buys all our horses and we're looking for future broodmares who are well bred. Anything they achieve on the racecourse is a bonus. We love our racing, but the dream is to build up our own stud farm and to have an Oaks winner so early is unbelievable.

"On the Monday before the Oaks she scoped badly and on the Wednesday she coughed. We nearly pulled her out, but on the Thursday she scoped clean and we let her take her chance. It was probably the best thing that could have happened as we went with lowered expectations. We thought a top-six finish would be great as she wasn't 100 per cent, but Johnny [Murtagh] gave her a fantastic ride. To have an Oaks winner is brilliant, especially with Maybe on her pedigree page. She's from an exciting family and we're delighted to own her."

British Flat owners

		Highest earning horse	Wins-runs	Winners-horses	Win and place prize-money £
1	K Abdullah	Frankel	55-279	42-103	2,738,284
2	Godolphin	Blue Bunting	105-638	83-264	2,476,306
3	Hamdan Al Maktoum	Entifaadha	93-585	72-172	1,074,536
4	M Tabor	Pour Moi	21-98	17-54	1,012,340
5	Mrs John Magnier	Pour Moi	19-100	16-60	962,156
6	Dr Marwan Koukash	Our Jonathan	75-479	42-80	865,601
7	Derrick Smith	Pour Moi	18-88	15-51	855,328
8	Lady Rothschild	Nathaniel	9-40	6-16	759,637
9	Sheikh Hamdan Bin Mohammed Al Maktoum	Namibian	67-473	42-89	731,400
10	Andrew Tinkler	Tell Dad	28-217	19-44	617,708
11	Khalifa Dasmal	Dream Ahead	8-53	6-14	491,763
12	B E Nielsen	Masked Marvel	10-42	6-13	424,475
13	The Queen	Carlton House	13-92	10-27	388,400
14	Mrs J Wood	Strong Suit	14-11	7 9-27	356,315
15	Cheveley Park Stud	Regal Realm	27-189	22-57	319,784
16	Mrs Angie Bailey	Bogart	12-58	6-6	311,794
17	Coupede Ville Partnership	Coupe De Ville	4-6	1-11	297,533
18	HRH Princess Haya of Jordan	Joviality	23-138	20-36	292,611
19	Jaber Abdullah	Factory Time	23-196	18-51	290,454
20	Nick & Olga Dhandsa & John & Zoe Webster	Samitar	4-19	3-4	277,212
21	Saeed Manana	Nideeb	13-195	10-61	254,534
22	J C Smith	Highland Knight	21-150	16-38	245,096
23	H E Sheikh Sultan Bin Khalifa Al Nahyan	Vita Nova	16-77	12-22	234,440
24	Simon Gibson	Society Rock	1-11	1-3	233,995
25	Saleh Al Homaizi & Imad Al Sagar	Green Destiny	7-34	3-11	233,140
26	Mrs Fitri Hay	Fame And Glory	10-104	9-37	208,021
27	Normandie Stud Ltd	Duncan	6-32	5-10	195,896
28	Owen Promotions Limited	Brown Panther	8-31	4-6	188,792
29	Pearl Bloodstock Ltd	Dever Dream	9-60	8-22	188,031
30	John Stocker	Barbican	12-63	5-7	184,733

Irish Flat owners

		Highest earning horse	Wins-runs	Winners-horses	Win and place prize-money €
1	Michael Tabor	Maybe	33-149	24-47	1,314,525
2	D Smith, Mrs J Magnier, M Tabor	Treasure Beach	2-3	2-3	1,180,000
3	Mrs John Magnier	Roderic O'Connor	35-193	28-57	1,079,555
4	Mrs J S Bolger	Banimpire	32-301	24-8	873,517
5	K Abdullah	Famous Name	12-36	6-15	597,220
6	Derrick Smith	Together	18-110	17-34	588,825
7	H H Aga Khan	Alanza	29-161	21-47	531,620
8	Anamoine Limited	Snow Fairy	12-58	9-15	469,690
9	Moyglare Stud Farm	Sense Of Purpose	16-74	11-23	340,030
10	Godolphin	Blue Bunting	1-3	1-3 1	297,000
11	M Tabor, D Smith & Mrs John Magnier	Seville	1-4	1-4 1	260,500
12	Lady O'Reilly	Rose Bonheur	13-80	8-19	203,280
13	Smith/Magnier/Tabor/ DatoTan/TunkuYahaya	So You Think	2 2	1 1	100,150
14	Sean Jones	Casbah Rock	14-112	10-20	175,947
15	Dr R Lambe	Stunning View	6-55	6-21	172,220
16	Richard Barnes	Coral Wave	6-49	3-11	169,795
17	Jorg Vasicek	La Collina	2-7	1-2	159,300
18	J Connaughton	Dunboyne Express	2-16	2-3	154,560
19	David Keoghan	Lolly For Dolly	4-9	2-3	149,200
20	Mrs John Magnier, M Tabor & D Smith	Memphis Tennessee	1-8	1-8	138,680
21	Mrs Fitri Hay	Fame And Glory	3-5	2-2	125,700
22	Michael Tabor, Mrs John Magnier & Derrick Smith	Misty For Me	1-2	1-2	122,000
23	Hamdan Al Maktoum	Asheerah	7-73	7-20	119,725
24	Ballylinch Stud	Anam Allta	3-13	2-3	116,390
25	TanKai Chah	Dragon Pulse	2-4	1-1	113,590
26	Jaber Abdullah	Akeed Mofeed	7-45	6-16	112,155
27	Iona Equine Syndicate	Bay Knight	9-54	7-8	111,581
28	Maxwell Morris	Manieree	2-5	1-1	109,900
29	Peter Jones	Flowers Of Spring	4-10	2-3	108,350
30	Damian Lavelle	Seanie	3-8	2-3	107,500

Battle at the top

The top two were unchanged, with 2010 champion Khalid Abdullah (pictured) setting the pace again. Workforce, his top earner last year, did not really reward the decision to keep him in training at four, with only a Group 3 win to add to his Derby and Arc, but any disappointment was dispelled by the sheer joy of Frankel's brilliant campaign. Godolphin were competitive right from the start of the season, with top earner Blue Bunting giving them a first Newmarket Guineas since 2002.

On the up

Lady Rothschild was a newcomer to the top ranks thanks to King George and Queen Elizabeth Stakes winner Nathaniel. Stobart chief executive Andrew Tinkler more than trebled his number of winners, with dual Guineas runner-up Dubawi Gold chief among them, as he joined the top ten, having been outside the top 50 last year. The Queen had her highest placing in almost two decades and it would have been much better if her Derby hopes had been realised by Carlton House.

On the slide

Cheveley Park Stud, sixth last year, had a low-key season by their standards with a lower number of winners and a much-reduced prize-money haul. Highclere Thoroughbred Racing, tenth in 2010 with Harbinger horse of the year, could never hope to match that this time.

Battle at the top

Once again the table was dominated by the Ballydoyle owners in various guises (pictured, left to right, are Derrick Smith, John Magnier and Michael Tabor) with their team led by Classic winners Roderic O'Connor and Treasure Beach, along with 2012 Guineas favourite Maybe. The Bolger horses had an excellent year, headed by the tough Banimpire, and with the promise of more to come in 2012 from Dewhurst winner Parish Hall.

On the up

Sean Jones, a major owner in the Ger Lyons yard, is not in the big league but not many beat him on number of winners. Only just inside the top 50 in 2010, he jumped a long way up the table with the likes of four-time handicap winner Casbah Rock, whose rating rose by almost 30lb in little more than two months. Jorg Vasicek doesn't have many horses but has the happy knack of turning up a good one, this year winning the Group 1 Phoenix Stakes with La Collina to add to Termagant's success in the 2009 Moyglare Stud Stakes.

On the slide

Hamdan Al Maktoum, sixth in 2010, was well down the standings this time. His number of runners was much the same, but the winners halved. Lady O'Reilly had more winners this year but the quality was lacking – with no Group 1 winner to replace Chinese White – and she dropped out of the top ten.

JUST FOR FUN Name the 2011 beaten favourites in (a) 1,000 Guineas (b) Oaks (c) Derby (d) St Leger. Answer page 170

RACING POST ANNUAL 2012 153

LEADERS of the pack

Two-year-old colt

RACING POST RATINGS
119 Dabirsim
118 Parish Hall
118 Power
117 Dragon Pulse
117 Harbour Watch

DABIRSIM *below*
Trainer **Christophe Ferland**
Owner **Simon Springer**

The emergence of another Frankel was highly unlikely but the 2011 crop of two-year-old colts weren't even close in a muddled and messy division. Dabirsim was on top after going five races unbeaten, including a pair of Group 1 victories. The first was in the Darley Prix Morny over 6f at Deauville, where he beat dual Group winner Family One by three lengths to earn his top RPR of 119. He didn't need to repeat that form when stepped up to 7f for the Prix Jean-Luc Lagardere at Longchamp on Arc day, recording an RPR of 115 in beating Sofast by three-quarters of a length (the runner-up had been four lengths behind at Deauville).

Close behind Dabirsim on RPR were Parish Hall and Power, who were separated by half a length in the Group 1 Dubai Dewhurst Stakes at Newmarket in October. Parish Hall stepped up from a previous-best of 110 when winning that day, while Power's 117 in second place was just below the 118 he recorded when beating Dragon Pulse by half a length in the Group 1 Goffs National Stakes the previous month.

Two-year-old filly

RACING POST RATINGS
115 Elusive Kate
115 Wading
114 Maybe
114 La Collina
113 Best Terms

ELUSIVE KATE *below*
Trainer **John Gosden**
Owner **Magnolia Racing and Rachel Hood**
WADING
Trainer **Aidan O'Brien**
Owner **Mrs John Magnier, Michael Tabor and Derrick Smith**

As with the two-year-old colts division, there were promising performers but no standout leader. Elusive Kate set the standard with her three-length win from Fire Lily in the Group 1 Prix Marcel Boussac over 1m on Arc day, stepping up to an RPR of 115 from the 105 she had recorded when winning a Group 3 at Deauville. Fire Lily was a good benchmark, having been beaten a length and three-quarters by Maybe in the Group 1 Moyglare Stud Stakes at the Curragh and two lengths by Best Terms in the Jaguar Cars Lowther Stakes at York.

Maybe's trainer Aidan O'Brien produced a better performer on RPR when Wading joined Elusive Kate at the top of the leaderboard with an impressive two-length win in the Group 2 Vision.ae Rockfel Stakes at Newmarket in October.

Horse of the year

RACING POST RATINGS
139 Frankel
130 Canford Cliffs
130 Cirrus Des Aigles
130 Rewilding

Three-year-old colt

RACING POST RATINGS
139 Frankel
129 Dream Ahead
129 Excelebration
126 Nathaniel
126 Sea Moon
RPRs up to and including October 15

FRANKEL
Trainer **Sir Henry Cecil**
Owner **Khalid Abdullah**

Frankel had been forced to share champion two-year-old honours with Dream Ahead in the World Thoroughbred Racehorse Rankings – a decision many thought unfair (on RPR he was 2lb better) – but he left no doubt about his supremacy in 2011 as he blazed across the summer. Dream Ahead trained on impressively, winning three Group 1 contests and taking the scalp of Goldikova in the Prix de la Foret to post his career-best RPR of 129, but like the rest he was no match for Frankel. On the only occasion they met in 2011 he was beaten almost six lengths into fifth in the St James's Palace Stakes, but in truth that was not an accurate measure of either colt.

An RPR of 122 in the St James's Palace was Frankel's lowest of the season, but he had set the bar high – both for himself and others – with his breathtaking victory in the Qipco 2,000 Guineas. His six-length demolition earned an RPR of 133, up 7lb from his 126 peak figure as a two-year-old, and he was already in the superstar bracket. The St James's Palace at least kept his unbeaten run going, even if it was something of a struggle at the end, and then it was time to take on the older horses in the Qipco Sussex Stakes at Glorious Goodwood. He faced a formidable opponent in Canford Cliffs, but he hastened the four-year-old's retirement with another unstoppable display. This time he recorded an RPR of 137 in finishing five lengths clear of Canford Cliffs, who otherwise would have been the joint top-rated horse of the year.

Then came the Queen Elizabeth II Stakes on Champions Day, when he put himself alongside Dubai Millennium as the best in the history of Racing Post Ratings with an RPR of 139.

Among the three-year-old colts Frankel was 10lb ahead and it is notable that three of the next four in the rankings had taken him on at least once in his career and all had been beaten, a couple of them more than once.

Three-year-old filly

128 Danedream
123 Immortal Verse
122 Moonlight Cloud
121 Galikova
120 Blue Bunting
120 Shareta

DANEDREAM *below*

Trainer **Peter Schiergen**
Owner **Gestut Burg Eberstein and Teruya Yoshida**

Danedream was the leader of this division even before her runaway win in the Qatar Prix de l'Arc de Triomphe, although that only slightly diminished the surprise factor of her Longchamp romp against a top-quality all-aged field. The weight-for-age and sex allowances were significant as they put her on 8st 8lb, 11lb less than the older males, but still it was an impressive performance. Her RPR of 128 – only a pound behind Zarkava, the three-year-old filly who won the 2008 Arc – completed a remarkable rise from the 101 on which she started the season.

But the real story of Danedream was about the romance, not the facts and figures. In a division where most of the principals represented owner-breeder powerhouses such as the Wertheimer brothers, Godolphin and the Aga Khan, here was a cheaply bought filly who showed it was possible to live the dream even in the top Flat races.

Sprinter

125 Deacon Blues
124 Dream Ahead
124 Hoof It
122 Bated Breath
121 Prohibit
120 Sole Power

DEACON BLUES *below*

Trainer **James Fanshawe**
Owner **Jan and Peter Hopper, Michelle Morris**

A typically tight sprint division but it says something when the top-rated has never even competed in a Group 1, let alone won one.

Deacon Blues showed he had the talent for Group 1 sprinting, however, when he earned his division-topping RPR with a seven-length win in the Group 3 Phoenix Sprint Stakes at the Curragh in July. He was slightly below that level in winning the Group 2 British Champions Sprint at Ascot in October with an RPR of 123. Having had a top RPR of 99 as a three-year-old handicapper in 2010, he was gelded over the winter and made huge improvement.

Dream Ahead was best of the Group 1-winning sprinters, with a high of 124 for his Darley July Cup success and 122 for his narrow win in the Betfred Sprint Cup. His best mark came outside the sprint category when he recorded an RPR of 129 at 7f with his head victory over Goldikova in the Qatar Prix de la Foret.

Stayer

124 Masked Marvel
122 Saddler's Rock
121 Fame And Glory
121 Sea Moon
120 Opinion Poll

MASKED MARVEL

Trainer **John Gosden**
Owner **Bjorn Nielsen**

Masked Marvel (below) became one of the division leaders from the Classic generation with a three-length win in the Ladbrokes St Leger that put him ahead of fellow three-year-old Saddler's Rock, who had landed the Stobart Doncaster Cup the previous day. Fame And Glory, despite his Ascot victories in the Gold Cup and Long Distance Cup, lagged behind.

Masked Marvel disappointed after being supplemented for the Qatar Prix de l'Arc de Triomphe, finishing last of 16, but otherwise he had a progressive profile. He was reportedly not fully tuned up for his reappearance in the Bet365 Classic Trial at Sandown but earned an RPR of 111 and a place in the Investec Derby with a Listed victory at Goodwood on his next start. Eighth in the Derby, he won the Group 3 Bahrain Trophy over 1m5f at Newmarket with an RPR of 114 and was then put away for three months to wait for the Leger. In that time he had improved markedly and at Doncaster he proved he was a stayer with a touch of class.

Older horse

130 Canford Cliffs
130 Cirrus Des Aigles
130 Rewilding
129 So You Think
128 Workforce

CANFORD CLIFFS

Trainer **Richard Hannon**
Owner **The Heffer Syndicate, Michael Tabor and Derrick Smith**

CIRRUS DES AIGLES

Trainer **Corinne Barande-Barbe** Owner **Jean-Claude-Alain Dupouy**

REWILDING

Trainer **Mahmood Al Zarooni**
Owner **Godolphin**

A strong bunch of older horses lined up for the 2011 Flat season and they did not disappoint, putting in several memorable performances, even if the three-year-olds often held sway in the big races. Only Frankel bettered the RPR of 130 achieved by Canford Cliffs, Cirrus Des Aigles and Rewilding, with several other older horses close to that mark.

The three division leaders all achieved their best mark of the year at Ascot. Canford Cliffs (below) took a first-class renewal of the Queen Anne Stakes, Rewilding got the better of So You Think by a neck in the Prince of Wales's Stakes and Cirrus Des Aigles made it a three-way tie taking the Qipco Champion Stakes.

British Group 1 winners 2011

Race	Dist	Course	Month	Age	Winner	RPR	SP
2,000 Guineas	1m	Nmkr	Apr	3	Frankel	133	1-2
1,000 Guineas (F)	1m	Nmkr	May	3	Blue Bunting	116	16-1
Lockinge	1m	Newb	May	4+	Canford Cliffs	126	4-5
Coronation Cup	1m4f	Epsm	Jun	4+	St Nicholas Abbey	125	Evens
Oaks (F)	1m4f	Epsm	Jun	3	Dancing Rain	114	20-1
Derby	1m4f	Epsm	Jun	3	Pour Moi	123	4-1
King's Stand	5f	Asct	Jun	3+	Prohibit	121	7-1
Queen Anne	1m	Asct	Jun	4+	Canford Cliffs	130	11-8
St James's Palace	1m	Asct	Jun	3	Frankel	122	30-100
Prince Of Wales's	1m2f	Asct	Jun	4+	Rewilding	130	17-2
Gold Cup	2m4f	Asct	Jun	4+	Fame And Glory	119	11-8
Coronation (F)	1m	Asct	Jun	3	Immortal Verse	115	8-1
Golden Jubilee	6f	Asct	Jun	3+	Society Rock	119	25-1
Eclipse	1m2f	Sand	Jul	3+	So You Think	132	4-6
Falmouth (F&M)	1m	Nmkj	Jul	3+	Timepiece	116	16-1
July Cup	6f	Nmkj	Jul	3+	Dream Ahead	124	7-1
King George V& And Queen Elizabeth	1m4f	Asct	Jul	3+	Nathaniel	126	11-2
Sussex	1m	Gdwd	Jul	3+	Frankel	137	8-13
Nassau(F&M)	1m2f	Gdwd	Jul	3+	Midday	121	6-4
International	1m2f	York	Aug	3+	Twice Over	127	11-2
Yorkshire Oaks (F&M)	1m4f	York	Aug	3+	Blue Bunting	120	11-4
Nunthorpe	5f	York	Aug	2+	Margot Did	118	20-1
Sprint Cup	6f	Hayd	Sep	3+	Dream Ahead	122	4-1
St Leger	1m7f	Donc	Sep	3	Masked Marvel	124	15-2
Fillies' Mile	1m	Nmkr	Sep	2	Lyric Of Light	112	2-1
Sun Chariot (F&M)	1m	Nmkr	Sep	3+	Sahpresa	119	13-8
Cheveley Park (F)	6f	Nmkr	Sep	2	Lightening Pearl	110	3-1

British Group 2 winners 2011

Race	Dist	Course	Month	Age	Winner	RPR	SP
Mile	1m	Sand	Apr	4+	Dick Turpin	110	8-13
Jockey Club	1m4f	Nmkr	Apr	4+	Dandino	117	7-4
Duke Of York	6f	York	May	3+	Delegator	117	5-1
Dante	1m2f	York	May	3	Carlton House	118	11-4
Middleton (F&M)	1m2f	York	May	4+	Midday	123	11-10
Yorkshire Cup	1m6f	York	May	4+	Duncan	117	11-4
Temple	5f	Hayd	May	3+	Sole Power	121	8-1
Henry Ii	2m	Sand	May	4+	Blue Bajan	109	4-1
Coventry	6f	Asct	Jun	2	Power	110	4-1
Queen Mary (F)	5f	Asct	Jun	2	Best Terms	102	12-1
Windsor Forest (F&M)	1m	Asct	Jun	4+	Lolly For Dolly	115	11-1
Norfolk	5f	Asct	Jun	2	Bapak Chinta	106	6-1
Ribblesdale (F)	1m4f	Asct	Jun	3	Banimpire	111	3-1
King Edward Vii	1m4f	Asct	Jun	3	Nathaniel	120	11-4
Hardwicke	1m4f	Asct	Jun	4+	Await The Dawn	124	4-6
Lancashire Oaks (F&M)	1m4f	Hayd	Jul	3+	Gertrude Bell	108	9-2
July	6f	Nmkj	Jul	2	Frederick Engels	111	7-4
Princess Of Wales's	1m4f	Nmkj	Jul	3+	Crystal Capella	121	4-1
Cherry Hinton (F)	6f	Nmkj	Jul	2	Gamilati	107	14-1
Summer Mile	1m	Asct	Jul	4+	Dick Turpin	123	2-1
Superlative	7f	Nmkj	Jul	2	Red Duke	107	10-1
York	1m2f	York	Jul	3+	Twice Over	120	5-2
Lennox	7f	Gdwd	Jul	3+	Strong Suit	119	5-2
Vintage	7f	Gdwd	Jul	2	Chandlery	107	5-2
Goodwood Cup	2m	Gdwd	Jul	3+	Opinion Poll	114	9-2
King George	5f	Gdwd	Jul	3+	Masamah	117	4-1
Richmond	6f	Gdwd	Jul	2	Harbour Watch	115	Evens
Hungerford	7f	Newb	Aug	3+	Excelebration	126	5-4
Great Voltigeur	1m4f	York	Aug	3	Sea Moon	126	11-2
Lowther (F)	6f	York	Aug	2	Best Terms	112	11-1
Gimcrack	6f	York	Aug	2	Caspar Netscher	112	5-1
Lonsdale Cup	2m	York	Aug	3+	Opinion Poll	120	3-1
Celebration Mile	1m	Gdwd	Aug	3+	Dubawi Gold	119	3-1
Park Hill (F&M)	1m7f	Donc	Sep	3+	Meeznah	115	5-2
Doncaster Cup	2m2f	Donc	Sep	3+	Saddler's Rock	122	11-2

British Group 2 winners

Race	Dist	Course	Month	Age	Winner	RPR	SP
Flying Childers	5f	Donc	Sep	2	Requinto	110	100-30
May Hill (F)	1m	Donc	Sep	2	Lyric Of Light	111	9-1
Park	7f	Donc	Sep	3+	Premio Loco	113	15-8
Champagne	7f	Donc	Sep	2	Trumpet Major	111	7-1
Mill Reef	6f	Newb	Sep	2	Caspar Netscher	112	15-8
Joel	1m	Nmkr	Sep	3+	Ransom Note	118	4-1
Royal Lodge	1m	Nmkr	Sep	2	Daddy Long Legs	112	11-4

British Group 3 winners 2011

Race	Dist	Course	Month	Age	Winner	RPR	SP
Winter Derby (Aw)	1m2f	Ling	Mar	4+	Nideeh	112	9-4
Nell Gwyn (F)	7f	Nmkr	Apr	3	Barefoot Lady	104	14-1
Earl Of Sefton	1m1f	Nmkr	Apr	4+	Ransom Note	114	6-1
Craven	1m	Nmkr	Apr	3	Native Khan	111	8-11
John Porter	1m4f	Newb	Apr	4+	Indian Days	117	7-1
Greenham	7f	Newb	Apr	3	Frankel	124	1-4
Fred Darling	7f	Newb	Apr	3	Rimth	106	13-2
Gordon Richards	1m2f	Sand	Apr	4+	Kings Gambit	110	5-1
Classic Trial	1m2f	Sand	Apr	3	Genius Beast	110	8-1
Sagaro	2m	Asct	Apr	4+	Askar Tau	108	4-1
Palace House	5f	Nmkr	Apr	3+	Tangerine Trees	110	18-1
Dahlia	1m1f	Nmkr	May	4+	I'm A Dreamer	115	10-1
Huxley	1m2f	Chst	May	4+	Await The Dawn	125	8-11
Chester Vase	1m4f	Chst	May	3	Treasure Beach	111	7-2
Ormonde	1m5f	Chst	May	4+	St Nicholas Abbey	124	11-8
Dee	1m2f	Chst	May	3	Glen's Diamond	107	2-1
Derby Trial	1m3f	Ling	May	3	Dordogne	106	10-1
Chartwell (F&M)	7f	Ling	May	3+	Perfect Tribute	110	12-1
Musidora (F)	1m2f	York	May	3	Joviality	108	5-1
Brigadier Gerard	1m2f	Sand	May	4+	Workforce	127	Evens
John Of Gaunt	7f	Hayd	May	4+	The Cheka	114	6-1
Princess Elizabeth (F&M)	1m1f	Epsm	Jun	3+	Antara	108	11-8
Diomed	1m1f	Epsm	Jun	3+	Fanunalter	111	16-1
Jersey	7f	Asct	Jun	3	Strong Suit	117	11-1
Tercentenary	1m2f	Asct	Jun	3	Pisco Sour	113	20-1
Albany (F)	6f	Asct	Jun	2	Samitar	105	16-1
Queen's Vase	2m	Asct	Jun	3	Namibian	108	7-2
Chipchase	6f	Nwcs	Jun	3+	Genki	114	11-2
Criterion	7f	Nmkj	Jun	3+	Libranno	112	9-1
Coral Charge	5f	Sand	Jul	3+	Night Carnation	110	11-2
Bahrain Trophy	1m5f	Nmkj	Jul	3	Masked Marvel	114	2-1
Summer (F&M)	6f	York	Jul	3+	Ladies Are Forever	111	9-2
Hackwood	6f	Newb	Jul	3+	Deacon Blues	121	5-2
Princess Margaret (F)	6f	Asct	Jul	2	Angels Will Fall	104	9-2
Gordon	1m4f	Gdwd	Jul	3	Namibian	115	7-1
Molecomb	5f	Gdwd	Jul	2	Requinto	106	6-1
Lillie Langtry (F&M)	1m6f	Gdwd	Jul	3+	Meeznah	115	6-1
Glorious	1m4f	Gdwd	Jul	4+	Drunken Sailor	116	9-2
Oak Tree (F&M)	7f	Gdwd	Jul	3+	Chachamaidee	115	9-2
Sweet Solera (F)	7f	Nmkj	Aug	2	Discourse	112	5-2
Rose Of Lancaster	1m2f	Hayd	Aug	3+	Class Is Class	118	3-1
Sovereign	1m	Salisbury	Aug	3+	Side Glance	115	2-1
Geoffrey Freer	1m5f	Newb	Aug	3+	Census	118	4-1
Acomb	7f	York	Aug	2	Entifaadha	107	7-2
Strensall	1m1f	York	Aug	3+	Green Destiny	119	11-4
Solario	7f	Sand	Aug	2	Talwar	110	9-4
Winter Hill	1m2f	Wndr	Aug	3+	Prince Siegfried	116	14-1
Prestige	7f	Gdwd	Aug	2	Regal Realm	103	2-1
Supreme	7f	Gdwd	Aug	3+	Libranno	111	7-2
September (Aw)	1m4f	Kemp	Sep	3+	Modun	113	2-1
Sirenia (Aw)	6f	Kemp	Sep	2	Shumoos	103	9-4
Sceptre (F&M)	7f	Donc	Sep	3+	Alanza	112	11-4
Select	1m2f	Gdwd	Sep	3+	French Navy	116	2-1
Firth Of Clyde (F)	6f	Ayr	Sep	2	Roger Sez	109	14-1
Arc Trial	1m3f	Newb	Sep	3+	Green Destiny	121	2-1
World Trophy	5f	Nmkr	Sep	3+	Deacon Blues	120	5-4
Tattersall	7f	Nmkr	Sep	2	Crius	109	15-2
Oh So Sharp (F)	7f	Nmkr	Sep	2	Alsindi	103	5-1

Irish Group 1 winners 2011

Race	Dist	Course	Month	Age	Winner	RPR	SP
Irish 2,000 Guineas	1m	Curr	May	3	Roderic O'connor	120	7-2
Irish 1,000 Guineas (F)	1m	Curr	May	3	Misty For Me	115	5-1
Gold Cup	1m3f	Curr	May	4+	So You Think	127	1-7
Pretty Polly (F&M)	1m2f	Curr	Jun	3+	Misty For Me	120	100-30
Irish Derby	1m4f	Curr	Jun	3	Treasure Beach	122	7-2
Irish Oaks (F)	1m4f	Curr	Jul	3	Blue Bunting	116	5-2
Phoenix	6f	Curr	Aug	2	La Collina	113	33-1
Moyglare (F)	7f	Curr	Aug	2	Maybe	113	8-13
Matron (F&M)	1m	Leop	Sep	3+	Emulous	120	9-2
Irish Champion	1m2f	Leop	Sep	3+	So You Think	128	1-4
Irish St. Leger	1m6f	Curr	Sep	3+	Jukebox Jury	119	4-1
dead-heated with					Duncan	119	5-1
National	7f	Curr	Sep	2	Power	117	11-4

Irish Group 2 winners 2011

Race	Dist	Course	Month	Age	Winner	RPR	SP
Derby Trial	1m2f	Leop	May	3	Recital	118	1-2
Railway	6f	Curr	Jun	2	Lilbourne Lad	111	9-4
Royal Whip	1m2f	Curr	Aug	3+	Banimpire	115	4-5
Debutante (F)	7f	Curr	Aug	2	Maybe	112	5-4
Futurity	7f	Curr	Aug	2	Dragon Pulse	112	7-1
Blandford (F&M)	1m2f	Curr	Sep	3+	Manieree	112	9-1
Juddmonte Beresford	1m	Curr	Sep	2	David Livingston	115	7-2

Irish Group 3 winners 2011

Race	Dist	Course	Month	Age	Winner	RPR	SP
Park Express (F&M)	1m	Curr	Mar	3+	Lolly For Dolly	107	5-2
1,000 Guineas Trial (F)	7f	Leop	Mar	3	Empowering	104	11-2
2,000 Guineas Trial	1m	Leop	Mar	3	Dunboyne Express	99	5-4
Gladness	7f	Curr	Apr	4+	Lolly For Dolly	114	9-2
Ballysax	1m2f	Leop	Apr	3	Banimpire	104	14-1
Athasi (F)	7f	Curr	May	3+	Emiyna	106	5-2
Mooresbridge	1m2f	Curr	May	4+	So You Think	128	2-13
Amethyst	1m	Leop	May	3+	Famous Name	123	1-6
1,000 Guineas Trial (F)	1m	Leop	May	3	Ballybacka Lady	104	33-1
Blue Wind (F&M)	1m2f	Naas	May	3+	Banimpire	107	5-2
Greenlands	6f	Curr	May	3+	Hitchens	115	11-4
Equestrian (F&M)	1m	Curr	May	4+	Emulous	113	11-4
Gallinule	1m2f	Curr	May	3	Alexander Pope	110	3-1
Ballycorus	7f	Leop	May	3+	Bewitched	113	6-1
Ballyogan (F&M)	6f	Leop	Jun	3+	Radharcnafarraige	103	14-1
Noblesse (F&M)	1m4f	Cork	Jun	3+	Banimpire	107	7-4
International	1m2f	Curr	Jun	3+	Famous Name	123	4-5
Curragh Cup	1m6f	Curr	Jun	3+	Red Cadeaux	114	7-2
Grangecon Stud (F)	6f	Curr	Jun	2	Experience	99	Evens
Sapphire	5f	Curr	Jun	3+	Invincible Ash	110	9-2
Brownstown (F&M)	7f	Fair	Jun	3+	Emulous	112	9-4
Silver Flash (F)	7f	Leop	Jul	2	Maybe	106	2-7
Minstrel	7f	Curr	Jul	3+	Across The Rhine	111	12-1
Kilboy Estate (F&M)	1m1f	Curr	Jul	3+	Manieree	105	7-1
Anglesey	6f	Curr	Jul	2	Fire Lily	103	11-4
Meld	1m1f	Leop	Jul	3+	Famous Name	123	4-9
Tyros	7f	Leop	Jul	2	Remember Alexander	105	7-1
Thanks (F&M)	1m4f	Cork	Jul	3+	Pink Symphony	104	8-1
Ballyroan	1m4f	Leop	Aug	3+	Sense Of Purpose	108	6-1
Phoenix Sprint	6f	Curr	Aug	3+	Deacon Blues	125	4-11
Desmond	1m	Leop	Aug	3+	Future Generation	108	3-1
Dance Design (F&M)	1m1f	Curr	Aug	3+	Bible Belt	111	15-8
Flying Five	5f	Curr	Aug	3+	Amour Propre	114	15-8
Round Tower	6f	Curr	Aug	2	Lightening Pearl	112	6-4
Kilternan	1m2f	Leop	Sep	3+	Galileo's Choice	111	13-2
Renaissance	6f	Curr	Sep	3+	Bewitched	112	13-8
Solonaway	1m	Curr	Sep	3+	Cityscape	121	2-5
Denny Cordell (F&M)	1m1f	Gwpk	Sep	3+	Flowers Of Spring	105	11-2
Weld Park (F)	7f	Curr	Sep	2	Coral Wave	105	4-1

Richest handicaps in Britain 2011

Value	Race	Dist	Course	Month	Winner	RPR	SP
131k	Ebor	1m6f	York	Aug	Moyenne Corniche	99	25-1
100k	Cambridgeshire	1m1f	Nmkr	Sep	Prince Of Johanne	91	40-1
97k	Ladbrokes Mobile	1m4f	Asct	Sep	Barbican	100	16-1
97k	John Smith's Cup	1m2f	York	Jul	Green Destiny	99	6-1
92k	Northumberland Plate	2m	Nwcs	Jun	Tominator	90	25-1
78k	Totesport Mile	1m	Gdwd	Jul	Boom And Bust	94	22-1
75k	Ayr Gold Cup	6f	Ayr	Sep	Our Jonathan	105	11-1
62k	Chester Cup	2m3f	Chst	May	Overturn	99	11-2
62k	Lincoln	1m	Donc	Apr	Sweet Lightning	104	16-1
62k	Royal Hunt Cup	1m	Asct	Jun	Julienas	93	12-1
62k	Britannia	1m	Asct	Jun	Sagramor	93	8-1
62k	Wokingham	6f	Asct	Jun	Deacon Blues	98	15-2
62k	Summer Double Leg 1	7f	Asct	Jul	Bronze Prince	89	16-1
62k	Summer Double Leg 2	7f	Gdwd	Aug	Eton Rifles	97	5-1
62k	Totesport.Com	6f	Nmkj	Jul	Coeus	88	9 1
62k	Stewards' Cup	6f	Gdwd	Jul	Hoof It	111	13-2
53k	Victoria Cup	7f	Asct	May	Hawkeyethenoo	96	15-2
52k	Bond Tyres Trophy	6f	York	Jun	Lexi's Hero	95	20-1
52k	Fly London Southend Airport	7f	Asct	Sep	Smarty Socks	95	11-2
50k	Edinburgh Cup	1m4f	Muss	Jun	Eternal Heart	87	11-2
47k	'Dash'	5f	Epsm	Jun	Captain Dunne	105	13-2
47k	Dubai Duty Free	1m2f	Newb	Sep	Taqleed	92	12-1
44k	Challenge	1m	Sand	Jul	Highland Knight	89	10-1
44k	Great St Wilfrid	6f	Ripn	Aug	Pepper Lane	95	11-1
42k	Melrose	1m6f	York	Aug	Parlour Games	89	9-1
37k	Silver Bowl	1m	Hayd	May	Sagramor	85	15-2
37k	Old Newton Cup	1m4f	Hayd	Jul	Halicarnassus	97	14-1
37k	Portland	6f	Donc	Sep	Nocturnal Affair	101	14-1
32k	Old Borough Cup	1m6f	Hayd	Sep	Bauer	100	16-1
32k	Cesarewitch Trial	2m2f	Nmkr	Sep	Cosimo De Medici	84	13-2
32k	Dash	6f	York	Jul	Hoof It	105	3-1
31k	Buckingham Palace	7f	Asct	Jun	Manassas	95	12-1
31k	Duke Of Edinburgh	1m4f	Asct	Jun	Fox Hunt	99	12-1
31k	Ascot	2m4f	Asct	Jun	Veiled	88	11-2
31k	King George V	1m4f	Asct	Jun	Brown Panther	91	4-1
31k	Totepool	6f	Asct	Jul	Noble Citizen	87	33-1
31k	Bunbury Cup	7f	Nmkj	Jul	Brae Hill	93	11-1
31k	Sportingbet.Com	1m2f	Nmkj	Jul	Fulgur	89	7-1

Richest handicaps in Ireland 2011

Value	Race	Dist	Course	Month	Winner	RPR	SP
59k	Topaz Mile	1m	Galw	Jul	Stunning View	98	7-1
52k	Irish Cambridgeshire	1m	Curr	Aug	Castle Bar Sling	90	20-1
44k	Sprint	6f	Curr	Jun	Six Of Hearts	102	16-1
41k	Rockingham	5f	Curr	Jul	Captain Carey	92	5-1
41k	September	7f	Leop	Sep	Below Zero	95	4-1
39k	Autumn Fillies	1m4f	Leop	Sep	Goldplated	82	20-1
39k	Galwaycity (Qr)	2m	Galw	Jul	Fosters Cross	77	10-1
39k	Finest Surprise	1m4f	Curr	Jun	Gimli's Rock	91	7-1
36k	Ladbrokes	7f	Galw	Jul	Rock Critic	92	10-11
34k	Summer Fillies	7f	Curr	Jun	Future Generation	96	9-1
32k	Ulster Derby	1m5f	D Royal	Jun	Banksters Bonus	100	9-2
32k	United Arab Emirates	1m4f	Curr	May	Bob Le Beau	103	10-1
31k	Guinness	1m4f	Galw	Jul	Clare Glen	88	14-1
31k	Tennis Championship	1m	Curr	Jun	Moran Gra	98	14-1
31k	Irish Lincolnshire	1m	Curr	Mar	Drombeg Dawn	85	25-1

Results up to and including September 30, 2011

THE BIGGER PICTURE

The Warren Hill gallops on a misty April morning in Newmarket. Horses trained in the town won four of the five British Classics in 2011 **Edward Whitaker**

'The **best day of my life**. It's **something you dream of**'

MY BIG MOMENT *Three jockeys look back on festival highlights*

Emmet Mullins had his first Cheltenham Festival winner on Sir Des Champs in the Martin Pipe Conditional Jockeys' Handicap Hurdle, a win made all the sweeter as it helped his uncle Willie secure the trainers' title at the festival

"It was awesome, just a massive release of excitement. Winning on an Irish favourite at the festival, the atmosphere hits you straight away. I'd been over with the horse all week and he was quietly fancied. In a conditional jockeys' race you know they might go too fast and I wanted to drop him out at the start, but I got quite a long way back. He didn't jump great down the back and was hampered by the pile-up at the top of the hill.

"The owners had said to look after him for next year if I was too far back going to the last, but he just took off when he started passing beaten horses and it was great to get up for the win."

Derek O'Connor, six-times Irish point-to-point champion, broke his duck at the Cheltenham Festival with victory in the National Hunt Chase on Chicago Grey and two days later added the Foxhunter Chase on Zemsky

"I love Irish racing, Punchestown and the festivals. To be honest I'd never really fallen in love with Cheltenham, but the experience of having a winner there is unbelievable. The reception when you wear the tricolour and go in the winner's enclosure is just the best feeling in the world. When I got back home people who knew nothing about racing would come up and congratulate me.

"Paul Carberry was a huge influence. He said Chicago Grey's jumping can let him down sometimes and told me exactly how to ride him. I owe a lot of that success to him. Zemsky's was a dramatic race. Everyone says Baby Run would have won if he hadn't fallen – I don't know. It was particularly special to ride a winner for Ronnie Bartlett. He has a huge input in Irish point-to-point racing and at the grassroots level."

Willy Twiston-Davies got the thrill of his young life when winning the John Smith's Fox Hunters at the age of 16 on Baby Run, trained by his father Nigel – a victory that more than made up for the disappointment of being unseated two fences out when leading on the same horse at the festival

"It was a brilliant day, the best day of my life. It meant so much to win over the National fences, it's something you dream of as a kid. It was particularly emotional because of what happened at Cheltenham – that made it even better. And it was great when people pointed out I'm the youngest to win over the National fences.

"I didn't feel any pressure beforehand just because it's Aintree. Dad trusted me, he just said to let him go wherever he feels comfortable and to respect the fences. Baby Run jumped brilliantly. He was long at Becher's and had no trouble all the way round."

Clockwise from left Willy Twiston-Davies negotiates Aintree with Baby Run, Emmet Mullins celebrates his festival success on Sir Des Champs and Derek O'Connor heads to the Cheltenham winner's enclosure

British jump jockeys

Final standings 2010-11

		Wins-runs	Strike rate	Profit/loss to £1 stake	Win and place prize-money £
1	Tony McCoy	218-885	25%	-163.86	1,871,512
2	Richard Johnson	151-784	19%	-41.74	1,442,328
3	Jason Maguire	95-490	19%	-44.59	1,233,427
4	Paul Moloney	79-531	15%	-50.22	606,000
5	Paddy Brennan	78-535	15%	-42.80	780,685
6	Graham Lee	77-606	13%	-153.57	599,951
7	Tom O'Brien	74-466	16%	+2.60	483,222
8	Brian Hughes	65-541	12%	-176.36	456,369
9	Tom Scudamore	63-556	11%	-207.24	717,038
10	Barry Geraghty	61-235	26%	-23.32	1,225,057
	Aidan Coleman	61-491	12%	+12.74	431,821
12	Sam Twiston-Davies	59-487	12%	-7.00	505,693
13	Dougie Costello	47-366	16%	-44.71	444,400
14	Daryl Jacob	56-427	13%	-88.46	686,869
15	Robert Thornton	52-375	14%	-170.84	586,471
16	Jamie Moore	47-417	11%	-19.02	311,307
17	Nick Scholfield	42-323	13%	-47.88	270,747
18	Wayne Hutchinson	41-284	14%	+12.80	322,457
19	Felix de Giles	39-245	16%	+14.17	204,265
	Leighton Aspell	39-448	9%	-12.83	230,719
21	Jimmy Derham	36-319	11%	-83.49	203,009
	Sam Thomas	36-340	11%	-73.18	406,644
23	James Reveley	35-304	12%	-18.89	240,288
	Andrew Tinkler	35-328	11%	-82.60	217,757
	Richie McLernon	35-354	10%	-46.53	210,855
	Denis O'Regan	35-378	9%	-170.87	229,459
27	Barry Keniry	34-295	12%	-53.82	154,116
28	David Bass	33-234	14%	-22.43	243,664
29	Timmy Murphy	32-283	11%	-91.52	424,209
30	Noel Fehily	31-150	21%	-5.44	375,317

Irish jump jockeys

Final standings 2010-11

		Wins-runs	Strike rate	Profit/loss to £1 stake	Win and place prize-money €
1	Paul Townend	80-509	16%	-171.68	1,673,161
2	Davy Russell	76-404	19%	-51.89	1,553,538
3	Paul Carberry	68-510	13%	-180.72	1,284,799
4	Andrew McNamara	64-587	11%	-220.84	1,056,645
5	Barry Geraghty	50-321	16%	-64.97	1,150,940
6	Andrew Lynch	47-589	8%	-285.53	832,499
7	Ruby Walsh	45-192	23%	-35.49	914,117
8	Bryan Cooper	37-425	9%	-126.62	577,605
9	Davy Condon	34-408	8%	-127.53	586,038
10	Mr Patrick Mullins	31-131	24%	-38.68	309,312
	Tom Doyle	31-296	10%	+41.88	417,078
12	David Casey	28-368	8%	-150.46	579,561
13	John Cullen	26-414	6%	-124.39	321,655
14	Niall Madden	25-319	8%	-96.92	336,962
	Mick Darcy	25-336	7%	-114.14	332,843
16	Miss Nina Carberry	24-169	14%	-79.67	401,553
17	Mr Mikey Fogarty	23-155	15%	-2.75	190,442
18	Keith Donoghue	22-260	8%	-67.65	224,328
	Eddie O'Connell	22-281	8%	-66.87	240,532
	Alan Crowe	22-317	7%	-168.25	337,043
21	Robbie Power	20-287	7%	-134.07	628,778
	Mark Walsh	20-287	7%	-195.35	287,812
23	Shay Barry	19-227	8%	-89.15	299,221
	Patrick Mangan	19-353	5%	-145.25	281,258
25	Brian O'Connell	18-357	5%	-136.65	265,132
26	Mr Robbie McNamara	17-93	18%	+27.82	315,350
	Philip Enright	17-348	5%	-147.00	337,179
28	Paddy Flood	16-160	10%	-60.87	260,847
29	Emmet Mullins	15-147	10%	-57.63	276,312
	Matty Bowes	15-180	8%	-23.50	163,996
	Barry Cash	15-248	6%	-113.75	156,754

Battle at the top

Everyone knows the score by now: Tony McCoy first, Richard Johnson second. McCoy's 16th consecutive title was secured more decisively than in recent seasons, with his highest score and biggest margin of victory since the record-breaking days with Martin Pipe.

On the up

Paul Moloney rose to fourth, from 12th the previous season, with a personal-best of 79 thanks mainly to his successful association with Evan Williams. Tom O'Brien jumped to seventh from 23rd with 74 winners, more than double his previous season's score and his best since his century in 2006-07. Brian Hughes was the other newcomer to the top ten, from 17th, with a near 50 per cent rise in his total. Twenty-five of his 65 winners were supplied by Howard Johnson.

On the slide

Denis O'Regan dropped from tenth to 23rd, with his number of winners almost halving following his split with Howard Johnson. Ruby Walsh and Robert Thornton (seventh and eighth respectively the previous season) dropped back because of injury-hit seasons.

Punters' friend

Daryl Jacob had a particularly fruitful partnership with David Arbuthnot, with a 33 per cent strike-rate.

High strike-rate

Barry Geraghty (pictured) was best among the top jockeys for the third consecutive season since teaming up with Nicky Henderson, although this was the first time he had a level-stake loss on his mounts.

Battle at the top

A new champion as Paul Townend made the most of Ruby Walsh's long injury layoff with a hatful of winners for Willie Mullins. Forty-nine winners for the champion trainer, at a 29 per cent strike-rate, laid the foundations for his success at the age of 20. Davy Russell, runner-up to Walsh for the previous four seasons, had to settle for second again.

On the up

Bryan Cooper was champion conditional with a record total in his breakthrough season with Dessie Hughes, little more than 18 months after his first winner over jumps for his trainer-father Tom. Paul Carberry put his problems of the previous season behind him to take a familiar high position, up from 13th. Davy Condon had his first top-ten finish, up from 19th the season before, with a seasonal-best.

On the slide

David Casey finished outside the top ten for the first time in more than a decade, with fewer than half the number of winners he had when fourth in 2007-08. Nina Carberry, down from eighth, and Paddy Flood, who dropped from ninth in an injury-hit season, were the others to drop out of the top ten.

Punters' friend

Robbie McNamara (pictured) was well in profit overall and his association with Dermot Weld paid big dividends as the pair enjoyed a 46 per cent strike-rate.

'It was **awesome, brilliant**. You've got to enjoy the **good days**'

MY BIG MOMENT
Three trainers on the thrill of making their owners happy

Brian Ellison began 2011, in which he would also win the Ebor, with his first top-level triumph when Marsh Warbler won the Grade 1 Coral Future Champions Finale Juvenile Hurdle at Chepstow in January

"You never know how they [ex-Flat horses] will go, but he schooled really well before his first race and I was surprised when he was beaten – he ran as if he'd never seen a hurdle in his life. But he bolted up in his next two starts and we really fancied him at Chepstow. He must have heavy ground and that's what we got.

"When he won it was awesome, brilliant. It was great for the owners, Dan Gilbert and Kristian Strangeway. We didn't pay a lot of money for Marsh Warbler and he went and won a big race. He then went to Cheltenham and things didn't happen for him. The ground was against him and he pulled a muscle in his back. There's plenty of disappointment in racing, so you've got to enjoy the good days. There are a few we've got that I'm fond of and he's one of them."

Paul Flynn, a Cheltenham Festival-winning jockey who now trains in County Longford, saddled his biggest winner when 20-1 shot Moon Dice landed the Guinness Galway Hurdle in July for the Three Friers Cross Syndicate

"It was a great day and it beat riding a Cheltenham Festival winner. It was a great boost to the yard and to everyone in the area as well. There are only seven members of the syndicate

Clockwise from top Holmwood Legend wins the Byrne Group Plate, Moon Dice takes the Galway Hurdle and and Marsh Warbler lands the Finale at Chepstow

but all their families, friends and anyone who knew them were there. It was the most I've seen in a winner's enclosure in a long time. There must have been 350 people.

"He won at Limerick the time before and I told the boys to lump on. That was their payday for the year and after that it was left to me to do whatever I liked with him for the rest of the

season. He works very well and felt like a good horse to me all the time, even if he hadn't always run like that. I was confident of him running well, but we'd have been happy with fifth or sixth.

"I didn't realise before the race how much it was worth, I couldn't believe the prize-money. It didn't last very long because we had a big session

afterwards. If we had as many winners as Dermot Weld does at Galway we'd still be there now. We definitely enjoyed ourselves."

Pat Rodford, with only ten horses in his Somerset stable and just one Cheltenham Festival runner before this year, sent out Sparky May to finish second to Quevega in the David Nicholson Mares' Hurdle and two days later won the Byrne Group Plate with Holmwood Legend. After 25 years as a trainer, he then retired and handed over to his assistant Keiran Burke, who rode Holmwood Legend

"When Holmwood Legend won it was an incredible day as Sparky May was the one all the fuss had been about. We had Racing Post and national press coverage with her and were delighted to finish second to the best mare around. That was the pressure over and the whole reason Holmwood Legend went was that the owner [Brian Derrick] wanted a day out.

"We didn't have any expectations. If he had finished in the first six we would have been pleased and still had an enjoyable day. I was absolutely flabbergasted when he won so well and it didn't register until later, then you realise how big an occasion it was. It was special to have a winner at Cheltenham for Brian, as we grew up in the same village and played football together. It was the icing on the cake to an already successful season and was my swansong. Kieran was a big part of it and hopefully he can continue things as a trainer."

British jumps trainers
Final standings 2010-11

		Wins-runs	Strike rate	Profit/loss to £1 stake	Win and place prize-money £
1	Paul Nicholls	134-583	23%	-77.99	2,424,059
2	Nicky Henderson	153-612	25%	-77.66	2,210,465
3	Donald McCain	100-588	17%	-169.14	1,286,133
4	Philip Hobbs	86-556	15%	-154.06	1,163,050
5	David Pipe	65-504	13%	-99.39	999,941
6	Nigel Twiston-Davies	97-711	14%	+20.40	988,425
7	Alan King	84-600	14%	-180.82	901,328
8	Jonjo O'Neill	94-750	13%	-160.11	861,735
9	Evan Williams	90-595	15%	-75.90	647,447
10	Tim Vaughan	91-563	16%	-133.61	574,061
11	Howard Johnson	60-368	16%	-30.83	524,194
12	Willie Mullins	4-35	11%	-12.92	483,874
13	Colin Tizzard	41-328	13%	-37.11	436,281
14	Peter Bowen	60-384	16%	+14.82	396,961
15	Ferdy Murphy	29-321	9%	-124.12	392,034
16	Gordon Elliott	35-123	28%	+46.24	365,015
17	Nick Williams	17-116	15%	+17.71	352,498
18	Tom George	18-224	8%	-103.27	341,862
19	Lucinda Russell	41-343	12%	-117.50	323,902
20	Gary Moore	45-390	12%	-30.36	304,186
21	Venetia Williams	38-372	10%	-83.62	264,405
22	Sue Smith	40-361	11%	-25.21	258,496
23	Charlie Longsdon	44-233	19%	+53.80	258,091
24	Emma Lavelle	30-206	15%	-41.04	257,910
25	Paul Webber	28-203	14%	-14.92	256,817
26	Henry de Bromhead	2-11	18%	+7.50	228,601
27	Brian Ellison	21-108	19%	+21.06	223,406
28	Milton Harris	32-311	10%	-34.83	222,213
29	Neil Mulholland	21-206	10%	-66.67	202,968
30	Martin Lynch	0-1	0%	-1.00	201,590

Irish jumps trainers
Final standings 2010-11

		Wins-runs	Strike rate	Profit/loss to £1 stake	Win and place prize-money €
1	Willie Mullins	106-467	23%	-119.06	2,412,247
2	Noel Meade	53-314	17%	-44.36	1,134,027
3	Dessie Hughes	52-475	11%	-124.92	987,203
4	Gordon Elliott	62-407	15%	-91.82	829,263
5	Edward O'Grady	47-352	13%	-90.84	787,453
6	Jessica Harrington	33-369	9%	-155.69	775,269
7	Colm Murphy	24-180	13%	-14.74	592,138
8	Paul Nolan	31-263	12%	-58.58	569,179
9	Charles Byrnes	29-155	19%	+4.95	566,330
10	Dermot Weld	16-51	31%	+30.16	364,385
11	Henry de Bromhead	19-183	10%	-98.20	363,219
12	John Joseph Hanlon	24-280	9%	-135.14	350,983
13	Tony Martin	21-221	10%	-107.97	310,250
14	John Kiely	20-119	17%	+4.90	299,085
15	Michael Hourigan	16-236	7%	-147.12	294,983
16	Charlie Swan	20-261	8%	-139.75	278,311
17	Mouse Morris	14-164	9%	-73.42	275,072
18	Eoin Griffin	12-126	10%	-26.00	274,637
19	Arthur Moore	6-146	4%	-96.87	230,727
20	Robert Tyner	12-121	10%	-29.00	211,345
21	Christy Roche	14-145	10%	-22.90	209,418
22	Eoin Doyle	20-136	15%	-20.77	202,350
23	Oliver McKiernan	6-69	9%	+14.50	187,051
24	Adrian Maguire	8-89	9%	-34.25	179,382
25	Paul Flynn	12-127	9%	-46.92	176,782
26	Tom Taaffe	3-104	3%	-71.00	167,706
27	Philip Rothwell	13-370	4%	-252.38	162,480
28	Colin Bowe	15-87	17%	+44.13	160,637
29	Francis Flood	11-190	6%	-77.50	159,992
30	James Lambe	14-194	7%	-86.37	155,580

Battle at the top

The top two has not changed in three seasons, but the gap was much smaller this time as Nicky Henderson (pictured) threw down a concerted challenge. Paul Nicholls was crowned champion for the sixth consecutive season, but with his lowest prize-money haul since the first of those titles. Henderson was top by number of winners for the second season running.

On the up

Donald McCain jumped from his previous-best of eighth the season before as he recorded his first century of winners, headed by Grand National hero Ballabriggs. Nigel Twiston-Davies had a career-best 97 winners, up from 70 the previous season, although he dropped two places in the table. The only newcomer to the top ten was Tim Vaughan, up from 13th.

On the slide

Howard Johnson was the only trainer to drop out of the top ten and, although he fell only to 11th, that was before his four-year ban and subsequent retirement.

Punters' friend

The underrated Charlie Longsdon more than doubled his previous best score and was in profit for the fourth time in his five seasons with a licence.

High strike-rate

Gordon Elliott once again excelled with his raiders, with a 28% strike-rate and a solid profit, and broke his Cheltenham Festival duck with two winners.

Battle at the top

Once again it was a case of Willie Mullins first, the rest nowhere. Mullins took his fourth consecutive championship with more than double the prize-money haul of Noel Meade, who has finished runner-up every season since Mullins wrested the title from his grasp. It was a fourth consecutive century of winners for Mullins but his lowest total during that run.

On the up

Gordon Elliott (pictured) had a great season on both sides of the water and in Ireland jumped into the top echelon, continuing a rapid rise that has taken him from 44th to 25th, 14th and now fourth in the past four seasons. Colm Murphy and Charles Byrnes both returned to the top ten, while Dermot Weld had his best jumps campaign in years.

On the slide

Charlie Swan finished outside the top ten for the first time since 2002-03, with his number of winners falling below 30 for the first time in that period. Tony Martin, Henry de Bromhead and Mouse Morris were the others to drop out of the top ten.

Punters' friend

Former champion point-to-point trainer Colin Bowe has made a tremendous impression in his first two seasons with a full licence and those who followed him from the start have made a tidy profit.

High strike-rate

Dermot Weld was best with 31 per cent. Notably, that was matched by the collective strike-rate of the top four British trainers – Paul Nicholls, Nicky Henderson, Donald McCain and Philip Hobbs – on their occasional sorties to Ireland.

JUST FOR FUN Who is missing from this result: 1 Ballabriggs, 2 Oscar Time, 3 ???, 4 State Of Play? Answer page 170

'It was an **extremely special** moment, truly **unbelievable**'

MY BIG MOMENT *Three owners on the day it all came right*

Ronnie Bartlett, whose company sponsors the Albert Bartlett Novices' Hurdle, finally got to receive a prize at the Cheltenham Festival after the Ian Ferguson-trained Zemsky won the Foxhunter Chase

"It was a dream come true. I've been going to the festival since the mid-1980s and had my first runner there in 1991. I've been a hunting man all my life and it's the ultimate race to win.

"The first time we sent Zemsky to Nicky Henderson he sent him back and said he wouldn't win a bumper. We went back pointing and he won two point-to-points. Nicky came to the yard and said if there was one horse he could have back it would be Zemsky, and that's when he won his two novice hurdles.

"We always thought he was a good horse. He just went off the boil when he went chasing initially but he got his confidence back in point-to-points. I suppose it sums up racing – we had those higher expectations in the early days but it didn't happen, so you get even greater pleasure when the success comes once your expectations are lower."

Bensalem won the Stewart Family Spinal Research Handicap Chase at the Cheltenham Festival for owners John Duggan and Alan Marsh, a year after falling two out in the same race and having recovered from life-threatening illness in the interim. Marsh tells the story

"He came back from his summer in Ireland, where he stayed with

Clockwise from above Simon Clarke (left) with Nacarat at Aintree, Zemsky and Derek O'Connor after the Foxhunter and Bensalem on his way to victory at Cheltenham

John, and John's nephew Paul, who looks after him over there, travelled with him. When they arrived back at Alan King's yard, something was amiss and Alan took him straight to the vets. He had travel sickness, which developed into pneumonia. We spoke to Alan and Jeremy Swann [the vet] and it seemed unlikely he would survive. We were advised it would be best to take an early decision for the horse's sake as he was in so much pain. I went for a long drive to sort my mind out, it was such a tough decision. But then Alan and Jeremy felt there were signs he'd pull through, though he wouldn't race again, and we all came to the same decision. I'm glad we did.

"Everyone worked wonders to get him back and Cheltenham was fantastic. Choc [Robert Thornton] gave him a great ride. He learned from the previous year's mistakes and brought him wide down the hill so that he didn't get unsighted again. To win the race, after everything he'd been through, was an extremely special moment. I will never forget that day, it was truly unbelievable and all credit goes to Alan, his team, Paul Duggan and Jeremy Swann."

Simon Clarke, owner of Nacarat, was thrilled when the Tom George-trained ten-year-old gained a deserved first Grade 1 success in the Totesport Bowl at Aintree

"It's a dream come true just to own a horse who might be capable of winning a Grade 1, let alone having one that actually does it. He's a great horse to own, he tries so hard. The three times he's had his ground in a big race he's won the Racing Post Chase, the Charlie Hall and the Totesport Bowl. But even when it hasn't been his ground, he has always tried his heart out.

"Aintree was always the plan after he'd run at Kempton. Before the race I was nervous, like always, but I had a good feeling because we knew he had his ground. All the talk beforehand was about Denman, so we were hopeful, not expectant. The atmosphere after he won was just unbelievable. For me it's definitely on a par with Cheltenham.

"I've got to pay tribute to Tom and his team. I really enjoy having horses with them and it's a great team effort. We bought him from France and it was Tom's father-in-law who found him for me. You can't really describe the thrill of owning a racehorse like him. It's a mix of nerves, excitement, expectation, joy and relief. I'm so lucky to have had that experience. You could try for a lifetime before you experience something like that again."

British jumps owners — Final standings 2010-11

		Highest earning horse	Wins-runs	Winners-horses	Win and place prize-money £
1	Trevor Hemmings	Ballabriggs	32-204	21-59	951,635
2	John P McManus	Don't Push It	84-650	60-165	818,918
3	Robert Waley-Cohen	Long Run	3-15	2-6	624,260
4	The Stewart Family	Big Buck's	14-74	7-19	549,563
5	Andrea & Graham Wylie	Tidal Bay	46-242	33-80	439,553
6	Mrs Diana L Whateley	Menorah	16-67	9-19	425,452
7	Clive D Smith	Master Minded	4-18	1-6	302,272
8	T G Leslie	Peddlers Cross	15-88	11-19	295,596
9	Walters Plant Hire Ltd	Oscar Whisky	22-83	14-30	273,190
10	Gigginstown House Stud	Carlito Brigante	6-29	5-22	262,511
11	Michael Buckley	Finian's Rainbow	15-47	8-17	242,416
12	Ann & Alan Potts	Sizing Europe	5-20	5-10	235,733
13	Paul K Barber	Denman	12-32	8-9	183,028
14	Simon W Clarke	Nacarat	3-30	2-8	177,281
15	D A Johnson	Poker De Sivola	12-99	10-30	173,765
16	Potensis Limited	Silviniaco Conti	10-26	5-7	165,117
17	John Wade	Always Right	22-156	13-44	164,448
18	Paul Murphy	Carole's Legacy	9-30	6-9	153,984
19	Paul Duffy Diamond Prtnrs	Diamond Harry	4-14	3-4	140,695
20	Jimmy Nesbitt Partnership	Riverside Theatre	2-3	1-1	138,817
21	R E R Williams	Courella	36-200	20-45	131,785
22	Mrs Jean R Bishop	Cue Card	5-14	4-4	125,731
23	J Hales	Al Ferof	6-32	4-10	124,184
24	Chris Giles	Zarkandar	5-22	3-6	116,376
25	Our Friends in the North	Imperial Commander	1-4	1-2	112,660
26	S Munir	Grandouet	9-66	7-19	110,057
27	Mrs Rose Boyd	Hurricane Fly	1-1	1-1	105,469
28	George Creighton	Hurricane Fly	1-1	1-1	105,469
29	Jared Sullivan	Gauvain	8-28	6-7	103,874
30	Alan Peterson	Massini's Maguire	6-34	4-11	101,795

Irish jumps owners — Final standings 2010-11

		Highest earning horse	Wins-runs	Winners-horses	Win and place prize-money €
1	John P McManus	Finger Onthe Pulse	78-660	53-173	1,504,221
2	Gigginstown House Stud	Quito De La Roque	70-442	44-95	1,308,870
3	Mrs S Ricci	Zaidpour	10-44	7-13	348,990
4	George Creighton	Hurricane Fly	5-15	2-3	306,710
5	D J Sharkey	Realt Dubh	5-8	1-1	241,100
6	Dr R Lambe	Majestic Concorde	7-56	6-16	231,340
7	Mrs A F Mee	Hidden Cyclone	10-52	5-10	213,252
8	Patrick Joseph Redmond	Big Zeb	3-7	1-2	191,795
9	Redgap Partnership	Follow The Plan	6-68	4-13	190,801
10	Barry Connell	Pineau De Re	12-104	9-32	188,297
11	Hammer & Trowel Syndicate	Quevega	1-9	1-3	174,600
12	Mrs A Dunlop	Organisedconfusion	2-8	1-3	161,200
13	Mrs Violet O'Leary	Golden Silver	4-12	1-3	157,840
14	T G Leslie	Overturn	1-1	1-1	152,500
15	J P Dunne	Roberto Goldback	4-26	3-7	142,960
16	G Burke	Western Charmer	5-45	5-10	139,555
17	Barry Healy	Alfa Beat	5-7	1-1	138,460
18	John J Brennan	Darwins Fox	8-49	7-14	132,375
19	Mrs Tracey O'Hare	Sweet Shock	11-59	5-11	131,700
20	E Duignan	Johnny McGeeney	7-42	5-14	128,530
21	Thomas Barr	Torphichen	7-26	4-7	126,710
22	Top Of The Hill Syndicate	Solwhit	2-11	2-2	123,535
23	E A P Scouller	Bostons Angel	3-12	1-2	120,070
24	Mrs M Brophy	Voler La Vedette	4-17	2-4	113,955
25	Molley Malone Syndicate	Oscars Well	3-4	1-1	113,725
26	Patrick Wilmott	Sailors Warn	6-43	6-11	112,390
27	Mrs Diana L Whateley	Captain Chris	2-4	2-4	111,750
28	James F Mernagh	Golden Sunbird	5-19	2-5	109,630
29	D Cox	Tranquil Sea	4-39	2-12	108,831
30	Michael O'Flynn	China Rock	5-49	3-12	108,655

Battle at the top

Trevor Hemmings (pictured) landed his first title thanks to John Smith's Grand National winner Ballabriggs, making him the only man apart from JP McManus and David Johnson to finish top in the past decade. The National proved decisive, with McManus's 2010 winner Don't Push It third this time.

On the up

Robert Waley-Cohen doesn't have many horses but his very good one, Long Run, and Grand National runner-up Oscar Time, who he owns in partnership, took him from 62nd the season before. Dai Walters also rose from the depths thanks mainly to Aintree Hurdle winner Oscar Whisky, while Diana Whateley moved up from 14th with the promise of better to come from talented trio Menorah, Wishfull Thinking and Captain Chris. Michael O'Leary's Gigginstown House Stud, having enjoyed a wonderful festival season at Cheltenham and Punchestown, rose from 24th into the top ten

On the slide

David Johnson, five times champion and never out of the top five in the previous decade, slumped to 15th from fourth the previous season. Our Friends in the North dropped from seventh as Imperial Commander lost his Gold Cup crown and Caroline Mould, despite the promise of Sprinter Sacre, was down from sixth as Khyber Kim underperformed.

Battle at the top

JP McManus (pictured) was knocked off his perch in Britain but regained his crown in Ireland from Gigginstown House Stud, which had ended his long reign at the top the previous season. It was a close-run affair, with Gigginstown enjoying an even better season this time, but in the end McManus's superior firepower made the difference. The big two were almost a million euros clear of the rest.

On the up

George Creighton, 19th the previous year, rose to fourth after the exploits of Hurricane Fly. Derek Sharkey was a newcomer to the top ten thanks to top novice chaser Realt Dubh – his father Des owns Noble Prince, who was beaten three times by Realt Dubh but had his big payday at Cheltenham in the Jewson Novice Chase. Barry Connell, up from 15th, fired plenty of ammunition and hit the target more times than anyone else outside the big two.

On the slide

Violet O'Leary, so long a regular in the upper reaches of the table, slipped down from third. Golden Silver carried her famous colours with distinction but was her only winner. Eamonn Duignan dropped from ninth but had the satisfaction of a homebred Punchestown festival winner with Johnny McGeeney.

WE ARE THE

Champions

Champion 2m4f+ Hurdler
BIG BUCK'S

Trainer **Paul Nicholls**
Owner **The Stewart family**

RACING POST RATINGS
178 Big Buck's
171 Grands Crus
165 Mourad
165 Oscar Whisky
165 Thousand Stars

HOW HE DID IT With effortless ease, extending his winning run to 12 since returning to hurdles in January 2009 after his Hennessy mishap and winning at both the Cheltenham and Aintree festivals for the third year in a row

WHAT MADE IT SPECIAL The sheer eye-popping class as he twice saw off young pretender Grands Crus with aplomb

HIGH POINT The 5l victory from Grands Crus at Aintree earned him an RPR of 178, the best of his career

LOW POINT The last one of those was back in the 2008 Hennessy

WHAT THEY SAID "Dan [Skelton, assistant trainer] said he's probably the best we've ever trained and ability-wise he might well be right. You can't argue with his record. He's phenomenal" – Nicholls

WHAT NEXT A 13th straight win would match the great Bula's run of successes and then a record fourth World Hurdle beckons

Champion 2m4f Chaser
MASTER MINDED

Trainer **Paul Nicholls**
Owner **Clive Smith**

RACING POST RATINGS
176 Master Minded
172 Poquelin
172 Riverside Theatre
168 Albertas Run
168 Kalahari King

HOW HE DID IT Ended the doubts about his effectiveness at 2m4f with an impressive 9l victory over dual Ryanair Chase winner Albertas Run in the Grade 1 Melling Chase at Aintree

WHAT MADE IT SPECIAL The high-performance engine, electric jumping and utter dominance – it was like the old Master Minded at Aintree and racegoers loved it

HIGH POINT Recorded his best RPR in two and a quarter years at Aintree – and the joint third-best of his career

LOW POINT Finishing eighth of 11 in the Queen Mother Champion Chase, beaten 31 lengths

WHAT THEY SAID "It's obvious he wants a trip now. Looking back, he should have gone for the Ryanair rather than the Champion Chase" – Nicholls

WHAT NEXT Aintree raised hopes of a bold bid for the King George, with the option of a drop back to the Ryanair later

Champions
Clockwise from main picture, Sizing Europe, Spirit Son, Master Minded, Hurricane Fly and Long Run

Champion 2m Chaser
SIZING EUROPE

Trainer **Henry de Bromhead**
Owner **Ann and Alan Potts**

RACING POST RATINGS
176 Sizing Europe
175 Big Zeb
174 Twist Magic
173 Master Minded
171 Somersby

HOW HE DID IT Won only once in the 2010-11 season but it came when it mattered most in the Queen Mother Champion Chase at Cheltenham and was enough to edge a tight division

WHAT MADE IT SPECIAL His Champion Chase victory was the highlight of a memorable second day of the Cheltenham Festival for Irish-trained horses, who won the first six races on the card

HIGH POINT The way he surged clear up the hill at Cheltenham, putting 5l between him and Big Zeb

LOW POINT Defeat as 5-4 favourite on his reappearance at Punchestown during the failed early-season experiment over 3m

WHAT THEY SAID "We've had a lot of very good days and a couple of dodgy days with him but God, he was good at Cheltenham" – De Bromhead

WHAT NEXT? Connections are still keen to try longer trips, but there's always the Champion Chase down the line

Champion 2m Hurdler
HURRICANE FLY

Trainer **Willie Mullins**
Owner **George Creighton**

RACING POST RATINGS
173 Hurricane Fly
170 Peddlers Cross
165 Menorah
165 Oscar Whiskly
165 Solwhit
165 Thousand Stars

HOW HE DID IT Carried all before him with an unbeaten run in five Grade 1 races in 2010-11, culminating with impressive wins in the Champion Hurdles at Cheltenham and Punchestown

WHAT MADE IT SPECIAL The superb hurdling technique, high cruising speed, boundless stamina and killer turn of foot

HIGH POINT Cheltenham was good, but his Rabobank Champion Hurdle victory at Punchestown was his best performance on RPR

LOW POINT Okay, so he can get buzzed up before a race and can race freely. But, really, what's not to like?

WHAT THEY SAID "He's very hyper, but he's a lot more mature now and at Punchestown he was just awesome" – Mullins

WHAT NEXT He'll have some new challengers but started the season a best-priced 7-4 for a repeat win in the Champion Hurdle at Cheltenham

Champion Novice Hurdler
SPIRIT SON
Trainer **Nicky Henderson**
Owner **Michael Buckley**

RACING POST RATINGS
160 Spirit Son
155 Al Ferof
153 Bobs Worth
153 Oscars Well
152 Cue Card

HOW HE DID IT Stamped himself the top novice with a 13l demolition of Cue Card in the Grade 2 Mersey Novices' Hurdle at Aintree – the crowning performance in a highly progressive first season that brought four wins from five starts

WHAT MADE IT SPECIAL Barely six months after his racecourse debut he was mixing it at the top level at Cheltenham and Aintree

HIGH POINT The runaway success at Aintree on his first try at 2m4f, stretching his superiority over Cue Card by 8¹/₂l from their Cheltenham Festival running

LOW POINT His only defeat when 2l runner-up to Al Ferof in the Supreme Novices' Hurdle at Cheltenham, where he hung right on the run-in

WHAT THEY SAID "Cheltenham probably came six months early and I promise you he has massive improvement. He was sensational at Aintree" – Henderson

WHAT NEXT Quoted as short as 8-1 for the Champion Hurdle pre-season and his mix of speed and stamina bodes well for further progress in his second campaign

Champion Novice Chaser
WISHFULL THINKING
Trainer **Philip Hobbs**
Owner **Diana Whateley**

RACING POST RATINGS
167 Wishfull Thinking
166 Captain Chris
165 Realt Dubh
164 Noble Prince
163 Finian's Rainbow
163 Time For Rupert

HOW HE DID IT Edged a tight division from his stablemate Captain Chris after a commanding win under top weight in a handicap chase at the Punchestown festival, following up a 10l Grade 2 victory over Medermit at Aintree

WHAT MADE IT SPECIAL His bold jumping and gutsy front running was a sight to behold as he ran his rivals ragged at Punchestown and Aintree

HIGH POINT Punchestown, where he conceded 20lb or more to his 16 rivals and came home 4¹/₂l clear of subsequent Galway Plate winner Blazing Tempo

LOW POINT The first-fence fall on his debut at Aintree, which proved to be no indication of his jumping ability

WHAT THEY SAID "It's hard to know what his best trip really is. Earlier in the season we thought he wanted three miles but he's got loads of pace as well and hopefully we've got both options with him" – Hobbs

WHAT NEXT The King George was in the thoughts of connections by the end of the season, with the fallback option of the top chases at his proven distance of 2m4f

Champion 3+ Chaser
LONG RUN
Trainer **Nicky Henderson**
Owner **Robert Waley-Cohen**

RACING POST RATINGS
183 Long Run
181 Denman
174 Imperial Commander
174 Kauto Star
172 Riverside Theatre
172 Tidal Bay
172 What A Friend

HOW HE DID IT At the age of six, and after just six starts in Britain, put himself alongside the greats by landing the Cheltenham Gold Cup and King George VI Chase in the same season, recording RPRs in the 180s each time with winning distances of 7l and 12l respectively

WHAT MADE IT SPECIAL Take your pick: his youth, his amateur rider, a first Gold Cup for Nicky Henderson. Most of all, his sheer class

HIGH POINT The sight of him going head to head with Denman and Kauto Star, in the best Gold Cup in years, will live long in the memory

LOW POINT Defeat in the Paddy Power Gold Cup on his reappearance, which at the time fuelled doubts over his suitability to Cheltenham

WHAT THEY SAID "The Gold Cup is a war and there is no quarter given. What marks out a horse like Long Run is that he fights, he wants it and he has courage" – Sam Waley-Cohen, rider

WHAT NEXT The sky's the limit at his age and plans will revolve around the King George and Gold Cup for years to come

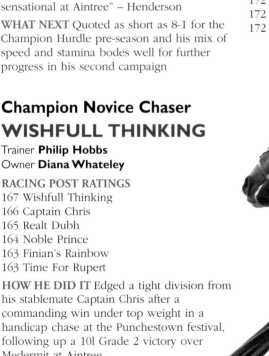

Running them ragged Wishfull Thinking flies to victory at Aintree

British Grade 1 winners 2010-11

Race	Dist	Course	Month	Age	Winner	RPR	SP
Betfair Ch	3m	Hayd	Nov	5+	Imperial Commander	172	10-11
Fighting Fifth Hdl	2m1f	Newb	Nov	4+	Peddlers Cross	161	9-4
Tingle Creek Ch	2m1f	Chlt	Dec	4+	Master Minded	173	10-11
Long Walk Hdl	3m1f	Newb	Dec	4+	Big Buck's	167	2-13
Challow Nov Hdl	2m5f	Newb	Dec	4+	Backspin	147	5-1
Finale Juvenile Hdl	2m1f	Chep	Jan	4	Marsh Warbler	140	8-1
Tolworth	2m1f	Sand	Jan	4+	Minella Class	143	6-4
King George VI Ch	3m	Kemp	Jan	5+	Long Run	181	9-2
Christmas Hdl	2m	Kemp	Jan	5+	Binocular	164	13-8
Victor Chandler Ch	2m1f	Asct	Jan	5+	Master Minded	171	4-7
Challengers Nov Ch	2m5f	Sand	Feb	5+	Medermit	155	5-2
Ascot Ch	2m6f	Asct	Feb	5+	Riverside Theatre	172	11-10
Champion Hdl	2m1f	Chlt	Mar	4+	Hurricane Fly	170	11-4
Supreme Nov Hdl	2m1f	Chlt	Mar	4+	Al Ferof	155	10-1
Arkle Challenge Trophy Ch	2m	Chlt	Mar	5+	Captain Chris	166	6-1
Queen Mother Champion Ch	2m	Chlt	Mar	5+	Sizing Europe	176	10-1
RSA Ch	3m1f	Chlt	Mar	5+	Bostons Angel	158	16-1
Neptune Invest' Nov Hdl	2m5f	Chlt	Mar	4+	First Lieutenant	151	7-1
Champion Bumper	2m1f	Chlt	Mar	4-6	Cheltenian	138	14-1
Ryanair Ch	2m5f	Chlt	Mar	5+	Albertas Run	168	6-1
World Hdl	3m	Chlt	Mar	4+	Big Buck's	166	10-11
Cheltenham Gold Cup Ch	3m3f	Chlt	Mar	5+	Long Run	183	7-2
JCB Triumph Hdl	2m1f	Chlt	Mar	4	Zarkandar	147	13-2
Albert Bartlett Nov Hdl	3m	Chlt	Mar	4+	Bobs Worth	153	15-8
Liverpool Hdl	3m1f	Aint	Apr	4+	Big Buck's	178	4-6
Anniversary Hdl	2m1f	Aint	Apr	4	Zarkandar	147	4-6
Bowl Ch	3m1f	Aint	Apr	5+	Nacarat	168	7-2
Melling Ch	2m4f	Aint	Apr	5+	Master Minded	176	11-2
Sefton Nov Hdl	3m1f	Aint	Apr	4+	Saint Are	145	33-1
Aintree Hdl	2m4f	Aint	Apr	4+	Oscar Whisky	165	6-1
Maghull Nov Ch	2m	Aint	Apr	5+	Finian's Rainbow	161	10-11

British Grade 2 winners 2010-11

Race	Dist	Course	Month	Age	Winner	RPR	SP
Old Roan Ch Lmtd H'cap	2m4f	Aint	Oct	4+	Monet's Garden	165	12-1
Persian War Nov Hdl	2m4f	Chep	Oct	4+	Reve De Sivola	148	6-5
Old Roan Ch (H'cap)	2m4f	Aint	Oct	4+	Monet's Garden	165	4-1
Persian War Nov Hdl	2m4f	Chep	Oct	4+	Silviniaco Conti	160	7-2
John Smith's Hdl	3m1f	Weth	Oct	4+	Fair Along	159	6-1
Bet365 Charlie Hall Ch	3m1f	Weth	Oct	5+	Nacarat	160	6-1
Haldon Gold Cup Ch (H'cap)	2m2f	Extr	Nov	4+	Tchico Polos	153	3-1
Rising Stars Nov Ch	2m5f	Winc	Nov	4+	Wishfull Thinking	140	5-4
Elite Hdl (H'cap)	2m	Winc	Nov	4+	Nearby	151	11-2
Sharp Nov Hdl	2m1f	Chlt	Nov	4+	Cue Card	152	8-13
JCB Triumph Hdl Trial	2m1f	Chlt	Nov	3	Sam Winner	141	4/1
November Nov Ch	2m	Chlt	Nov	4+	Ghizao	158	13-2
Hyde Nov Hdl	2m5f	Chlt	Nov	4+	Champion Court	135	5-1
Amlin 1965 Ch	2m3f	Asct	Nov	4+	Master Minded	174	5-6
Ascot Hdl	2m4f	Asct	Nov	4+	Silviniaco Conti	163	100-30
Worcester Nov Ch	3m	Newb	Nov	4+	Aiteen Thirtythree	153	13-2
Berkshire Nov Ch	2m4f	Newb	Nov	4+	Cois Farraig	131	10-1
Long Distance Hdl	3m1f	Newb	Nov	4+	Big Buck's	160	2-7
Relkeel Hdl	2m5f	Chlt	Dec	4+	Karabak	161	5-1
International Hdl	2m1f	Chlt	Dec	4+	Menorah	157	7-4
Bristol Nov Hdl	3m	Chlt	Dec	4+	Mossley	142	3-1
Peterborough Ch	2m4f	Newb	Dec	4+	Tartak	156	11-4
Dipper Nov Ch	2m5f	Chlt	Jan	5+	Hell's Bay	156	16-1
Leamington Nov Hdl	2m5f	Warw	Jan	4+	Court In Motion	147	6-4
Warfield Mares' Hdl	3m	Asct	Jan	4+	Sparky May	149	7-1
Holloway's Hdl (H'cap)	2m4f	Asct	Jan	4+	Tiger O'Toole	137	40-1
JCB Triumph Hdl Trial	2m1f	Chlt	Jan	4	Local Hero	132	15-8
Argento Ch	3m2f	Chlt	Jan	5+	Neptune Collonges	169	11-2
Cleeve Hdl	3m	Chlt	Jan	5+	Grands Crus	171	2-1
Classic Nov Hdl	2m5f	Chlt	Jan	4+	Bobs Worth	153	7-2
Towton Nov Ch	3m1f	Weth	Feb	5+	Wayward Prince	151	5-6

British Grade 2 winners 2010-11

Race	Dist	Course	Month	Age	Winner	RPR	SP
Kingmaker Nov Ch	2m	Warw	Feb	5+	Finian's Rainbow	152	2-5
Game Spirit Ch	2m1f	Newb	Feb	5+	French Opera	162	7-2
Aon Ch	3m	Newb	Feb	5+	Noland	150	13-2
Winter Bumper	2m1f	Newb	Feb	4-6	Ericht	125	11-10
Rendlesham Hdl	3m	Hayd	Feb	4+	Cross Kennon	160	8-1
Reynoldstown Nov Ch	3m	Asct	Feb	5+	Master Of The Hall	148	6-5
Prestige Nov Hdl	3m	Hayd	Feb	4+	Back In Focus	142	16-1
Kingwell Hdl	2m	Winc	Feb	4+	Mille Chief	159	15-8
Dovecote Nov Hdl	2m	Kemp	Feb	4+	Sire De Grugy	141	11-4
Adonis Juvenile Hdl	2m	Kemp	Feb	4	Zarkandar	141	8-1
Pendil Nov Ch	2m5f	Kemp	Feb	5+	Captain Chris	147	2-5
National Spirit Hdl	2m4f	Font	Feb	4+	Celestial Halo	153	6-4
Premier Kelso Nov Hdl	2m2f	Kelso	Mar	4+	Bold Sir Brian	131	20-1
David Nicholson Mares' Hdl	2m4f	Chlt	Mar	4+	Quevega	157	5-6
Jewson Nov Ch	2m4f	Chlt	Mar	5+	Noble Prince	164	4-1
Manifesto Nov Ch	2m4f	Aint	Apr	5+	Wishfull Thinking	163	9-4
Top Nov Hdl	2m1f	Aint	Apr	4+	Topolski	149	11-2
Mildmay Nov Ch	3m	Aint	Apr	5+	Quito De La Roque	151	6-1
Mersey Nov Hdl	2m4f	Aint	Apr	4+	Spirit Son	160	3-1
Champion Open NHF	2m1f	Aint	Apr	4-6	Steps To Freedom	130	12-1
Silver Trophy Ch (H'cap)	2m5f	Chlt	Apr	5+	Poquelin	167	11-10
Scottish Champion Hdl (Hcap)	2m	Ayr	Apr	4+	Sanctuaire	150	9-2
Future Champion Nov Ch	2m4f	Ayr	Apr	5+	Gilbarry	152	8-1
Celebration Ch	2m	Sand	Apr	5+	French Opera	159	2-1

Irish Grade 1 winners 2010-11

Race	Dist	Course	Month	Age	Winner	RPR	SP
Champion Ch	3m	DRoy	Nov	5+	Kauto Star	164	4-7
Dobbins & Madigans Hdl	2m	Punc	Nov	4+	Solwhit	161	11-10
Hatton's Grace Hdl	2m4f	Fairy	Dec	4+	Hurricane Fly	164	11-4
Drinmore Nov Ch	2m4f	Fairy	Dec	4+	Jessies Dream	156	7-2
John Durkan Ch	2m4f	Fairy	Dec	5+	Tranquil Sea	161	5-2
Royal Bond Nov Hdl	2m	Fairy	Dec	4+	Zaidpour	150	4-7
Navan Nov Hdl	2m4f	Navan	Dec	4+	Oscars Well	148	9-4
Lexus Ch	3m	Leop	Dec	5+	Pandorama	169	7-2
Fort Leney Nov Ch	3m	Leop	Dec	5+	Bostons Angel	143	14-1
Paddy Power Dial-A-Bet Ch	2m1f	Leop	Dec	5+	Big Zeb	165	Evens
Festival Hdl	2m	Leop	Dec	4+	Hurricane Fly	164	8-11
Future Champions Nov Hdl	2m	Leop	Dec	4+	First Lieutenant	145	16-1
Bord Na Mona Nov Ch	2m1f	Leop	Dec	4+	Realt Dubh	146	10-1
Irish Champion Hdl	2m	Leop	Jan	4+	Hurricane Fly	169	4-9
Arkle Novice Ch	2m1f	Leop	Jan	5+	Realt Dubh	156	5-2
Hennessy Gold Cup	3m	Leop	Feb	5+	Kempes	167	5-1
Spring Juvenile Hdl	2m	Leop	Feb	4	Unaccompanied	132	5-2
Dr P J Moriarty Nov Ch	2m5f	Leop	Feb	5+	Bostons Angel	155	8-1
Deloitte Nov Hdl	2m2f	Leop	Feb	5+	Oscars Well	153	7-1
Powers Gold Cup	2m4f	Fairy	Apr	5+	Realt Dubh	166	9-2
Champion Ch	2m	Punc	May	5+	Big Zeb	175	9-4
Champion Nov Ch	3m1f	Punc	May	5+	Quito De La Roque	164	7-2
Champion Nov Hdl	2m	Punc	May	5+	Shot From The Hip	150	11-2
Guinness Gold Cup	3m1f	Punc	May	5+	Follow The Plan	160	20-1
Champion INH Flat	2m	Punc	May	4-7	Lovethehigherlaw	138	8-1
World Series Hdl	3m	Punc	May	4+	Quevega	162	8-11
Ryanair Novice Ch	2m	Punc	May	5+	Captain Chris	166	4-6
Champion Hdl	2m	Punc	May	4+	Hurricane Fly	171	1-2
Champion Nov Hdl	2m4f	Punc	May	4+	Spirit Of Adjisa	145	16-1
Champion 4yo Hdl	2m	Punc	May	4	Grandouet	148	5-2

Irish Grade 2 winners 2010-11

Race	Dist	Course	Month	Age	Winner	RPR	SP
Gowran Park Champion Ch	2m4f	GowP	Oct	5+	China Rock	142	13-8
Friends Of Tipperary Hdl	2m	Tipp	Oct	4+	Donnas Palm	150	5-4
WKD Core Hdl	2m	DRoy	Nov	4+	Gimli's Rock	142	10-1
Ladbrokes.com Ch	2m4f	DRoy	Nov	5+	The Nightingale	160	3-1
Fortria Ch	2m	Navan	Nov	5+	Big Zeb	160	8-15
Lismullen Hdl	2m4f	Navan	Nov	4+	Oscar Dan Dan	156	11-4
Clonmel Oil Ch	2m4f	Clon	Nov	5+	Tranquil Sea	163	10-11
Craddockstown Nov Ch	2m	Punc	Nov	4+	Realt Dubh	144	4-7
Monksfield Nov Hdl	2m4f	Navan	Nov	4+	Fully Funded	132	6-1
Hilly Way Ch	2m1f	Fairy	Dec	5+	Golden Silver	165	4-6
Tara Hdl	2m4f	Navan	Dec	4+	Rigour Back Bob	142	7-1
Christmas Hdl	3m	Leop	Dec	4+	Mourad	156	7-4
Greenmount Park Nov Ch	2m4f	Limk	Dec	4+	Mr Cracker	151	9-4
Future Champions INH Flat	2m	Leop	Dec	4-7	Jim Will Fix It	126	8-1
Juvenile Hdl	?m	Leop	Dec	3	Sailors Warn	131	12-1
Slaney Nov Hdl	2m4f	Naas	Jan	5+	Gagewell Flyer	139	6-1
Killiney Nov Ch	2m5f	Leop	Jan	5+	Magnanimity	148	9-4
Woodlands Park Nov.Ch	3m	Naas	Jan	5+	Quito De La Roque	152	11-10
Normans Grove Ch	2m1f	Fairy	Jan	5+	Golden Silver	166	2-11
Synergy Security Nov Hdl	2m4f	Leop	Jan	5+	Hidden Cyclone	144	7-4
Kinloch Brae Ch	2m4f	Thurl	Jan	6+	Follow The Plan	152	25-1
Galmoy Hdl	3m	GowP	Jan	5+	Mourad	167	4-9
Tied Cottage Ch	2m	Punc	Jan	5+	Golden Silver	170	3-1
Moscow Flyer Nov Hdl	2m	Punc	Jan	5+	Gagewell Flyer	146	13-8
Boyne Hdl	2m5f	Navan	Feb	5+	Voler La Vedette	154	9-4
Ten Up Nov Ch	3m	Navan	Feb	5+	Quito De La Roque	154	Evens
Flyingbolt Nov Ch	2m	Navan	Feb	5+	Saludos	145	5-2
Red Mills Trial Hdl	2m	GowP	Feb	4+	Dunguib	159	8-11
Red Mills Ch	2m4f	GowP	Feb	5+	Rubi Light	154	7-1
Paddypower.com Ch	2m	Naas	Feb	5+	Golden Silver	167	2-13
Nas Na Riogh Nov Ch	2m4f	Naas	Feb	5+	Roi Du Mee	149	6-4
Paddypower.com Nov Hdl	2m	Naas	Feb	4+	Dare To Doubt	134	7-2
Bobbyjo Ch	3m1f	Fairy	Feb	5+	The Midnight Club	156	11-10
Juvenile Hdl	2m	Fairy	Feb	4	Little Green	125	13-2
Michael Purcell Nov Hdl	2m4f	Thurl	Feb	5+	Hidden Cyclone	148	13-8
Webster Cup Ch	2m4f	Navan	Mar	5+	Hughies Grey	136	7-1
Hugh McMahon Nov Ch	3m	Limk	Apr	5+	Mr Cracker	150	4-1
EBF Mares Nov Hdl Final	2m4f	Fairy	Apr	4+	Knockfierna	143	6-1
Rathbarry & Glenview Studs Hdl	2m	Fairy	Apr	4+	Prima Vista	139	5-2
Keelings Irish Strawberry Hdl	2m4f	Fairy	Apr	5+	Voler La Vedette	154	11-8
Coolmore NH Sires Nov Hdl	2m4f	Fairy	Apr	4+	Lambro	143	6-1
Irish Daily Mirror Nov Hdl	3m	Punc	May	4+	Askanna	143	33-1

Big handicap chases in Britain 2010-11

Value	Race	Dist	Course	Month	Winner	RPR	SP
£535	Grand National	4m4f	Aint	Apr	Ballabriggs	150	14-1
£103	Scottish Grand National	4m1f	Ayr	Apr	Beshabar	146	15-2
£100	Hennessy Gold Cup	3m3f	Newb	Nov	Diamond Harry	156	6-1
£86	Paddy Power Gold Cup	2m5f	Chlt	Nov	Little Josh	146	20-1
£86	Vote A P Gold Cup	2m5f	Chlt	Dec	Poquelin	163	16-1
£80	Bet365 Gold Cup	3m6f	Sand	Apr	Poker De Sivola	136	11-1
£57	Racing Post	3m	Kemp	Feb	Quinz	144	8-1
£56	Becher	3m2f	Aint	Nov	Hello Bud	133	15-2
£56	Topham	2m6f	Aint	Apr	Always Waining	133	14-1
£56	United House Gold Cup	3m	Asct	Oct	Massini's Maguire	146	8-1
£46	Coral Welsh National	3m6f	Chep	Jan	Synchronised	150	5-1
£44	Victorchandler.com	2m6f	Asct	Jan	Tatenen	137	22-1
£44	Grand National Trial	3m4f	Hayd	Feb	Silver By Nature	149	10-1
£43	Stewart Family Spinal	3m1f	Chlt	Mar	Bensalem	143	5-1
£43	Byrne Group Plate	2m5f	Chlt	Mar	Holmwood Legend	130	25-1
£43	Grand Annual	2m1f	Chlt	Mar	Oiseau De Nuit	145	40-1
£42	Midlands Grand National	4m2f	Uttx	Mar	Minella Four Star	133	25-1

Big handicap chases in Britain 2010-11

Value	Race	Dist	Course	Month	Winner	RPR	SP
£37	Badger Ales Trophy	3m2f	Winc	Nov	Meanus Dandy	126	5
£37	Grand Sefton	2m6f	Aint	Nov	Frankie Figg	130	10-1
£34	John Smith's	3m1f	Aint	Apr	Prince De Beauchene	138	10-1
£34	Red Rum	2m	Aint	Apr	Silk Drum	141	9-1
£34	Classic	3m5f	Warw	Jan	West End Rocker	133	10-1
£34	Summer Plate	2m7f	MRas	Jly	Grand Slam Hero	129	9-1
£31	Zeturf.com	2m5f	Chlt	Oct	Edgbriar	137	14-1
£30	Fulke Walwyn Kim Muir	3m2f	Chlt	Mar	Junior	134	10-3
£29	Grimthorpe	3m2f	Donc	Mar	Always Right	130	9-2
£29	Morson Group	3m4f	Chlt	Nov	Midnight Chase	146	8-1
£29	Tom Wragg Trophy	3m	Uttx	May	Auroras Encore	139	12-1
£29	Centenary Nov	2m5f	Chlt	Mar	Divers	132	10-1
£29	Prelude	2m7f	MRas	Sep	Silmi	124	16-1
£29	English Summer National	3m4f	Uttx	Jun	Ouzbeck	142	14-1

Big h'cap chases in Ireland 2010-11

Value	Race	Dist	Course	Month	Winner	RPR	SP
£121	Irish Grand National	3m5f	Fairy	Apr	Organisedconfusion	132	12-1
£107	Galway Plate	2m6f	Galw	Jly	Finger Onthe Pulse	138	22-1
£95	Paddy Power	3m	Leop	Dec	Majestic Concorde	144	33-1
£85	Kerry National	3m	Listl	Sep	Alfa Beat	137	6-1
£50	Thyestes	3m	Gowp	Jan	Siegemaster	145	16-1
£49	Munster National	3m	Limk	Oct	Golden Kite	128	20-1
£49	Troytown	3m	Navan	Nov	Jack The Bus	119	9-1
£43	Guinness	2m4f	Punc	May	Scotsirish	150	7-1
£42	Leopardstown	2m5f	Leop	Jan	Rare Bob	145	10-1
£42	Dan Moore Memorial	2m1f	Fairy	Apr	Idarah	131	25-1
£40	Mick The Tent Memorial	2m5f	Punc	May	Wishfull Thinking	159	11-4
£32	Cork Grand National	3m4f	Cork	Oct	Streets Of Gold	120	11-1
£29	Midlands National	2m6f	Kilb	Jly	Golden Kite	122	11-2

Big h'cap hurdles in Britain 2010-11

Value	Race	Dist	Course	Month	Winner	RPR	SP
£57	Greatwood	2m1f	Chlt	Nov	Menorah	151	6-1
£43	Swinton	2m1f	Hayd	May	Eradicate	132	16-1
£43	Fixed Brush	3m	Hayd	Nov	Grands Crus	132	6-4
£40	Pertemps Final	3m	Chlt	Mar	Buena Vista	138	20-1
£40	Coral Cup	2m5f	Chlt	Mar	Carlito Brigante	142	16-1
£40	County	2m1f	Chlt	Mar	Final Approach	139	10-1
£34	Totesport Trophy	2m1f	Newb	Feb	Recession Proof	134	12-1
£34	Imperial Cup	2m1f	Sand	Mar	Alarazi	126	10-1
£34	Fred Winter Juvenile	2m1f	Chlt	Mar	What A Charm	115	9-1
£29	Smithythehorse.com	3m1f	Aint	Apr	Battle Group	137	16-1
£29	EBF Nov Final	2m4f	Sand	Mar	Skint	128	10-1
£28	Lanzarote Hdl	2m5f	Kemp	Jan	James De Vassy	144	8-1
£28	Martin Pipe Con' Jockeys'	2m5f	Chlt	Mar	Sir Des Champs	134	9-2

Big h'cap hurdles in Ireland 2010-11

Value	Race	Dist	Course	Month	Winner	RPR	SP
£133	Galway	2m	Galw	Jly	Overturn	145	6-1
£52	MCR	2m	Leop	Jan	Final Approach	123	6-1
£43	www.thetote.com	2m4f	Punc	May	Truckers Delight	122	11-1
£34	www.thetote.com	2m	Fairy	Apr	Jack Cool	136	5-1
£32	EBF Novice Series Final	3m	Fairy	Apr	Baracas	119	33-1
£29	Lartigue	2m	Listl	Sep	Sword Fish	108	14-1
£29	Freshways	2m6f	Galw	Jly	Silverhand	125	8-1

THE BIGGER PICTURE

The Queen tours the Irish National Stud in May as part of her historic state visit to Ireland, which also included visits to Coolmore Stud and the Aga Khan's Gilltown Stud **Getty**

A fantastic set of prizes is on offer to eight winners of the *Racing Post Annual* quiz. The first two winners will each win a year's free membership worth £208 to Racing Post Members' Club, plus a copy of *Racing Post* photographer Edward Whitaker's new photographic book *Beyond The Frame*, rrp £30.
Six runners-up will each receive a copy of *Beyond The Frame*.

HOW TO ENTER

▸▸ Entries, which must be received by midnight, Friday, January 20, 2012, should be sent to RP Annual Quiz, Raceform, Compton, Newbury, RG20 6NL

▸▸ Include your name, address, daytime telephone number and, where possible, your email address

▸▸ Or email your answers to Rpannual@ racingpost.com

▸▸ Only one entry per household

▸▸ The first two all-correct entries chosen at random will be the winners of a Members' Club subscription and *Beyond The Frame* book. The next six runners-up will each receive a *Beyond The Frame* book. In the event of no all-correct entry, the winner and runners-up will be chosen at random from amongst those with the highest scores

▸▸ The judges' decision is final. There are no alternative prizes. All prizes are non-transferable and not exchangeable for cash

▸▸ *Racing Post* employees or their relatives are not eligible

▸▸ Entrants must be aged 18 or over

▸▸ By entering the quiz you have automatically opted to receive emails from *Racing Post* and selected third parties

▸▸ Normal *Racing Post* rules apply. For a copy please telephone customer services on 01635 898781 or visit racingpost.com

THE BIG QUIZ

National service

1 Who completed a full house of Grand National wins with the victory of Synchronised in the Welsh version at Chepstow in January?

2 **Which two horses were awarded joint top-weight when the handicap for the John Smith's Grand National was unveiled?**

3 Donald McCain's first Grand National victory with Ballabriggs came how many years after his father's last with Amberleigh House?

4 **Which horse made the frame in the John Smith's Grand National for the third year in a row?**

5 Which Welsh-trained horse won the Scottish National at Ayr under Richard Johnson?

Off and on

6 **Which traditional Boxing Day highlight was postponed until January 15, owing to bad weather?**

7 What caused the Totesport Trophy Hurdle at Newbury to be postponed in February?

8 **Name the highlight of the jumps season at Doncaster which had to be abandoned due to a frozen track in January for the second year in a row.**

Gone but not forgotten

9 Which dual Breeders' Cup winner, described as 'a great, great racehorse' by her jockey Freddy Head, died at the age of 27 in January?

10 **The only horse to win the Racing Post Chase twice died in the spring – can you name him?**

11 Which former lightweight jockey, who served as a body double for actor Rupert Grint in a Harry Potter film, died in June?

12 **Owner, breeder and trainer Arthur Budgett died in June – can you name his two Derby winners?**

Cheltenham hits and misses

13 Which defending champion was forced to miss the Cheltenham Festival owing to fears that he would fail a drugs test?

14 **Which luckless jockey missed the festival after breaking his leg in a fall at Stratford the day before?**

15 Sam Waley-Cohen won the Cheltenham Gold Cup on Long Run – who was the last amateur rider to win the race before him?

16 **Which two former winners were placed in the Cheltenham Gold Cup behind Long Run?**

17 Which Cheltenham Festival winner had also scored at Royal Ascot nine months earlier?

18 **Who was top jockey at the Cheltenham Festival for the fourth year in a row and the sixth time overall?**

Landmarks (not all good)

19 Which horse passed £1 million in prize-money earnings when landing his seventh Grade 1 victory in the Victor Chandler Chase at Ascot?

20 **A protest against poor prize-money at which track led to Britain's first walkover for four years in April and forced another race later in the month to be abandoned after failing to attract a single entry?**

46-50 Identify the missing horse in each picture

34 **On which course did Overturn win the inaugural Scottish Hydro Summer Champion Hurdle in the presence of the Prince of Wales?**

Fame and fortune

35 Which top golfer part-owns Stewards' Cup winner Hoof It?

36 **Which Premier League footballer was the owner of a winner at York on Ebor day?**

37 Which trainer was knighted in the Queen's Birthday Honours list?

38 **What did Jessica Lodge's first winner under rules at Exeter in March mean to heating engineer Steve Whiteley?**

Legends of the turf

39 Who announced he was giving up training, 30 years after winning the Derby as a teenager on Shergar?

40 **Which US Hall Of Fame jockey, the first woman to ride in an American Triple Crown race, took part in the Leger Legends race at Doncaster?**

41 Tony McCoy was champion jump jockey again in the 2010-11 season – how many times in a row has he won the title?

Significant others

42 **What was significant about the victories of One Lucky Lady at Bath in August and Blaise Chorus at Kempton two days later?**

43 Which jumps trainer had 13 winners in a five-day spell in August?

44 **In which race did the French and Irish Derby winners go head to head in July – and both fail to make the first two?**

45 How many Group 1 races did Canford Cliffs win before his retirement due to injury in the summer?

46-50 **See picture panel**

---

21 Who rode the 500th winner of her career on Efistorm at Windsor in the summer?

Classic winners (and one non-winner)

22 **By what distance did Frankel land the 2,000 Guineas, the biggest winning margin in the race since 1947?**

23 Which trainer won his first British Classic when Blue Bunting took the 1,000 Guineas?

24 **Which English-born Leeds United fan trained Kentucky Derby winner Animal Kingdom?**

25 Which trainer has had two runners in Epsom Classics and won with both – Shaamit in the Derby in 1996, Dancing Rain in the Oaks this June?

26 **Pour Moi was retired due to injury in the summer – which was the last Derby winner before him who failed to race again after Epsom?**

27 Which horse started favourite for both the Investec Derby and the Dubai Duty Free Irish Derby but won neither?

Notable firsts

28 **Which Newmarket trainer won the William Hill Spring Mile at Doncaster with his first runner in Britain?**

29 Which horse gave Khalid Abdullah his first winner in the Juddmonte International at York, a race he has sponsored for 22 years?

30 **Which course staged the world's first meeting with all races restricted to women riders?**

31 Which former jump jockey rode his first Royal Ascot winner on Prohibit in the Group 1 King's Stand Stakes?

32 **Which course staged the first meeting of the 2011 British Flat turf season?**

33 Which jockey's commitment to ride elsewhere allowed Hayley Turner the chance to ride her first Group 1 winner on Dream Ahead in the July Cup?

"Emotional
Nightmare
Gutted
Leave me alone
I set my boxer shorts on fire"

"I can't say I thought Paul was a future champion – when he was with me he was useless"
Former trainer Terry Caldwell, the first mentor to champion Flat jockey Paul Hanagan

"It was like going to a job interview and then puking all over yourself"
Rich Ricci, owner of Leopardstown winner Day Of A Lifetime, on his horse's erratic effort in the 2010 Champion Bumper at Cheltenham

"He did my bathroom for me and if he thinks I'm paying now he's mad"
A friend of plumbing and heating engineer Steve Whiteley, the man who netted a record-shattering £1,445,671.20 on the Tote Jackpot

"I'm the husband now and he's the wife"
Noel Quinlan, taking over the trainer's licence from brother Mick

"We kept hitting the crossbar, but I was starting to think the crossbar was getting bigger"
Trainer Philip Kirby, ending a 148-day spell without a winner

"If he asked me to marry him I definitely would"
Trainer Jennie Candlish, hugging stable star Cross Kennon after victory at Haydock

"I'm well aware I was only an average rider, but I'm an old average rider now"
A modest Warren Marston decides to retire at 40 "still in one piece" after a 23-year, 700-winner career that embraced two Cheltenham Festival winners, a Becher Chase and a Racing Post Chase

"He was probably worried about me poking his eye out with one of my elbows"
Marston again, on being told he was the only jockey Tony McCoy feared in a finish

"We love each other the best but we have separate beds because in my dreams I'm back riding in races. I throw myself about all over the place when I'm asleep"
Willie Snaith, 60 years married to Sylvia, who rode in the Derby for the Queen 57 years ago and has clearly never lost the racing bug

"It's very emotional for me. I feel like pushing the wife over to one side of the bed and putting him in the middle"
Owner Paul Barber, after Denman's gallant second in the Gold Cup

"I must say I don't find the idea of seduction by Phil Smith a very appealing one"
Robert Waley-Cohen's response to the BHA handicapper's bid to tempt him into running Gold Cup hero Long Run in the Hennessy

"This lot have had such a great day they'd have run for an Easter egg"
Trainer Richard Phillips on the Pak Jack Partnership, owner of the eponymous winner at an 'under-tariffed' Wetherby meeting

"You win one Grand National and think it's the greatest moment of your life, but it's like going to bed with a good-looking woman – once you've been there you want to go back again"
The late Ginger McCain, four times a National winner as a trainer, after son Donald's victory with Ballabriggs

"One evening, for a bet, I set my boxer shorts on fire. Unfortunately I was wearing them at the time and the scars took weeks to heal"
Betfair head of media Tony Calvin recalling wild days at the Racing Post on the occasion of the paper's 25th anniversary

"I make that nought from two. After making such a bold statement, isn't it time for a new chairman?"
BHA critic James Given recalls being approached at the sales by Paul Roy, who asked to be judged on the outcome of the levy negotiations and the sale of the Tote

"I can probably be a little intense sometimes. I didn't blame him for running away from me"
Aidan O'Brien after Jamie Spencer lands the Gold Cup for his erstwhile Ballydoyle employers on Fame And Glory

"It was great to win the race but I was gutted on the way back because people kept shouting 'Well done Kieren'"
Eddie Ahern, a late replacement for the indisposed Kieren Fallon on Veiled in the Ascot Stakes

"At first we were a bit like two strange dogs sniffing each other's bottoms. But although people kept telling me he was unreliable, money-grubbing and difficult to deal with, I found none of this to be true"
Luca Cumani speaks as he finds in singing the praises of his jockey Kieren Fallon

"I used to have an office in Racing Welfare but I hardly used it and I'd get a bollocking for dirtying their carpets when I came back from the gallops"
Newmarket chaplain Graham Locking finds it easier to get his message across from a car park on Warren Hill

"There are about 15 of us and they have brought along wives, ex-lovers and hitchhikers"
John Storey, of Gale Force Five, on why the winner's enclosure was rather crowded after the Plumpton success of Health Is Wealth

"I feel a certain sympathy with Denis Thatcher, although I do it without the gin and tonic"
Trainer James Fanshawe says he fully supports his activist wife Jacko, a Newmarket councillor

"I just wish in the last furlong I could have got hold of him and hit him, but I didn't have the bottle because I would have thrown myself off"
Rodger Sargent, who rode Nemo Spirit in the charity Flat race at the Cheltenham Festival wearing his spectacles. "Apparently I finished second," he said

"If I go to Hong Kong and hit seven times I get ten years in jail because they think I'm not trying"
Gerald Mosse contrasts Britain's new whip rules with the approach elsewhere

"I was wondering when you were coming"
What the Queen said to Tony McCoy at his OBE investiture, the champion having been prevented from collecting a previous MBE by riding commitments

"It's not really the end of the world. It just feels like it"
A dejected Tom Dascombe as Michael Owen's Royal Ascot winner Brown Panther blows out in the German Derby

'It's great for Hayley, but Vettel would not win around Monaco in a mini, would he?'
Trainer David Simcock, ensuring Dream

Ahead has his fair share of the credit after Hayley Turner's historic July Cup victory at Newmarket

"The ambulance is older than me"
Jamie Spencer, as an ambulance delays proceedings at Yarmouth by failing to start – a day after holding things up for 20 minutes at the course with a flat tyre

"I've got to talk to the telly – leave me alone!"
Golf agent Chubby Chandler on the phone to Lee Westwood on being approached by Derek Thompson after their Hoof It won the £50,000 Sky Bet Dash at York

"I can't, I've got a sore toe"
A plaintive Frankie Dettori declines the crowd's invitation to perform a flying dismount after Goodwood Cup victory on Opinion Poll

"Newmarket moving the July Cup to the Saturday is a complete nightmare. They have paid absolutely no attention to the bullfighting calendar"
Sir Mark Prescott on the conflict between festival and fiesta

"Lucian was desperate to paint Lester Piggott but Lester wanted either money or the finished work in return"
Victor Chandler on one that got away for the late Lucian Freud, master artist and passionate racing fan

"It's great that the George Baker, George Baker, George Baker, George Baker thing is off our backs"
Trainer George Baker – who else? – as the horse of the same name, part-owned and ridden by men of the same name, scores at Leicester

"I managed to uncouple the battery but I could smell petrol. I wasn't happy about that, because I was sitting on the petrol tank"
Trainer Brian Gubby, who returned to the spotlight with Son Of The Cat at Glorious

Goodwood, recalls a crash in Sicily during his previous incarnation as a racing driver

"I had no idea they'd be so strong for such small men"
Librarian Lesley Evans, at Folkestone to enjoy her first racecourse experience, on shaking hands with Eddie Ahern

"Racing is a marvellous sport, full of intrigue, fascination and a bit of skulduggery. It's too serious these days. It should be fun"
A valediction from Barry Hills on the final day of his 42-year training career

"I reckon I'm in the best shape I've been in since I foaled. I'd like to hear a few of the guys I'll ride against at Doncaster say that"
US great Julie Krone, mother to five-year-old Lorelei, before winning the Leger Legends race aboard Invincible Hero

"Do you have £20 for me because now I have no money to pay for the taxi?"
Christophe Soumillon to Nick Luck on Racing UK after a whip ban cost him his £52,000 prize-money for winning the Qipco Champion Stakes on Cirrus Des Aigles

"I've only had him a couple of weeks and I haven't had enough time to improve him, but I've had enough time to ** him up"**
David Elsworth, saddling Eton Rifles to score a first win for Graham Wylie since Howard Johnson lost his licence

"He's got a new spy programme out. It's very good. Well, it's quite good. I actually fell asleep during it, but I didn't tell him that"
Trainer Jonathan Portman on meeting actor Bill Nighy at Epsom

"Ouch! I'm thinking it's just bruised, but going for a double check. Gutted I didn't wax my legs before I went racing"
Hayley Turner tweets after the fall at Bath that left her with a broken ankle

19

Mickael Barzalona's age when he landed the Derby – the youngest winning jockey since Walter Swinburn on Shergar in 1981

£265m

The price Betfred paid to take over the Tote

6min29.7sec

Long Run's record winning time in the Cheltenham Gold Cup

13

Irish-trained winners at the Cheltenham Festival – a record

£59.53m

The total yield from bets on British horseracing in 2010-11, the lowest since the turn of the century and a drop of more than 34% in two years

14

The Tatling's age when he won a 5f handicap at Yarmouth in June, making him the oldest Flat winner in Britain since Redoubtable, also 14, in 2005

THE essential A-Z
OF 2011

A is for age, a topic much discussed all year, and the youngsters held sway with Long Run defeating the old guard over jumps and Frankel leading the three-year-old charge on the Flat.

B is for Betfred. An ever-increasing presence in the bookmaking world thanks to their purchase of the Tote after a long-running and, at times, bitter sale process.

C is for Champions Day. Racing For Change's grand spectacle for the end of the Flat season was finally unveiled with massive prize-money and lukewarm reaction in some quarters.

D is for De Sousa. Previously just some Brazilian who rode well in sprints up north, Silvestre de Sousa forged a strong alliance with Mark Johnston to become one of the most sought-after riders.

E is for Easterby, specifically the inimitable Mick. Despite turning 80 there were no signs of slowing down, especially with Hoof It keeping his name in lights.

F is easy. We don't mean for easy, we mean F is easy because it can only be for Frankel. A horse for the ages, not just this year.

G is for Grand National. The headlines should have been only for Ballabriggs, Donald McCain and Jason Maguire but that wasn't the case. Let's hope that, after the modifications to the course, the next one is remembered for the right reasons.

H is for Hills. After a tremendous career Barry Hills, aka Mr Combustible, retired. The training licence went to son Charlie, who made a cracking start. Watch out Richard Hannon . . .

I is for Il est tres bon. "He's a young rider with a huge future," said Simon Crisford when asked why Mickael Barzalona was riding for Godolphin. One UAE Derby win, a Prix Saint-Alary success and a Derby victory later, we can all agree that's not a bad assessment.

J is for Johnson. Disgraced trainer Howard Johnson retired in August after being banned for four years for running a horse that had been de-nerved and for administering steroids to three horses. It saw the end of the Johnson-Graham Wylie alliance that produced triple World Hurdle winner Inglis Drever. Wylie remains but at a much reduced level.

K is for knighthood. Not one dissenting voice was heard when plain old Henry Cecil became Sir Henry Cecil in June. Along with a Cheltenham Festival winner and Frankel, it was quite some year for Cecil.

L is for Long Run. He started the year as the baddy when he won the King George that was meant to go to Kauto Star. After an epic Gold Cup at Cheltenham, however, he rightly became recognised as the new star of jump racing.

M is for medication. After many years with its head in the sand, US racing made steps to join the worldwide racing community by banning raceday medication for juvenile stakes races and for Breeders' Cup races.

N is for Newbury, which had one of the darkest days of the year with the electrocution of Fenix Two and Marching Song in the paddock.

O is for Oh My God! BBC racing presenter Rishi Persad was rather overcome when greeting his hero Bobby Flay, the celebrity chef, in the paddock at Royal Ascot.

P is for Peter Toole. The young jockey showed tremendous courage to battle back from serious head injuries sustained in a fall at Aintree.

Q is for the Queen. Her Majesty had Derby favourite Carlton House but the fairytale was not to be, as Stephen Fry recounted on QI: "It's winning, it's winning, it's going to win the Derby. Oh, bollocks! It came third and a Frenchman won."

R is for Rewilding. Three runs in 2011 provided us with brilliance and tragedy as Godolphin's star landed the Dubai Sheema Classic and Prince of Wales's Stakes in awesome style before breaking down fatally in the King George.

S is for Swinburn. Three-time Derby-winning jockey Walter Swinburn handed in his training licence at the end of the season after his father-in-law and principal patron Peter Harris scaled back his racing interests.

T is for tariffs. The controversial Horsemen's Group levels for minimum prize-money generated heated debate, a walkover, a boycott and plenty of sniping. Where it ends up next year we can only guess.

U is for underfunding. Racing continued to struggle with low prize-money despite high attendances. With the levy on the slide, racing's share of betting-shop interest falling and exports of British horses to other countries increasing, something must be done.

V is for Vefa Ibrahim Araci. The Turkish industrialist took racing into the High Court when he was granted an injunction to stop Kieren Fallon riding in the Derby after the jockey broke a contract to partner Native Khan.

W is for whip. Never before has the whip been under such scrutiny with high-profile cases involving Ballabriggs in the Grand National and Rewilding at Royal Ascot. The issue did not go away after major changes to the whip rules with Richard Hughes and Christophe Soumillon two of the big names to voice opposition.

X is for Battle of the Exes. Yes, pin-up girl Chantal Sutherland took on former fiance Mike Smith in a match race at Del Mar with no holds barred. "There's something about Mike that makes you want to kick his butt," said Sutherland. But it was Smith who did said kicking as he eased to victory.

Y is for why, why, why Delilah? Newmarket celebrated 25 years of Newmarket Nights and the star name was Sir Tom Jones. After-racing concerts have come a long way from the Bootleg Beatles.

Z is for zero. Yards travelled by Memory in the 1,000 Guineas at Newmarket after she refused to race. The leading juvenile filly of the previous season pulled the same stunt at Newmarket's July course and Goodwood before she was retired for being a bad girl.

JUST FOR FUN My first name follows November, my second comes after Victor. Which Grade 1-winning hurdler of 2011 am I? Answer page 170

Best of twitter 'I now have a tash, spots and a hairy chest'

HORSERACING burst into the Twittersphere with a vengeance this year. Some of it was serious, with all manner of breaking news on there, including the Racing Post's Twitter feed. But racing's tweeting fraternity also gave us the chance to peer into the sometimes confusing, often seedy, always entertaining world of some of our favourite stars – equine as well as human. Here's our rundown of the most prolific and amusing Tweeters of the year

Hayley Turner @*hayleyturner123* Group 1-winning jockey and racing's Queen of Twitter
Sample tweet: I left my paper lying around in the girls room at Chepstow, I now have a tash, spots and a hairy chest. Thanks @cathygannon353

Denman @*TheRealDenman* Former Gold Cup winner, but you might know him as The Tank. Neigh
Sample tweet: Just seen Frankel. Must concede quite like the cut of his jib. Denman-esque in way galloped them into the ground. Not as handsome tho. Neigh

Ger Lyons @*gerlyonsracing* Cycling philosopher who trains a few horses
Sample tweet: Don't sweat the small stuff, in 100yrs time, will all this really matter.

Michael Owen *themichaelowen* Football star and racing lover
Sample tweet: I apologise now if you don't like racing but my next 15 tweets are dedicated to my pride and joy and those who have made today so special!!!

Andrew Duff @*andrewduff01* Struggling Arsenal fan and amateur rider
Sample tweet: Winner always buys the dinner but driver never does!! @ninacarberry is both mmmm wat should I do???

Richard Pugh @*pughp2p*
Point-to-point journalist, just don't mention the golf
Sample tweet: Off to Stradbally to deliver racecards then on to limerick for a type of racing where they pay the jockeys! What will they think of next

Kim Bailey @*kimbaileyracing* Trainer and entertainer, as long as he hasn't finished second
Sample tweet: So many ladies trying to go to the loo that they now using the gents. Welcome to Market Rasen

Pat Flynn @*patflynnracing* Waterford trainer who loves his 140 characters
Sample tweet: The Dalai Lama is in Kildare today, I wonder would he buy a nice racehorse. He comes across a very nice fellow and a good craic

Gary Carroll @*garyfcarroll* Champion apprentice who proves cheek goes a long way
Sample tweet: Was just asleep in bed when dusty wakes me n says were leavin at 2.20, not 3.20! If I didn kill him den I never will!! >:)

Matt Chapman @*mcyeeehaaa* ATR presenter who does exactly what it says on the tin
Sample tweet: Boom! Just hit 5000 followers. Not bad for a small-time freelance satellite TV presenter. Welcome to the party everyone. Yeeehaaa!

Bryan Cooper @*92bryan92* Champion conditional. Often bored, more often sleeping, always witty
Sample tweet: Sitting here watching homeward bound with my 2 dogs.. They might learn not to run away after watching it.. That's how exciting my day off is

Jamie Codd @*coddjj* Jockey who gives as good as he gets, but has anyone worked out what his profile picture is?
Sample tweet: Has someone moved our little island south somewhere?? Wheres all the rain gone?

And the winners are . . .

Tweeter of the Year (human)
Since joining Twitter in June, **Cathy Gannon** (@cathygannon353) has single-handedly opened the world's eyes to the unusual habits of Hayley Turner. The fact that Turner also happens to be her biggest rival for leading female jockey probably has nothing to do with Gannon begging her followers to get Turner pregnant or outing Turner as a porn-watching, dope-smoking lunatic.
Sample tweet: "I'm driving by Stonehenge and Hayley Turner is sunbathing on top of the stones with loads of youngsters smoking pot."

Tweeter of the Year (equine)
No-one has provided such an in-depth behind-the-scenes commentary as **Possol** (@Possol_10), who has kept his followers entertained with his fervent dislike of next-door neighbour Pickamus, news of how he spent the winter brewing cider and his observations that there are a few too many "little people" in Newmarket.

Follow the Racing Post on Twitter @racing_post

Best of the web What we've loved watching this year

Get away
Want to escape from the torrent of sarcasm and smartarsery that characterises much of the web? Does simple, good-natured comedy with a racing theme actually exist? Yes, it does. *tinyurl.com/carousel2*

Something for the attention span, sir?
Jeremy Noseda's YouTube channel makes for a good night in front of a screen if you've not yet fully migrated to bite-sized media. Best is a four-part documentary on his career with interviews and great archive footage. *tinyurl.com/noseda*

Weird world of the weighing room
Hayley Turner's slightly madcap site is worth those of a dozen other personalities put together, asking important questions of her colleagues such as 'Would you rather kiss a ladyboy or be locked in a dark room for a month?' *hayleyturner.com*

Ownership for the impecunious
Or the impatient, as the admirable team of trainer Rod Millman and jockey son James launched the People's Horse, aka Tweet Lady, who has – amazingly – already won two races. The concept is great – follow Tweet Lady (@peopleshorse) on Twitter and you're in. *thepeopleshorse.co.uk*

Take a closer look at your friends
Ever thought you could lose yourself in the crowd? No chance. HD's got nothing on the amazing gigapan photos of big-race crowds on the Qipco Champions Series website, which you can blow up to reveal all – and possibly more. *tinyurl.com/gigapan1*

Two fabulous Edward Whitaker limited edition prints to be won

Two winners will receive one of these two beautiful limited edition prints valued at more than £400 each. The two prints are framed and signed, number one of a series of only 12, by the *Racing Post*'s award-winning photographer Edward Whitaker. They are mounted in a mahogany stain wooden frame, measuring 22"x30"

Simply answer this question:

WHO WON THE 2011 BETFRED SPRINT CUP AT HAYDOCK IN A THREE-WAY PHOTO-FINISH?

A) HOOF IT
B) DREAM AHEAD
C) BATED BREATH

Frankel (Tom Queally) beats Canford Cliffs (Richard Hughes) to win the Sussex Stakes, Glorious Goodwood, July 27, 2011

The runners in the novice chase take the fence at the top of the hill. The race was won by Tullamore Dew, Plumpton, January 2, 2011

Edward Whitaker's new book of racing photographs *Beyond The Frame* is now published at the special price of £25 (RRP £30) from www.racingpost.com/shop or from all leading bookshops

BEYOND THE FRAME
GREAT RACING PHOTOGRAPHS
EDWARD WHITAKER

HOW TO ENTER

▸ Entries, which must be received by midnight, Friday, January 20, 2012, should be sent to Prints competition, Raceform, Compton, Newbury, RG20 6NL

▸ Postal entries must be typed or written clearly, with the answer to the question above

▸ Include your name, address, daytime telephone number and, where possible, your email address

▸ Or email your answers to rpannual@racingpost.com

▸ Only one entry per household

▸ The first two correct entries chosen at random will be the winners and will receive one of the two prints reproduced above

▸ The judges' decision is final. There are no alternative prizes. All prizes are non-transferable and not exchangeable for cash

▸ Racing Post employees or their relatives are not eligible

▸ Entrants must be aged 18 or over

▸ By entering the quiz you have automatically opted to receive emails from *Racing Post* and selected third parties

▸ Normal *Racing Post* rules apply. For a copy please telephone customer services on 01635 898781 or visit racingpost.com

Strange
but true

Life-saving, age-defying, mind-boggling . . . this year's collection of the oddest tales from the far corners of the racing world

Americans love a suffix to be added to their surname, but few can have been as pointless as the 'Sr' attached to jockey Frank Amonte when he rode in a minor claiming event at Suffolk Downs in September.

At the age of 76, Amonte was America's oldest jockey – maybe the world's oldest jockey – and he narrowly missed making racing history when he was beaten into second place at the Boston track.

The amazing Amonte had his first ride at the Fair Grounds in New Orleans in 1951. Sixty years and a triple heart bypass later – and after spells in Cuba, California, New York and Florida – he pitched up at Suffolk Downs determined to enter the record books.

"I do it because I love it," he said. "I'd love to win one at my age so I can be in the Guinness Book of Records as the oldest jockey to win a thoroughbred race. And if I quit, my wife will make me get a job!"

In a 21-year career featuring a catalogue of injuries, to go with more than 3,000 victories, American rider Clinton Potts has developed something of a reputation as a jinxed jockey. He suffered his worst injuries yet at Easter, when he was rushed to hospital with a badly ruptured spleen, a broken right wrist, a lacerated kidney, two broken ribs, two broken vertebrae in his back, torn ligaments in his right hip and a sacral fracture.

The cause this time? Potts fell out of a tree trying to rescue a cat.

Australian-based jockey Wanderson d'Avila was at the centre of a bizarre legal action after weighing in light on a winner at the Gold Coast in February.

The horse was disqualified and Brazilian-born D'Avila suspended from riding for one month – after which the makers of SensaSlim Solution agreed to pay Aus$12,500 for loss of earnings and costs, and also apologised for misleading literature.

D'Avila's solicitor said the company's literature claimed it "sprayed away hunger" but made no specific mention of potential weight loss.

SensaSlim managing director Peter O'Brien seemed quite pleased with the outcome. "We

France staged an unusual match race in the summer when the trotter Othello Bourbon was taken on by Tour de France cyclist Thomas Voeckler at Les Sable d'Olonne on a Wednesday evening.

More than 7,000 turned up to watch the best of three heats and both Voeckler – who finished fourth in Le Tour – and sulky* driver Eric Raffin posed for photos and signed autographs.

Othello Bourbon took the decider by a neck, much to Voeckler's chagrin. "I am disappointed, but perhaps a little less so than to have missed out on a podium finish in the Tour," he said.

*For the less initiated, the reference to Raffin being a sulky driver refers to his mode of transport, not his mood.

could hardly argue against what Mr D'Avila was saying," he said. "It is probably a world-first settlement for a product working too well."

Former jockey John Shear gained his 15 minutes of fame when he saved a little girl from serious

injury at Santa Anita, where he is employed as a paddock guard.

British expatriate Shear was featured on national US news after gaining hero status when he threw himself between a runaway horse and the six-year-old.

Shear was taken to hospital with internal bleeding and a fractured pelvis. Surgery, though, was

Insult was added to injury for Jimmy Quinn when the jockey did not turn up for the Czech Derby in June. The Czech authorities fined him Czk2,000 (about £76) for "failure to comply with an agreed commitment", which seemed a tad harsh in the circumstances.

Quinn had fractured a wrist and elbow, three ribs and his coccyx after two racecourse falls within the space of 24 hours the previous week.

"Jimmy would have had a job to ride," suggested his agent Gavin Horne.

deemed unnecessary. "My dad does 35 push-ups a day, eats well and stays fit," said his son Mike. "I think that's the reason he's recovering so quickly."

Which was quite a story, given John Shear was 90 at the time. He has been employed at Santa Anita since December 1961.

Christophe Soumillon has been known to fall foul of the French stewards on occasion, particularly with reference to his fondness for the whip – which wasn't a problem when he dropped his stick en route to victory aboard Oranais at Clairefontaine. "I hope I'm not going to be punished for abusive use of the hand," he suggested.

THE BIG

Boxing had Klitschko v Haye but racing had a better clash of the heavyweights as Sizing Europe and Big Zeb traded blows at Cheltenham and Punchestown. Their people relive those battles and look forward to a renewal of hostilities

Words by Nick Pulford

The sparring

Sizing Europe and Big Zeb met for the first time over fences in the Grade 2 Boylesports.com Tied Cottage Chase at Punchestown in January, but it was far from the blockbuster clash many had expected. Sizing Europe, dropping back after trainer Henry de Bromhead's unsuccessful experiment with stepping up a division to 3m, was out on his feet on the heavy ground and trailed home a well-beaten third, while odds-on favourite Big Zeb was floored by a sucker punch from Golden Silver.

The defeat still smarts for Big Zeb's trainer Colm Murphy. "There's no question who was the best horse on the day. He definitely needed the run, but the main reason he lost is that we committed him too early."

The first title bout

True champions come good on the big occasion and in the Sportingbet.com Queen Mother Champion Chase at Cheltenham the only two that mattered were title-holder Big Zeb and Sizing Europe, winner of the junior crown in the Arkle 12 months earlier. The return to his favourite arena was a major factor, De Bromhead says. "We really want to be turning on the gas with him four out and at Cheltenham it helps him that he's got the hill to roll away down."

Sizing Europe was out in front by the seventh and went from strength to strength in the finish, with Big Zeb unable to land a blow.

"He was beaten fair and square," admits Barry Geraghty, Big Zeb's rider. "Turning in I thought I'd get him. I threw everything at my fella at the second-last and I knew when Sizing Europe wasn't coming back to us that we were in trouble."

Preparation was the key for Sizing Europe. "In the ten days coming up to Cheltenham he really came to himself in his work and schooling," recalls jockey Andrew Lynch. "Henry had him ready for the big day and we were quietly confident he'd be bang there."

FIGHT

TALE OF THE TAPE

SIZING EUROPE		BIG ZEB
9	Age	10
26	Races run	26
12	Races won	11
46%	Strike-rate overall	47%
12	Chases run	19
7	Chases won	9
58%	Chase strike-rate	47%
1	Champion Chase wins	1
4	Grade 1 wins	5
1011	Cheltenham record	F12
1F241113232	Punchestown record	21F2121
1	Fell	4
176	Best RPR chase	175
168	Best RPR hurdles	148
2 wins	Head to head	1 win

The second title bout

With Lynch injured, Timmy Murphy was recruited for Sizing Europe in the Boylesports.com Champion Chase at Punchestown but this time it was Big Zeb's day. Sizing Europe was in front earlier than at Cheltenham, but it wasn't a good thing. "The pacemaker wasn't able to go the gallop – he'd have liked to be taken along for a bit," says Murphy.

The change of venue made a difference too, according to De Bromhead. "At Punchestown you're at the bottom of the hill at the point when we want to step it up and then you have to force him uphill. That makes him prone to a speed horse."

So it proved, but only after Big Zeb was against the ropes briefly after a mistake with four to go. "For a second I was worried," Geraghty admits, "but it wasn't a bad mistake and five or six strides later he was picking up for me."

It was close at the end, but Big Zeb's strong finish swung the verdict. "I put it down to the ground," Geraghty says. "He wants genuine good ground to be at his best. Then he's able to use his speed."

The rematch

"They've been racing against each other since they were five-year-olds and we know we're in for a good race when they meet. The public know it too," De Bromhead says.

When the rematch will come is hard to know, with Sizing Europe's corner testing him again at longer distances. "The options are limited in bang-on 2m races," his trainer says, "although we know he loves two miles on good ground around Cheltenham."

Big Zeb is more of a specialist in the 2m division and the question is when age might catch up with him. "The plan is the same as last year but he's ten coming 11 and we might have to tweak the plan a little bit," Murphy says. "We hope he's got another season at the top.

"Hopefully we won't have to take on Sizing Europe, but we're not frightened of him, that's for sure. They'll be every bit as afraid of Big Zeb as we are of him." Sounds like fighting talk.

THE
BIGGER
PICTURE

On the beach in a 6f handicap at Laytown in
September as the Ken Condon-trained Smoky
Cloud leads all the way under apprentice Danny
Mullins **Patrick McCann**

'It was a huge hit to us, our worst result of the year'

SYNCHRONISED

Welsh National, Chepstow, January 8

THE McCoy factor. Just three weeks after winning BBC Sports Personality of the Year in a landslide vote and with racing's Christmas and New Year having been hit hard by the weather, Tony McCoy was still the name on everybody's lips when it came to the rescheduled Coral Welsh National.

McCoy had slayed his Aintree demons on Don't Push It the previous year and now he was out to land the one major National missing from his roll of honour. Popular in the ante-post market, Synchronised was backed into 9-2 favouritism from his ante-post price of 7-1 before settling at an SP of 5-1. His comfortable win, by two and three-quarter lengths, is thought to have cost the bookmaking industry more than £1 million.

Coral spokesman David Stevens says: "AP has been the punters' favourite for more than 15 years and his profile was at an all-time high. He'd said the Welsh National was the one race left that he wanted to win and punters took the hint. For them it was the best possible start to 2011.

JUNIOR

Fulke Walywn Kim Muir Handicap Chase, Cheltenham, March 17

This was by far the worst result of the Cheltenham Festival for the bookies, with the David Pipe-trained eight-year-old landing a monster gamble under amateur Jamie Codd. Pricewise played a big part, tipping Junior at 7-1 on the morning of the race, but this was a wholesale gamble that harked back to yesteryear.

Junior was backed to large sums at every price, returning the 100-30 favourite and swinging the festival in the punters' favour as he stormed home by 24 lengths.

Betfred's George Primarolo says: "Results had been going the bookies' way on the third day of the festival but a gamble had been brewing on Junior and his price had halved to 7-2 by the time the Kim Muir came around. It takes a serious chunk of money to do that at the festival and the money was well and truly landed as Junior ran out one of the easiest winners of the week."

FAME AND GLORY

Gold Cup, Royal Ascot, June 16

Despite being far from impressive in winning his opening two races of 2011, both by half a length when heavily odds-on, Fame And Glory was strongly supported for the Ascot Gold Cup.

The 2009 Irish Derby winner was the class act of the field, but the question was whether he would handle the 2m4f trip – six furlongs further than he had ever gone before. Punters had no doubt and smashed into Aidan O'Brien's colt as if a fifth Group 1 success was a foregone conclusion. It was, with Fame And Glory pulling three lengths clear of Opinion Poll.

"We were left licking our wounds after that one, it cost us alone more than £2 million," says Paddy Power's Andrew Moore. "We wanted to lay Fame And Glory and, with the price war at its height during Royal Ascot, we were forced to go 13-5. We got filled up at that price and again at 5-2, but the money kept coming. Within an hour he was 9-4, another hour later he was 2-1 and with the firms all full, the on-course boys were running for cover.

"He went from 2-1 to 11-8 very quickly. He was the one big horse of the week with name recognition that was a punter-friendly price and, although we've been through some recession, it was like the good old days, people having £500 and £1,000 bets. It was a huge hit to us, our worst result of the year."

BROWN PANTHER

King George V Handicap, Royal Ascot, June 16

Black Thursday for the bookmakers at Royal Ascot culminated in the runaway success of Brown Panther. Less than two hours after Fame And Glory stuck the knife in, Brown

In the money
Clockwise from top left: Hoof It (right), Synchronised (left), Junior, Brown Panther and Fame And Glory

Panther provided the twist.

Punters, with money in their pockets from the successes of favourites Banimpire and Fame And Glory, piled into Manchester United striker Michael Owen's homebred colt, who had an exciting profile having won three of his four career starts.

Brown Panther, subsequently second in the St Leger, was a handicap good thing off a mark of 91, as he proved in winning by six lengths.

"It takes a serious amount of money to move a horse from a morning price of 7-1 to an SP of 4-1 at a meeting like Royal Ascot," says Kate Miller of William Hill. "The scale of support in what looked like a competitive 18-runner handicap for progressive types was astonishing. He made a bad day a terrible one. Brown Panther alone cost us £1 million."

HOOF IT

Sky Bet Dash, York, July 23

Hoof It was one of the most popular and successful sprinters of the summer, going from useful handicapper (RPR of 94) to top-class handicapper (RPR 119) with his Blue Square Stewards' Cup success and then to Group 1 contender as he finished an incredibly close third in the Betfred Sprint Cup.

Add in some colourful and popular connections – owned by top golfer Lee Westwood and his manager Chubby Chandler, trained by the octogenarian Mick Easterby and ridden by the mercurial Kieren Fallon – and all the ingredients were there for a nationwide gamble.

The moment came in the Sky Bet Dash, when he was supported into 3-1 from a morning price of 5-1. Hoof It had topweight of 9st 10lb but nothing could stop him as he sped home by three-quarters of a length.

Ladbrokes' David Williams says: "He's the handicap horse who has done most damage to us this year. Every time he won, we tried to take him on next time to get our money back. It started as a scratch but after York it was an open wound. All told, he must have cost us more than £2 million."

'I don't even like champagne'

Exeter racegoer Steve Whitelcy became an instant millionaire when he landed a record Tote Jackpot but he's in no rush to spend it

Words by Nick Pulford

Steve Whiteley tied the knot this summer with Jill, his partner of 12 years. Money wasn't the reason they hadn't got married sooner, it was just something they hadn't got round to. They might get round to a few more things now, after Whiteley became the biggest winner in Tote Jackpot history on an unforgettable day at Exeter in March.

Not that Whiteley, 62, is a spend, spend, spender. He is happy to stay in his old house in North Tawton, Devon, and has invested most of his £1,445,671.20 windfall in a manner that would meet with approval from the financial specialists employed to guide big winners on the National Lottery. "You either spend it or look after it," he says. "The first thing you have to think about is how long you're going to live. If you live to be 90, you could end up being skint."

The Whiteleys may not be in the same league as the Scottish couple who scooped £161m on the Euromillions draw this

summer, but they can look forward to a long and happy married life – perhaps even a honeymoon at some point. Their wedding, held at a small pub on Dartmoor, was "fair" – which in Devon parlance indicates it was pretty darn good - but they did not rush straight off to see the Pyramids or cruise round the world. "A cruise has been mentioned, but I've been too busy working," says Whiteley.

Working? Yes, Whiteley has carried on the day job as a plumbing and heating engineer three or four days a week, sometimes five. Like most plumbers, he is a hard man to pin down. It takes a fortnight to arrange an interview with the Annual, although he is generous with his time once he does take a few moments out of his busy life.

He admits he was worn out by the

totepool

The joy of six How Whiteley became a millionaire

Race 1 Semi Colon 2-1 'I don't usually do the favourites but it was a McCoy one and I thought he was going to win at least one race that day and that might be the one' *Tickets remaining after leg 1: 363,285.13*

Race 2 Black Phantom 12-1 'The jockey was Nick Scholfield, who used to live in North Tawton, or his father did anyway' *Tickets remaining: 9,076.75*

Race 3 Ammunition 16-1 'I just liked the sound of that' *Tickets remaining: 571*

Race 4 Mr Bennett 16-1 'I've got a mate in Australia whose surname is Bennett' *Tickets remaining: 7*

Race 5 Lundy Sky 5-1 'Well, of course, Lundy Island is just off the coast of Devon' *Tickets remaining: 1*

Race 6 Lupita 12-1 'I just picked her because of the girl's name. It's not a name of any special significance to me, I just liked it' *Tickets remaining: 1*

Jackpot: £1,445,671.20 Accumulated odds: 879,137-1

---

media whirlwind that greeted his big win, but it was some story. Everywhere you look these days people are trying to win a million pounds in all sorts of unusual ways: playing roulette with Ant and Dec, telling Chris Tarrant they'd like to phone a friend or stopping the money dropping down a chute with correct answers to Davina McCall's questions.

Nobody, surely, would expect to go to Exeter races on a nondescript Tuesday in March – exactly a week before the opening of the Cheltenham Festival – and return home a millionaire. Certainly not Whiteley, who arrived at the racecourse on his over-60s bus pass and with a free entry voucher in his pocket.

But in the space of two and a half hours Whiteley went from ordinary racegoer to record Tote Jackpot winner by being the only punter to select all six winners. His payout was almost three times bigger than the previous record. The pot had been building up for nine days and was generating huge interest and publicity, not that Whiteley was aware of it.

"Four of us usually go to the first meeting of the year at Exeter. We just jumped on the bus and off we went. One of the guys told us about the Jackpot rollover and we all decided to have a go. I'd never done it before and they said it was 50p a horse, so I put two horses in every race, thinking it would be six quid. But the lady at the window said it came to £32 and I did a new one, where I had two horses in the third race and one in all the others. It cost £2."

The first race went to the Tony McCoy-ridden 2-1 favourite Semi Colon but the next three winners had double-figure starting prices, which vastly reduced the number of punters holding a live ticket.

"I bumped into someone I knew and, when I told him I'd had four winners, he said, 'There's only seven of you left'," Whiteley recalls. "After the fifth there was only one ticket left and the Tote put it through the machine to check it was mine."

Once it was confirmed, the nerves were jangling. By then, of course, he was left with the selection he had made at the start of the afternoon and a Jackpot-clinching victory looked unlikely. His hopes rested on Lupita, joint-seventh favourite in a field of 13 and partnered by 7lb claiming amateur Jessica Lodge, who had never ridden a winner under rules. Nor had Lupita won in 28 attempts over jumps.

"I watched the race outside, near the finish line," Whiteley says. "Nobody thought it had a chance of winning and when it got a bit of a bump two out I thought, 'That's it, it won't win now'." He stopped watching and didn't see Lupita jump the last about a length behind the leader, Only Hope. But then, with his friends yelling "it's going to win, it's going to win", Whiteley looked up just in time to see Lupita pass the post three-quarters of a length in front. It was the day's closest finish.

"After that it was a bit of a blur. People were shaking my hand, then I was interviewed on the telly and we all went in the winner's enclosure. We had photographs taken and were given a bottle of champagne. I don't even like champagne. The way I won my money, at the racecourse with everybody there, you can't avoid the publicity. The phone went at six o'clock the next morning. We had BBC, Radio 4 – I was still in bed when I did that interview – Sky, all the papers."

The media attention was a brief inconvenience, but the bigger problem was the people who were after his money, not just his story. "People warn you about the begging letters, but I only had about six of them. I had more people offering me financial advice, something like 40."

Whiteley already had a trusted financial adviser and, with his mortgage paid off, felt financially secure. "Plumbing and heating is not exactly a poor man's job," he says. Retirement is not too far away now, even if he is in no rush to become a monied man of leisure. "Hopefully one day I'll get round to spending some of it," he says. "You've got to have a go at it some time."

When he does, perhaps he'll raise a glass to Jessica Lodge and Lupita. But it won't be with champagne.

JUST FOR FUN What, in 2011, linked Long Run, Fame And Glory, Kempes and Our Jonathan? Answer page 170

things we liked

5

Words by Peter Thomas

All those lovely older horses

Youth and promise are exciting qualities in a racehorse, but they mean far less when there's no age or achievement to measure them against. Which is why, after the crushingly premature retirement of Sea The Stars at the end of his Classic campaign, the owners of some of 2010's stellar performers are to be warmly congratulated for keeping them in training.

How much less of a year it would have been without the acid tests provided by Workforce, So You Think, Canford Cliffs, Sarafina, St Nicholas Abbey, Snow Fairy, Twice Over, Midday, Goldikova and their ilk, who, for reasons veering between sporting altruism and naked commercialism, were all given the chance to thrill us for another season.

It's like being in a room full of pouting starlets – who are fine up to a point but still rather lacking in substance – and all of a sudden seeing Felicity Kendal, Mother Teresa, Fiona 'Rear of the Year' Bruce and Kylie Minogue come sashaying through the door, with their button-nosed self-sufficiency, Nobel Peace Prize, intellectual eyebrows and sequinned hot pants, to provide a benchmark for their juniors to aspire to.

Sir Henry Cecil and Sir Mick Easterby

In a sporting world whose more interesting cracks and crevices are increasingly hidden from public view by the wallpaper of public relations, it was refreshing to see two of the game's finest individuals restored to their rightful status as maverick maestros.

Cecil's knighthood may have arrived a little too late to catch him in his numerical pomp, but with Frankel living up to even the most outlandish expectations and the great man still pleasing the crowds with his dandyish dress sense and mischievous humour, the honour was as warmly received by the sport's followers as it was by the man himself.

Easterby may never be officially honoured by Her Majesty, for

Continues, page 194

Back for more Older stars (from top) So You Think and Workforce in the Eclipse at Sandown; Canford Cliffs at Royal Ascot; Sarafina at Longchamp; St Nicholas Abbey and Midday in the Coronation Cup at Epsom

Racing legends From left, Mick Easterby (left) greets Sir Henry Cecil; Ginger McCain; Michael Jarvis

fear of him upsetting the corgis, but the emergence of Hoof It as a contender for champion sprinter provided us with a welcome opportunity to pay our own renewed tribute to this true original.

It's fair to say that his exceedingly roomy trousers, working man's braces and flat cap are no match for Sir Henry's Gucci loafers and Hermes ties, but Spittin' Mick has the kind of bluff northern charm that should be harnessed by Racing For Change, the Yorkshire Tourist Board and the Campaign for Plain English.

Free racing

It's hard to imagine, but apparently there are people out there who have never been racing and aren't too bothered about it. What they really need is a full psychological evaluation and a large cattle prod applied to their backsides to move them towards the turnstiles, but in this age of political correctness gone mad we may have to make do with putting an arm round their shoulder and offering them a few comforting words along the lines that they can go racing for no charge, if they pick their moment.

Everybody loves a gift, that's for sure, so Racing For Change's free racing week in the spring was never going to be a hard sell. Loads of people turned up to get something for nothing, you won't be surprised to hear, and it turns out that most of the penny-pinching weasels were either first-timers or occasional racegoers who, almost to a man, didn't say they wouldn't return.

It remains to be seen how many of the freeloaders will dip into their wallets and pay to come again, but as a common-sense application of the bleedin' obvious this was surely a project worth trying.

Economic revolution

A new approach to the finances of racing was long overdue, if only because everybody must have been fed up to the back teeth with listening to the interminable droning of the annual levy negotiation.

What seems to have happened in 2011, albeit in rather piecemeal fashion, is that the sport has been dragged kicking and whinnying into the free market, with each vested interest flexing its muscles and baring its teeth as a prelude to what will surely be several fascinating years of carnage.

The Horsemen's Group threw the first flurry of punches, with its tariff-system assault on the racecourses followed quickly by a call for bookmakers to open their wallets to fund the 'third tier' races that are widely viewed as money-draining fodder for the betting shops. But the BHA, the betting exchanges, the racecourses, the High Street layers and Uncle Tom Cobley are all swinging away merrily, in the courts, the newspapers and the boardrooms.

It is a fight that may be 'to the death' for some, but the theory is that at the final bell we'll have a leaner, fitter sport, trained on hard economics, that is built to survive in the modern financial environment. Unless the whole thing develops into a 53-round bare-knuckle fight and everybody collapses.

Proper champions

When all is said and done, the one thing everybody agrees on is that great horses are what make racing great and we had them in magnificent abundance this year.

First there was Long Run, who took what looked a great Cheltenham Gold Cup and turned it into his own property. In opposition were the winners of the previous four renewals, all of them crowd-pleasers and feasible contenders for the title, but the Waley-Cohens' young prince shunted them all aside in a fashion that suggested a long and bountiful reign to come.

Then came Frankel, with a mighty weight of expectation on his shoulders but proving equal to the task of lifting the Flat season to heights we had hardly dared imagine.

Wasn't it nice to be able to stop the bickering for a while and talk about proper horses for a change?

And five things we didn't like

Sad losses
Ginger McCain and Michael Jarvis were two of the most different and most special people I've had the privilege to encounter in racing. One was an outspoken but loveable rascal, the other an understated but loveable gent, and to lose them both within days of each other was a terrible shame.

Howard Johnson
Steroids are one thing, but severing nerves in the legs of active racehorses is cruel, dangerous and immoral. Johnson may not have known the rules about running palmar neurectomy patients in races, but then nor did I and I could still tell it was wrong – as could the beaks who banned him for a total of four years for his offences.

The Grand National
How could one of racing's biggest showpieces turn into such a wobbly-legged, tarpaulin-covered PR debacle? Dead horses on the telly, tired horses made to look like heart-attack contenders and a whip debate that got everybody hot under the collar: it was as if the sport had handed a loaded gun to the animal rights lobby and held out a foot.

The sale of the Tote
After an eternity of dithering the Government decreed that the Tote would go on the market, then sold off the last item in racing's crown jewels to a bookmaker. The sport is guaranteed a cut of the proceeds and a short-term piece of the action – after that, who knows? I don't mean to sound gloomy, but . . .

Negative vibes
Having watched for 40 years, I can't recall a more exciting card in Britain than Qipco Champions Day, yet still the gloom-mongers persisted in picking holes in it ad nauseam. British racing is being forced to the margins and most people agree that change is required, but as soon as change is mooted many of them fly into a reactionary rage.